Mastering D3.js

Bring your data to life by creating and deploying complex data visualizations with D3.js

Pablo Navarro Castillo

PUBLISHING

BIRMINGHAM - MUMBAI

Mastering D3.js

First published: August 2014

Production reference: 1180814

Published by Packt Publishing Ltd.
Livery Place
35 Livery Street
Birmingham B3 2PB, UK.

ISBN 978-1-78328-627-0

www.packtpub.com

Cover image by Artie Ng (artherng@yahoo.com.au)

Credits

Author

Pablo Navarro Castillo

Reviewers

Andrew Berls

Simon Heimler

Lars Kotthoff

Nathan Vander Wilt

Commissioning Editor

Edward Gordon

Acquisition Editors

Nikhil Chinnari

Mohammad Rizvi

Content Development Editor

Sankalp Pawar

Technical Editors

Indrajit A. Das

Humera Shaikh

Copy Editors

Dipti Kapadia

Deepa Nambiar

Stuti Srivastava

Project Coordinator

Harshal Ved

Proofreaders

Simran Bhogal

Maria Gould

Ameesha Green

Paul Hindle

Indexers

Hemangini Bari

Mariammal Chettiyar

Rekha Nair

Priya Subramani

Production Coordinator

Arvindkumar Gupta

Cover Work

Arvindkumar Gupta

About the Author

Pablo Navarro Castillo is a mathematical engineer and developer. He earned his Master's degree in Applied Mathematics from École des Mines de Saint-Etienne in France. After working for a few years in operations research and data analysis, he began to work as a data visualization consultant and developer.

He has collaborated with Packt Publishing as a technical reviewer for *Data Visualization with D3.js* and *Data Visualization with D3.js Cookbook*. In 2014, he founded Masega, which is a data visualization agency based in Santiago, Chile, where he currently works.

I wish to thank the Packt Publishing team for their collaboration in the inception and development of this book. I am also grateful to the technical reviewers, whose insightful comments and kind suggestions have been essential to improve the content and examples of every chapter.

To Miriam, for her patience and continuous support.

About the Reviewers

Andrew Berls is a Ruby and JavaScript developer who lives in Santa Barbara, CA. He has developed dashboards for www.causes.com using D3.js to visualize social networks and recently acted as a reviewer for *Data Visualization with D3.js Cookbook*, *Packt Publishing*. Andrew recently completed his degree in Computer Science at the University of California, Santa Barbara. When he's not programming, you can find him attempting to cook or hiking up a mountain.

Andrew regularly blogs about web technologies at *http://www.andrewberls.com*.

Simon Heimler is currently studying and working as a research assistant at the University of Applied Research in Augsburg in the field of Semantic Content Management. He has a degree in Interactive Media and over a decade of experience with web design and development.

Lars Kotthoff is a postdoctoral researcher at University College Cork, Ireland, where he uses artificial intelligence methods to make software faster and better. When he is not researching ways to make computers more intelligent, he plays around with JavaScript visualizations. He has extensive experience with D3.js.

Nathan Vander Wilt is a freelance software developer. He offers clients a wide range of expertise, including everything from creating HTML5 and native application interfaces to developing low-level control software for embedded and wireless systems. He especially enjoys solving problems such as peer-to-peer syncing or the many challenges of digital cartography. In order to stay sane in the suburbs, Nate also enjoys raising plants, fish, snails, honeybees, chickens, and rabbits with his family.

www.PacktPub.com

Support files, eBooks, discount offers, and more

You might want to visit www.PacktPub.com for support files and downloads related to your book.

Did you know that Packt offers eBook versions of every book published, with PDF and ePub files available? You can upgrade to the eBook version at www.PacktPub.com and as a print book customer, you are entitled to a discount on the eBook copy. Get in touch with us at service@packtpub.com for more details.

At www.PacktPub.com, you can also read a collection of free technical articles, sign up for a range of free newsletters and receive exclusive discounts and offers on Packt books and eBooks.

http://PacktLib.PacktPub.com

Do you need instant solutions to your IT questions? PacktLib is Packt's online digital book library. Here, you can access, read and search across Packt's entire library of books.

Why subscribe?

- Fully searchable across every book published by Packt
- Copy and paste, print and bookmark content
- On demand and accessible via web browser

Free access for Packt account holders

If you have an account with Packt at www.PacktPub.com, you can use this to access PacktLib today and view nine entirely free books. Simply use your login credentials for immediate access.

Table of Contents

Preface

D3 is an amazing library. On its website, there are hundreds of beautiful examples, visualizations, and charts created mainly with D3. Looking at the examples, we soon realize that D3 allows us to create an uncanny variety of visuals. We can find everything from simple bar charts to interactive maps.

The ability to create almost anything with D3 comes at a price; we must think about our charts at a more abstract level and learn how to bind data elements with elements in our page. This association between properties of our data items and visual attributes of the elements in our chart will allow us to create complex charts and visualizations.

In real-life projects, we will have to integrate components and charts created with D3 with other components and libraries. In most of the examples in this book, we will cover how to integrate D3 with other libraries and tools, creating complete applications that leverage the best of each library.

Through the examples of this book, we will cover reusable charts using external data sources, thereby creating user interface elements and interactive maps with D3. At the end, we will implement an application to visualize topics mentioned on Twitter in real time.

D3 is a great tool to experiment with visuals and data. I hope you will have fun following the examples in this book and creating your own visualizations.

What this book covers

Chapter 1, *Data Visualization*, provides us with examples of interesting visualization projects and references that help us learn more about data visualization. We also review some examples of historical relevance and discuss what makes D3 a good tool to create data-visualization projects.

Chapter 2, Reusable Charts, focuses on how to create configurable charts that can be used in several projects. In this chapter, we discuss how to use selections to manipulate elements in a web page and use this to create a reusable barcode chart from scratch. We also create a custom layout algorithm and use it to create a radial bar chart.

Chapter 3, Creating Visualizations without SVG, discusses the current state of SVG support in the browser market and provides some strategies to create visualizations that work in browsers that don't have SVG support. We create an animated bubble chart using div elements, learn how to detect whether the browser supports SVG, and use polyfills to render SVG figures using the HTML5 canvas element. We also learn how to create visualizations using D3 and canvas.

Chapter 4, Creating a Color Picker with D3, introduces concepts that allow us to create user interaction elements and controls. In this chapter, we use the D3 drag behavior and the reusable chart pattern to create a slider control. We use this control to create a color picker based on the CIE Lab color model, which is also a reusable chart.

Chapter 5, Creating User Interface Elements, discusses how to use event listeners to highlight elements in a chart. We also discuss how to create tooltips and how to integrate these tooltips with existing charts. We create an area chart and use the brush behavior to select a range in the chart.

Chapter 6, Interaction between Charts, discusses how to use Backbone to create structured web applications, separating data from its visual representation, and how to integrate D3 charts in this architecture. We will learn how to implement models, views, collections, and routes in order to keep a consistent application state. We will use this to create an application to explore the time series of stock prices using the area chart implemented in *Chapter 5, Creating User Interface Elements.*

Chapter 7, Creating a Charting Package, introduces the development workflow to create a charting package using D3. We introduce tools and best practices to implement, organize, and distribute the package. We will also create a sample project that uses the charting package as an external dependency.

Chapter 8, Data-driven Applications, provides us with an example of a web application and introduces tools to deploy visualization projects. We create an application that uses the World Bank data API to create a visualization of the evolution of indicators of human development. We will learn how to use GitHub pages to host our project and how to host a static website using Amazon S3.

Chapter 9, Creating a Dashboard, introduces concepts and best practices to create dashboards. We implement an example dashboard to monitor the performance of students in a class using D3 and custom charts.

Chapter 10, Creating Maps, discusses how to create vector maps using the geographic functions of D3. We will learn how to obtain geographic data and how to convert it to GeoJSON and TopoJSON formats, which are more suitable to be used with D3. We will create a choropleth map with D3 and use the TopoJSON library to visualize neighbors and boundaries between countries. We will also learn how to create a custom D3 layer to be used with Mapbox.

Chapter 11, Creating Advanced Maps, introduces some geographic projections and discusses how to configure projections to center and scale maps at specific locations. We also use the Orthographic projection to create a rotating globe. We also use a star catalog and the Stereographic projection to create a fullscreen star map. We will also learn how to use canvas to project raster images from Earth using the Orthographic projection.

Chapter 12, Creating a Real-time Application, introduces the concepts and tools that are used to create real-time applications. We will learn how to use Firebase to update the state of our applications in real time. We will also create a real-time application to explore the geographic distribution of geotagged tweets that match user-defined topics using Node, Socket.IO, and D3.

What you need for this book

The code bundle of this book was created using Jekyll, which is a static website generator. To run most of the examples in the code bundle, you will need a static web server and a modern web browser. The following list summarizes the main dependencies:

- A modern web browser
- D3 3.4
- Jekyll or other static web servers
- Text editor

Some chapters require you to install additional frontend libraries, such as Backbone, TopoJSON, Typeahead, and Bootstrap. Additional instructions on installing these libraries can be found in the corresponding chapters. In other chapters, we will use additional software to compile assets or process files. In those cases, installing the software is optional (the compiled files will be present as well), but it might be useful for you to install them for your own projects:

- Node and Node packages
- Git
- Make
- TopoJSON
- GDAL

Instructions to install these applications can also be found in the corresponding chapters.

Who this book is for

This book is for frontend programmers who want to learn how to create charts, visualizations, and interactive maps with D3. We will cover everything from creating basic charts to complex real-time applications, integrating other libraries and components to create real-life applications.

We assume that you know the fundamentals of HTML, CSS, and JavaScript, but we review the main concepts as needed.

Conventions

In this book, you will find a number of styles of text that distinguish between different kinds of information. Here are some examples of these styles, and an explanation of their meaning.

Code words in text, database table names, folder names, filenames, file extensions, pathnames, dummy URLs, user input, and Twitter handles are shown as follows:

"In the example file, we have a div element classed as `chart-example` and with the ID `chart`."

A block of code is set as follows:

```
divItems.enter()
    .append('div')
    .attr('class', 'data-item');
```

When we wish to draw your attention to a particular part of a code block, the relevant lines or items are set in bold:

```
chart.onClick = function(d) {
    // ...

    // Invoke the user callback.
    onColorChange(color);
};
```

Any command-line input or output is written as follows:

```
$ grunt vows
Running "vows:all" (vows) task
(additional output not shown)
Done, without errors.
```

New terms and **important words** are shown in bold. Words that you see on the screen, in menus or dialog boxes for example, appear in the text as follows:

"By clicking on **Create a Project**, we can access the map editor, where we can customize the colors of land, buildings, and other features; select the base layer (street, terrain, or satellite) and select the primary language for the features and locations in the map."

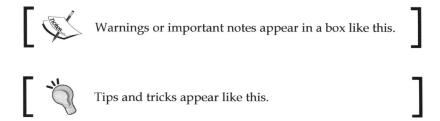

Warnings or important notes appear in a box like this.

Tips and tricks appear like this.

Reader feedback

Feedback from our readers is always welcome. Let us know what you think about this book—what you liked or may have disliked. Reader feedback is important for us to develop titles that you really get the most out of.

To send us general feedback, simply send an e-mail to feedback@packtpub.com, and mention the book title via the subject of your message.

If there is a topic that you have expertise in and you are interested in either writing or contributing to a book, see our author guide on www.packtpub.com/authors.

Customer support

Now that you are the proud owner of a Packt book, we have a number of things to help you to get the most from your purchase.

Downloading the example code

You can download the example code files for all Packt books you have purchased from your account at http://www.packtpub.com. If you purchased this book elsewhere, you can visit http://www.packtpub.com/support and register to have the files e-mailed directly to you.

Downloading the color images of this book

We also provide you a PDF file that has color images of the screenshots/diagrams used in this book. The color images will help you better understand the changes in the output. You can download this file from: `https://www.packtpub.com/sites/default/files/downloads/6270OS_Graphics.pdf`.

Errata

Although we have taken every care to ensure the accuracy of our content, mistakes do happen. If you find a mistake in one of our books—maybe a mistake in the text or the code—we would be grateful if you would report this to us. By doing so, you can save other readers from frustration and help us improve subsequent versions of this book. If you find any errata, please report them by visiting `http://www.packtpub.com/submit-errata`, selecting your book, clicking on the **errata submission form** link, and entering the details of your errata. Once your errata are verified, your submission will be accepted and the errata will be uploaded on our website, or added to any list of existing errata, under the Errata section of that title. Any existing errata can be viewed by selecting your title from `http://www.packtpub.com/support`.

Piracy

Piracy of copyright material on the Internet is an ongoing problem across all media. At Packt, we take the protection of our copyright and licenses very seriously. If you come across any illegal copies of our works, in any form, on the Internet, please provide us with the location address or website name immediately so that we can pursue a remedy.

Please contact us at `copyright@packtpub.com` with a link to the suspected pirated material.

We appreciate your help in protecting our authors, and our ability to bring you valuable content.

Questions

You can contact us at `questions@packtpub.com` if you are having a problem with any aspect of the book, and we will do our best to address it.

1
Data Visualization

Humans began to record things long before writing systems were created. When the number and diversity of things to remember outgrew the capacity of human memory, we began to use external devices to register quantitative information. Clay tokens were used as early as 8000-7500 BC to represent commodities like measures of wheat, livestock, and even units of man labor. These objects were handy to perform operations that would have been difficult to do with the real-life counterparts of the tokens; distribution and allocation of goods became easier to perform. With time, the tokens became increasingly complex, and soon, the limitations of the complex token system were identified and the system began to be replaced with simpler yet more abstract representations of quantities, thereby originating the earlier systems of writing.

Keeping records has always had a strong economic and practical drive. Having precise accounts of grains and pastures for the livestock allowed people to plan rations for the winter, and knowing about seasons and climate cycles allowed people to determine when to plant and when to harvest. As we became better at counting and registering quantitative information, trading with other nations and managing larger administrative units became possible, thereby providing us with access to goods and knowledge from other latitudes. We keep records because we think it's useful. Knowing what we have allows us to better distribute our assets, and knowing the past allows us to prepare for the future.

Today, we register and store more data than ever. Imagine that you want to go out for a morning cup of coffee. If you pay in cash, the date, price of the coffee, and the kind of coffee will be recorded before your coffee was actually prepared. These records will feed the accounting and stock systems of the store, being aggregated and transformed to financial statements, staff performance reports, and taxes to be paid by the store. Paying with credit card will generate a cascade of records in the accounting system of your bank. We measure things hoping that having the information will help us to make better decisions and to improve in the future.

History demonstrates that gathering and understanding data can help to solve relevant problems. An example of this is the famous report of John Snow about the Broad Street cholera outbreak. On August 31, 1854, a major outbreak of cholera was declared in the Soho district of London. Three days later, 127 people died from the disease. At the time, the mechanism of transmission of the cholera was not understood. The germ theory was yet to exist, and the mainstream theory was that the disease spread by a form of bad air. The physician, John Snow, began to investigate the case, collecting and classifying facts, recording deaths and their circumstances as well as a great number of testimonials. Refer to the following screenshot:

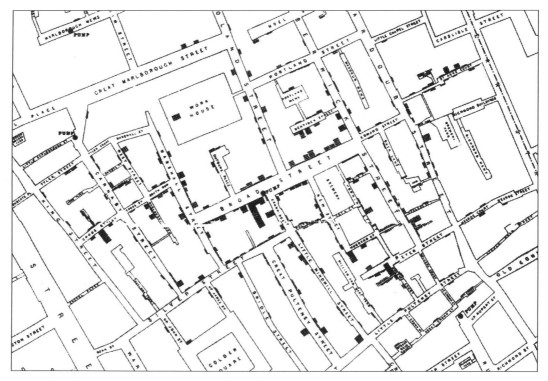

Details of the original map made for Snow, displaying the deaths by cholera in the Soho district

He gave special attention to the exceptions in the map and noticed that neither the workhouse inmates nor the brewery workers had been affected. The exceptions became further proof as he discovered that about 70 employees who worked in the brewery drank only beer made with water from a pump inside the walls of the brewery. In the workhouse, which also had its own water pump, only 5 out of 500 died, and further investigation revealed that the deceased were admitted when the outbreak had already begun. Although the map is convincing enough, Snow's original report contains more than 150 pages filled with tables and testimonials that support or raise questions about his theory. The local council decided to disable the pump by removing its handle, when the outbreak had already began to decline.

The report from John Snow is a great triumph of detective work and data visualization. He gathered information about the deaths and their circumstances and displayed them as data points in their geographic context, which made the pattern behind the causalities visible. He didn't stop at studying the data points; he also investigated the absence of the disease in certain places, faced the exceptions instead of quietly dismissing them, and eventually formed stronger evidence to support his case.

In this chapter, we will discuss what makes visual information so effective and discuss what data visualization is. We will comment about the different kinds of data visualization works, which gives a list of references to learn more about it. We will also discuss D3 and its differences with other tools to create visualizations.

Defining data visualization

Our brains are specially adapted to gather and analyze visual information. Images are easier to understand and recall. We tend to analyze and detect patterns in what we see even when we are not paying attention. The relation between visual perception and cognition can be used to our advantage if we can provide information that we want to communicate in a visual form.

Data visualization is the discipline that studies how to use visual perception to communicate and analyze data. Being a relatively young discipline, there are several working definitions of data visualization. One of the most accepted definitions states:

> *"Data visualization is the representation and presentation of data that exploits our visual perception in order to amplify cognition."*

The preceding quote is taken from *Data Visualization: A successful design process*, *Andy Kirk, Packt Publishing*.

There are several variants for this definition, but the essence remains the same—data visualization is a visual representation of data that aims to help us better understand the data and its relevant context. The capacity for visual processing of our brains can also play against us. Data visualization made without proper care can misrepresent the underlying data and fail to communicate the truth, or worse, succeed in communicating lies.

The kind of works that fall under this definition are also diverse; infographics, exploratory tools, and dashboards are data visualization subsets. In the next section, we will describe them and give some notable examples of each one.

Some kinds of data visualizations

There are countless ways to say things, and there are even more ways to communicate using visual means. We can create visualizations for the screen or for printed media, display the data in traditional charts, or try something new. The choice of colors alone can be overwhelming. When creating a project, a great number of decisions have to be made, and the emphasis given by the author to the different aspects of the visualization will have a great impact on the visual output.

Among this diversity, there are some forms that are recognizable. Infographics are usually suited with a great deal of contextual information. Projects more inclined to exploratory data analysis will tend to be more interactive and provide less guidance. Of course, this classification is only to provide reference points; the data visualization landscape is a continuum between infographics, exploratory tools, charts, and data art. Charles Minard's chart, which shows the number of men in Napoleon's 1812 Russian campaign, is shown in the following screenshot:

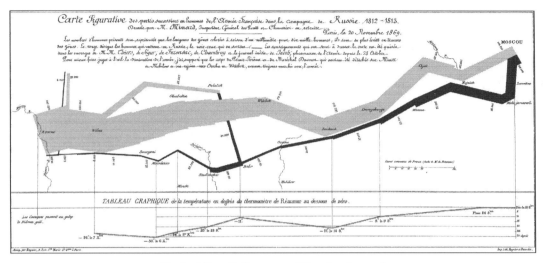

Charles Minard's flow map of Napoleon's march

It would be difficult to classify Charles Minard's figure as an infographic or as a flow chart because it allows for both. The information displayed is primarily quantitative, but it's shown in a map with contextual information that allows us to better understand the decline in the Napoleonic forces. There are several dimensions being displayed at once such as the number of soldiers, the geographic location of the soldiers during the march, and the temperature at each place. The figure does amazing work by showing how diminished the forces were when they arrived at Moscow and how the main enemy was the cold winter.

Infographics

Infographics is a form of data visualization that is focused on communicating and explaining one or more particular views of a subject. It usually contains images, charts, and annotations, which provides context and enhances the reader's capacity to understand the main display of information. The award-winning infography about the right whale (*La ballena Franca* in original Spanish), created by Jaime Serra and published in the Argentinian newspaper, *Clarin*, in 1995 is a great example of how infographics can be a powerful tool to enlighten and communicate a particular subject. This can be found at `http://3.bp.blogspot.com/_LCqDL30ndZQ/TBPkvZIQaNI/AAAAAAAAAik/OrjA6TShNsk/s1600/INFO-BALLENA.jpg`. A huge painting of the right whale covers most of the infography area. A small map shows where this species can be found during their migratory cycles. There are outlines of the right whale alongside other kinds of whales, comparing their sizes. The image of the whale is surrounded by annotations about their anatomy that explain how they swim and breathe. Bar charts display the dramatic decline in their population and how they are recovering at least in some corners of the globe. All these elements are integrated in a tasteful and beautiful display that accomplishes its purpose, which is to display data to inform the reader. The Right Whale, Jaime Serra, 1995, can be seen in the following image:

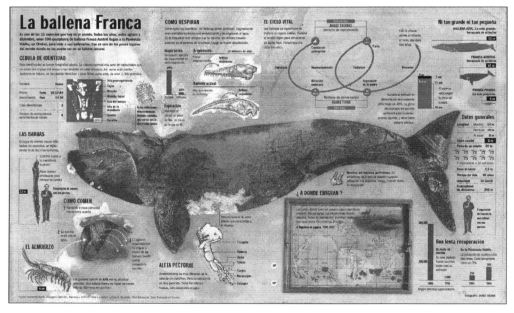

The Right Whale by Jaime Sierra

There are people who don't consider infographics as proper data visualization because they are designed to guide the reader through a story with the main facts already highlighted, as opposed to a chart-based data visualization where the story and the important facts are to be discovered by the reader.

Exploratory visualizations

This branch of data visualization is more focused on providing tools to explore and interpret datasets. These visualizations can be static or interactive. The exploration can be either looking at the charts carefully or to interact with the visualization to discover interesting things. In interactive projects, the user is allowed to filter and interact with the visualizations to discover interesting patterns and facts with little or no guidance. This kind of project is usually regarded as being more objective and data centered than other forms.

A great example is *The Wealth and Health of Nations*, from the Gapminder project (`http://www.gapminder.org/world`). The Gapminder World tool helps us explore the evolution of life in different parts of the world in the last two centuries. The visualization is mainly composed of a configurable bubble chart. The user can select indicators such as life expectancy, fertility rates, and even consumption of sugar per capita and see how different countries have evolved in regard to these indicators. One of the most interesting setups is to select life expectancy in the y axis, income per person in the x axis, and the size of the bubbles as the size of the population of each country. The bubbles will begin to animate as the years pass, bouncing and making loops as the life expectancy in each country changes. If you explore your own country, you will soon realize that some of the backward movements are related to economic crisis or political problems and how some countries that were formerly similar in their trends in these dimensions diverge. A visualization from Gapminder World, powered by Trendalyzer from `www.gapminder.org`, is shown in the following screenshot:

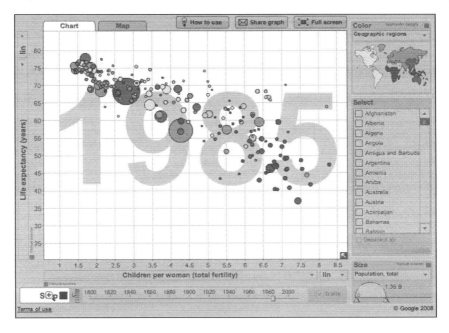

The time series for dozens of variables allow the user to explore this dataset, uncover stories, and learn very quickly about how countries that are similar in some regards can be very different in other aspects. The aim of the Gapminder project is to help users and policy makers to have a fact-based view of the world, and the visualization certainly succeeds in providing the means to better understand the world.

Dashboards

Dashboards are dense displays of charts that help us to understand the key metrics of an issue as quickly and effectively as possible. Business intelligence dashboards and website users' behavior are usually displayed as dashboards. Stephen Few defines an information dashboard as follows:

> *"A visual display of the most important information needed to achieve one or more objectives; consolidated and arranged on a single screen so the information can be monitored at a glance."*

The preceding quote can be found in *Information Dashboard Design: The Effective Visual Communication of Data, Stephen Few, O'Reilly Media.*

As the information has to be delivered quickly, there is no time to read long annotations or to click controls; the information should be visible, ready to be consumed. Dashboards are usually bundled with complementary information systems to further investigate issues if they are detected. The distribution of the space in a dashboard is the main challenge when designing them. Compact charts will be preferred in this kind of project, as long as they still allow for speedy decoding of the information. We will learn about designing dashboards in *Chapter 9, Creating a Dashboard*. An example dashboard from *Chapter 9, Creating a Dashboard*, showing the performance of students in a class can be seen in the following screenshot:

This classification mentions only some of the forms of data visualization projects; most parts of data visualizations won't fit exactly under these labels. There is plenty of room to experiment with new formats and borrow elements of infographics, dashboards, and traditional charts to communicate more effectively.

Learning about data visualization

Despite being a young discipline, there are great books on data visualization and information design. A successful data visualization practitioner should also know about design, statistics, cognition, and visual perception, but reading data visualization books is a good start.

Edward Tufte is an expert in information design and his works are a must-read in this field. They are filled with good and bad examples of information design and comments about how to better communicate quantitative information. They contain collections of images from ancient charts and visualizations, which explain their historic context and the impact they had. The discussion is not restricted to how to communicate quantitative information; there are examples ranging from natural history to architecture:

- *Visual Explanations: Images and Quantities, Evidence and Narrative*, Edward R. Tufte, Graphics Press

- *The Visual Display of Quantitative Information*, Edward R. Tufte, Graphics Press

- *Beautiful Evidence*, Edward R. Tufte, Graphics Press

- *Envisioning Information*, Edward R. Tufte, Graphics Press

Stephen Few is a data visualization consultant who specializes in how to display and communicate quantitative information, especially in business environments. His books focus on dashboard and quantitative information and provide actionable guidelines on how to effectively communicate data:

- *Information Dashboard Design: The Effective Visual Communication of Data*, Stephen Few, O'Reilly Series

- *Now You See It: Simple Visualization Techniques for Quantitative Analysis*, Stephen Few, Analytics Press

Alberto Cairo teaches visualization at the University of Miami. He has extensive experience in data journalism and infographics. His most recent book focuses on data visualization and how good infographics are made. He also has a strong presence on social media; be sure to follow him at http://twitter.com/albertocairo to be informed about infographics and data visualization:

- *The Functional Art: An introduction to information graphics and visualization*, Alberto Cairo, New Riders

Andy Kirk is a data visualization consultant and author. He recently published a book sharing his experiences in creating data visualizations. He gives guidelines to plan and make the creation of visualizations more systematic. The book is filled with actionable advice about how to design and plan our visualization projects. Andy's blog (`http://www.visualisingdata.com`) is a great source to be informed about the latest developments in the field:

- *Data Visualization: A Successful Design Process*, Andy Kirk, Packt Publishing

There isn't a universal recipe to create good data visualizations, but the experience and guidelines from experts in the field can help us to avoid mistakes and create better visualizations. It will take time to have the necessary skills to create great data visualizations, but learning from experienced people will help us make a safer journey. As with many other things in life, the key to learning is to practice, get feedback, and improve over time.

Introducing the D3 library

In 2011, I was working in a hedge fund, and most of my work consisted of processing and analyzing market data. It mostly consisted of time series, each row containing a timestamp and two prices: the bid and asking prices for stock options. I had to assess the quality of two years of market data and find whether there were errors or gaps between millions of records. The time series were not uniform; there can be hundreds of records in a couple of seconds or just a few records in an hour. I decided to create a bar chart that shows how many records there were in each hour for the two years of data. I created a Python script using the excellent packages NumPy and Matplotlib. The result was a folder with thousands of useless bar charts. Of course, the software was not to blame.

In my second attempt, I tried to create a heat map, where the columns represented hours in a week and the rows represented the weeks of a year. The color of each cell was proportional to the number of quotes in that hour. After tweaking the colors and the size of the cells, my first visualization emerged. Success! The pattern emerged. My coworkers began to gather around, recognizing and explaining the variations on market activity. The black columns at the end of the chart corresponded to weekends, when the market was closed. Mondays were brighter and had more activity than other days. Holidays were easy to spot after a quick consult to the holidays calendar for the year. More interesting patterns were also discernible; there was frantic activity at the beginning of the working day and a slight but noticeable decline at lunch. It was fun and interesting to recognize what we already knew.

However, besides the gaps explained by common sense, there were small gaps that couldn't be explained with holidays or hungry stock traders. There were hours with little or no activity; in the context of a year of market activity, we could see that it was something unusual. A simple heat map allowed us to find the gaps and begin to investigate the anomalies.

Of course, this first heat map required a better version, one that could allow the exploring of the dataset more easily. We needed an interactive version to know the exact date and time of the gaps and how many records there were in each hourly block. It should also highlight the weekends and holidays. This required better tools, something that allows for more interaction and that doesn't require Python's virtual environments and numerous packages to generate the graphics. This search led me to D3, and I began to learn.

There are several charting packages for web platforms, but D3 excels among them by its flexibility and strong features. A quick visit to the D3 home page (`http://www.d3js.org`) will amaze us with hundreds of examples of what can be done, from the humble bar chart to beautifully crafted interactive maps. Newcomers will soon realize that D3 is not a charting package, but is a tool to bind data items with DOM elements and associate data attributes with visual properties of the DOM elements. This could sound abstract, but this is all we need to create almost any chart.

A chart is a visual representation of a dataset. To create a chart, we must associate attributes of the data items with properties of graphic objects. Let's consider the following dataset:

x	y
2.358820	0.70524774
2.351551	0.71038206
...	...
3.581900	-0.426217726

This series of numbers doesn't have an intrinsic visual representation; we should encode the attributes of each record and assign them corresponding visual attributes. Using the most traditional representation for this kind of data, we can represent the rows as dots on a surface. The position of the dots will be determined by their x and y attributes. Their horizontal position will be proportional to the x attribute and their vertical position will be proportional to the y attribute. This will generate the following scatter plot:

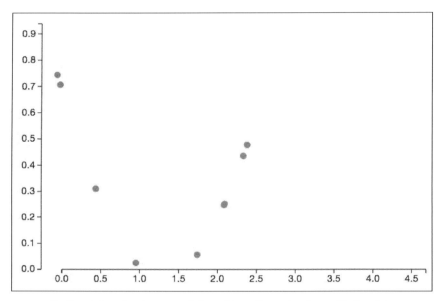

Scatter plot, a visual representation of two-dimensional quantitative data

To help the viewer trace back from position to data attributes, we can add axes, which are essentially annotations for the visual representation of the data. All charts work on the same principle, which is associate visual attributes to data attributes.

With D3, we can manipulate attributes of DOM elements based on attributes of the data items. This is the essence of creating charts. SVG stands for Scalable Vector Graphics, and in most browsers, SVG images can be included in the page and thereby become a part of the DOM. In most cases, we will use svg elements to create charts and other graphic elements. SVG allows us to create basic shapes as rectangles, circles, and lines as well as more complex elements as polygons and text. We can color the elements by assigning them classes and adding CSS styles to the page, or we can use the fill attribute of svg objects. D3 and SVG form a powerful combination, which we will use to create interactive charts and maps.

Of course, there is a price to pay to effectively use these powerful tools. We must learn and understand how browsers work and know our way with JavaScript, CSS, and HTML. One of the fundamentals of D3 is that it manipulates DOM elements, knowing little or nothing about the visual representation of the elements. If we want to create a circle, D3 doesn't provide a `createCircle(x, y, radius)` function, but rather we should append a circle svg element in a DOM node (the element with the container ID) and set their attributes:

```
// Appending a circle element to a DOM node
d3.select('#container').append('circle')
    .attr('cx', 10)
    .attr('cy', 10)
    .attr('r', 10);
```

Downloading the example code

You can download the example code files for all Packt books you have purchased from your account at http://www.packtpub.com. If you purchased this book elsewhere, you can visit http://www.packtpub.com/support and register to have the files e-mailed directly to you.

As D3 doesn't know anything else other than the fact that we are appending a DOM element, it is up to us to check whether the parent element is an svg element and that cx, cy, and r are valid attributes for a circle.

As we mentioned before, D3 doesn't have ready-to-use charts, but has several tools to make creating visualizations and charts easy. Binding data to DOM elements allows us to create from bar charts to interactive maps by following similar patterns. We will learn how to create reusable charts so that we don't have to code them each time we want to add a chart to a page. For big projects, we will need to integrate our D3-based charts with third-party libraries that support our need, which is out of the D3 scope. We will also learn about how to use D3 in conjunction with external libraries.

Fortunately, D3 has a great community of developers. Mike Bostock, the creator of D3, has created a nice collection of in-depth tutorials about the trickiest parts of D3 and examples demonstrating almost every feature. Users of the library have also contributed with examples covering a wide range of applications.

Summary

In this chapter, we gave a working definition of data visualization, one of the main fields of application of the D3 library.

This book is about D3 and how to create interactive data visualizations in real-life settings. We will learn about the inner working of D3 and create well-structured charts to be used and shared across projects. We will learn how to create complete applications using D3 and third-party libraries and services as well as how to prepare our development environment to have maintainable and comfortable workflows.

Learning D3 may take some time, but it's certainly rewarding. The following chapters are focused on providing the tools to learn how to use D3 and other tools to create beautiful charts that will add life to your data.

2
Reusable Charts

In this chapter, we will learn how to create configurable charts and layout algorithms and how to use these components. One important characteristic of configurable charts is that we can use them in different contexts without having to change the code. In this chapter, we will cover the following topics:

- Learn how to create reusable charts
- Create a reusable barcode chart
- Create a reusable layout algorithm
- Use the layout and the barcode chart

We will begin by defining what we understand by reusable charts and construct a reusable chart from scratch.

Creating reusable charts

A chart is a visual representation of a dataset. As datasets grow in complexity and number of elements, we might want to encapsulate the chart in a reusable piece of code to share it and use it in other projects. The success of the reusability of the chart depends on the choices made during the design process.

We will follow the proposal given in the article *Towards Reusable Charts* by Mike Bostock with some modifications. Charts created with this model will have the following attributes:

- **Configurable**: The chart appearance and behavior can be modified without having to change the code of the chart. The chart should expose an API that allows customization.

- **Repeatable**: A chart can be rendered in a selection that contains several elements, displaying independent visualizations in each node. The update process and the variables associated to the data items must be independent as well.

- **Composable**: A consequence of the previous attributes is that a chart can have inner charts as long as the inner charts follow the same conventions.

We must evaluate which aspects of the chart must be configurable and which aspects are fixed, because adding more flexibility increases the complexity of the chart.

There are other ways to implement reusability. For instance, the D3.Chart package by the Miso Project proposes a model that allows extension of the charts in terms of existing charts, add event-listening capabilities to the charts, and includes the mini framework D3.layer that allows us to configure life cycle events without changing the rendering logic of the chart.

We will begin by reviewing the creation and data-binding processes in D3 in order to construct a reusable chart step by step.

Creating elements with D3

In this section, we will review the mechanism of creation and manipulation of data-bound DOM elements using D3. To follow the examples in this section, open the `chapter02/01-creating-dom-elements.html` file and open the browser's Developer Tools.

We can use D3 to create and modify the elements in a web page. In the Developer Tools Console, we can create a new paragraph at the end of the body with a single command as follows:

```
> var p = d3.select('body').append('p');
```

Inspecting the document structure, we can see that an empty paragraph element was appended at the end of the body. The appended method returns a selection that contains the new paragraph element. Refer to the following screenshot:

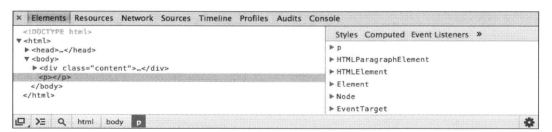

As we stored a reference to the paragraph selection in the p variable, we can use this reference to modify the content of the paragraph as follows:

```
> p.html('New paragraph.');
```

The text method will also return the paragraph selection, allowing us to use method chaining to modify the paragraph font color as follows:

```
> p.html('blue paragraph').style('color', 'blue');
```

The style method will once more return the paragraph selection.

Binding data

Before creating a chart, we will create a set of divs bound to a simple dataset and improve the example step-by-step in order to understand the process of creating a chart. We will begin with a data array that contains three strings and use D3 to create three corresponding div elements, each one with a paragraph that contains the strings. In the example file, we have a div element classed chart-example and with ID chart. This div element will be used as container for the divs to be created:

```
<div class="chart-example" id="chart"></div>
```

In the script, we define our dataset as an array with three strings:

```
var data = ['a', 'b', 'c'];
```

For each element, we want to append an inner div, and in each one of them, we append a paragraph. The container div can be selected using its ID:

```
var divChart = d3.select('#chart');
```

Next, we create a selection that contains the divs classed data-item and bind the data array to this selection:

```
var divItems = divChart.selectAll('div.data-item')
    .data(data);
```

Before invoking the data method, keep in mind that the inner divs don't exist yet, and the selection will be empty. We can check this by creating an empty selection:

```
// This will return true
> divChart.selectAll('p.test-empty-selection').empty()
```

The data() method joins the data array with the current selection. At this point, the data elements in the divItems selection don't have corresponding DOM nodes. The divItems.enter() selection stores placeholder DOM nodes for the elements to be created. We can instantiate new divs using the append method:

```
divItems.enter()
    .append('div')
    .attr('class', 'data-item');
```

As seen in the preceding example, the append method returns the created divs, and we can set its class directly. The divItems selection now contains three div elements, each one bounded to a data item. We can append a paragraph to each div and set its content:

```
var pItems = divItems.append('p')
    .html(function(d) { return d; });
```

The method-chaining pattern allows us to write the same sequence of operations in one single, compact statement:

```
d3.select('#chart').selectAll('div.data-item')
    .data(data)
    .enter()
    .append('div')
    .attr('class', 'data-item')
    .append('p')
    .html(function(d) { return d; });
```

The div elements and their corresponding paragraphs are created inside the container div. Refer to the following screenshot:

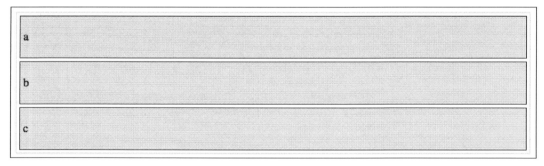

The creation of DOM elements by joining a data array with a selection of div elements

Encapsulating the creation of elements

We could add more elements on top of the previous elements, but the code would become confusing and monolithic. The `selection.call` method allows us to encapsulate the creation of the div contents as follows:

```
d3.select('#chart').selectAll('div.data-item')
    .data(data)
    .enter()
    .append('div')
    .attr('class', 'data-item')
    .call(function(selection) {
        selection.each(function(d) {
            d3.select(this).append('p').html(d);
        });
    });
```

The `call` method invokes its argument function, passing the current selection as the argument and setting the `this` context to the current selection.

The `selection.each` method invokes its own argument function, passing the bound data item to the function. The `this` context in the function is the current DOM element; in our case, it's the recently created div.

The argument of the call method can be defined elsewhere. We will define the `initDiv` function and use it to create the content of the div:

```
function initDiv(selection) {
    selection.each(function(data) {
        d3.select(this).append('p')
            .html(data);
    });
}
```

The `initDiv` function encapsulates the creation and configuration of the div contents; the code that creates the elements is more compact, shown as follows:

```
d3.select('#chart').selectAll('div.data-item')
    .data(data)
    .enter()
    .append('div')
    .attr('class', 'data-item')
    .call(initDiv);
```

Creating the svg element

We can use the same structure to create an svg element inside the inner div instead of the paragraph. We will need to define the width and height of svg as follows:

```
var width = 400,
    height = 40;
```

We will change the name of the initDiv function to the more appropriate name, chart, and replace the creation of the paragraph with the creation of svg and a background rectangle. Note that we are binding the svg selection to an array with a single element (the [data] array) and appending the svg and the rectangle only to the enter() selection as follows:

```
function chart(selection) {
    selection.each(function(data) {
        // Select and bind the svg element.
        var div = d3.select(this).attr('class', 'data-item'),
            svg = div.selectAll('svg').data([data]),
            svgEnter = svg.enter();

        // Append the svg and the rectangle on enter.
        svgEnter.append('svg')
            .attr('width', width)
            .attr('height', height)
            .append('rect')
            .attr('width', width)
            .attr('height', height)
            .attr('fill', 'white');
    });
}
```

The code to create the svg element in each div remains the same except for the name of the chart function, shown as follows:

```
d3.select('#chart').selectAll('div.data-item')
    .data(data)
    .enter()
    .append('div')
    .attr('class', 'data-item')
    .call(chart);
```

The barcode chart

A barcode chart displays a series of discrete events in a given time interval, showing the occurrence of each event with a small vertical bar. It uses the position of the bars as the principal visual variable, giving the reader a clear idea of the distribution of events in time. It might have a time axis or it might represent a fixed time interval. As it is a very compact display, a barcode chart can be integrated along with the text in a paragraph or in a table, giving context and allowing parallel comparison. Refer to the following screenshot:

An example of barcode charts in a table

In the previous section, we created an `svg` element using a charting function. In that implementation, the width and height are global variables, and as we all know, global variables are evil. A chart can have dozens of configurable values, and we can't depend on the user to define each one of them properly. To provide default values and encapsulate the chart-related variables, we will create a closure (the `chart` function) and define the variables in its private scope, as follows:

```
// Closure to create a private scope for the charting function.
var barcodeChart = function() {

    // Definition of the chart variables.
    var width = 600,
        height = 30;

    // Charting function.
    function chart(selection) {
        selection.each(function(data) {
            // Bind the dataset to the svg selection.
            var div = d3.select(this),
```

```
            svg = div.selectAll('svg').data([data]);

        // Create the svg element on enter, and append a
        // background rectangle to it.
        svg.enter()
            .append('svg')
            .attr('width', width)
            .attr('height', height)
            .append('rect')
            .attr('width', width)
            .attr('height', height)
            .attr('fill', 'white');
    });
    }

    return chart;
};
```

Note that the `barcodeChart` function returns an instance of the `chart` function, which will be used to create the chart later. Refer to the following code:

```
// The Dataset
var data = ['a', 'b', 'c'];

// Get the charting function.
var barcode = barcodeChart();

// Bind the data array with the data-item div selection, and call
// the barcode function on each div.
d3.select('#chart').selectAll('div.data-item')
    .data(data)
    .enter()
    .append('div')
    .attr('class', 'data-item')
    .call(barcode);
```

Accessor methods

The width and height are attributes of the `chart` function, and the `barcode` function has access to these variables. To allow the user to configure the `chart` attributes, we will add accessor methods to the chart. We will also add a `margin` attribute as follows:

```
var barcodeChart = function() {

    // Chart Variables.Attributes
```

```
var width = 600,
    height = 30,
    margin = {top: 5, right: 5, bottom: 5, left: 5};

function chart(selection) {
    // Chart creation ...
}

// Accessor function for the width
chart.width = function(value) {
    if (!arguments.length) { return width; }
    width = value;
    // Returns the chart to allow method chaining.
    return chart;
};

// Accessor functions for the height and the margin ...

return chart;
};
```

Note that when invoked without arguments, the accessor method will return the variable value. When setting the value, the accessor method will set the value and return the chart. This allows us to call other accessors using method chaining, as follows:

```
// Create and configure the chart.
var barcode = barcodeChart()
    .width(600)
    .height(25);
```

Chart initialization

In the `chart` function, we can use the `call` method to encapsulate the initialization code. We will add the `chart.svgInit` method, which will be in charge of setting the size of the `svg` element, create a container group for the chart, and add the background rectangle as follows:

```
// Initialize the SVG Element

function svgInit(svg) {
    // Set the SVG size
    svg
        .attr('width', width)
```

```
        .attr('height', height);

    // Create and translate the container group
    var g = svg.append('g')
        .attr('class', 'chart-content')
        .attr('transform', 'translate(' + [margin.top,
margin.left] + ')');

    // Add a background rectangle
    g.append('rect')
        .attr('width', width - margin.left - margin.right)
        .attr('height', height - margin.top - margin.bottom)
        .attr('fill', 'white');
};
```

In the chart function, we call the svgInit function that passes the appended svg element. The chart function is more compact. Refer to the following code:

```
function chart(selection) {
    selection.each(function(data) {
        // Bind the dataset to the svg selection.
        var div = d3.select(this),
            svg = div.selectAll('svg').data([data]);

        // Call thesvgInit function on enter.
        svg.enter()
            .append('svg')
            .call(svgInit);
    });
}
```

With the chart structure ready, we can proceed to draw the bars.

Adding data

We will generate a data array by repeatedly adding a random number of seconds to a date. To compute these random number of seconds, we will generate a random variable of exponential distribution. The details about how to generate the random variable are not important; just remember that the randomInterval function returns a random number of seconds as follows:

```
// Compute a random interval using an Exponential Distribution
function randomInterval(avgSeconds) {
    return Math.floor(-Math.log(Math.random()) * 1000 * avgSeconds);
};
```

We will create a function that returns an array with objects that have increasing random dates:

```
// Create or extend an array of increasing dates by adding
// a number of random seconds.
function addData(data, numItems, avgSeconds) {
    // Compute the most recent time in the data array.
    var n = data.length,
        t = (n > 0) ? data[n - 1].date : new Date();

    // Append items with increasing times in the data array.
    for (var k = 0; k < numItems - 1; k += 1) {
        t = new Date(t.getTime() + randomInterval(avgSeconds));
        data.push({date: t});
    }

    return data;
}
```

Invoking the function with an empty array as the first argument will generate the initial data with 150 elements, with an average of 300 seconds between each date:

```
var data = addData([], 150, 300);
```

The structure of the data array will be something like the following code:

```
data = [
    {date: Tue Jan 01 2013 09:48:52 GMT-0600 (PDT)},
    {date: Tue Jan 01 2013 09:49:14 GMT-0600 (PDT)},
    ...
    {date: Tue Jan 01 2013 21:57:31 GMT-0600 (PDT)}
]
```

With the dataset ready, we can modify the `chart` function to draw the bars. First, we compute the horizontal scale, select the container group, and create a selection for the bars. Refer to the following code:

```
function chart(selection) {
    selection.each(function(data) {
        // Creation of the SVG element ...

        // Compute the horizontal scale.
        var xScale = d3.time.scale()
            .domain(d3.extent(data, function(d) { return d.date;
                }))
```

```
        .range([0, width - margin.left - margin.right]);

    // Select the containing group
    var g = svg.select('g.chart-content');

    // Bind the data to the lines selection.
    var bars = g.selectAll('line')
        .data(data, function(d) { return d.date; });

    // Append the bars on the enter selection ...
    });
}
```

Each bar should be associated with a date, so we configure the key function to return the date. We append the line elements on enter and set the initial position and stroke of the bars as follows:

```
// Append the bars on the enter selection
bars.enter().append('line')
    .attr('x1', function(d) { return xScale(d.date); })
    .attr('x2', function(d) { return xScale(d.date); })
    .attr('y1', 0)
    .attr('y2', height - margin.top - margin.bottom)
    .attr('stroke', '#000')
    .attr('stroke-opacity', 0.5);
```

We set the stroke-opacity attribute to 0.5, so we can see the overlapping lines. Finally, the barcode chart has some bars, as shown in the following screenshot:

The first version of the barcode chart

Adding the date accessor function

The current implementation of the chart assumes that the dataset contains objects with the date attribute. This is an inconvenience, because the user could have a data array with the date information in an attribute named time, or the user might need to process other attributes to compute a valid date. We will add a configurable accessor for the date as follows:

```
var barcodeChart = function() {

    // Set the default date accessor function
```

```
    var value = function(d) { return d.date; };

    // chart function ...

    // Accessor for the value function
    chart.value = function(accessorFunction) {
        if (!arguments.length) { return value; }
        value = accessorFunction;
        return chart;
    };

    return chart;
};
```

We need to replace the references to d.date with invocations to the value method in the chart function as follows:

```
function chart(selection) {
    selection.each(function(data) {

    // Creation of the SVG element ...

    // Compute the horizontal scale using the date accessor.
    var xScale = d3.time.scale()
        .domain(d3.extent(data, value))
        .range([0, width - margin.left - margin.right]);
    // ...

    // Bind the data to the bars selection.
    var bars = g.selectAll('line').data(data, value);

    // Create the bars on enter and set their attributes, using
    // the date accessor function.
    bars.enter().append('line')
        .attr('x1', function(d) { return xScale(value(d)); })
        .attr('x2', function(d) { return xScale(value(d)); })
        // set more attributes ...
        .attr('stroke-opacity', 0.5);
```

A user who has the date information in the time attribute can use the chart by setting the value accessor without modifying the chart code or the data array:

```
// This will work if the array of objects with the time attribute.
var barcode = barcodeChart()
    .value(function(d) { return d.time; });
```

A barcode chart must represent a fixed time interval, but right now, the chart shows all the bars. We would like to remove the bars that are older than a certain time interval. We will then add the `timeInterval` variable:

```
// Default time interval.
var timeInterval = d3.time.day;
```

Add the corresponding accessor method:

```
// Time Interval Accessor
chart.timeInterval = function(value) {
    if (!arguments.length) { return timeInterval; }
    timeInterval = value;
    return chart;
};
```

Then, update the horizontal scale in the `chart` function:

```
// Compute the first and last dates of the time interval
var lastDate = d3.max(data, value),
    firstDate = timeInterval.offset(lastDate, -1);

// Compute the horizontal scale with the correct domain
var xScale = d3.time.scale()
    .domain([firstDate, lastDate])
    .range([0, width - margin.left - margin.right]);
```

The chart width represents the default time interval, and the user can set the time interval by using the `timeInterval` accessor method:

```
var barcode = barcodeChart()
    .timeInterval(d3.time.day);
```

The barcode chart length represents 24 hours. The dataset contains events covering about 11 hours as shown in the following barcode:

Updating the dataset

In most parts of the applications, the dataset is not static. The application might poll the server every couple of minutes, receive a stream of data items, or update the data on user request. In the case of a barcode chart, the new items will probably have more recent dates than the existing data items. The barcode chart is supposed to display the most recent item at the right-hand side of the chart, moving the old bars to the left-hand side. We can do this by updating the position of the bars as follows:

```
// Create the bars on enter ...

// Update the position of the bars.
bars.transition()
    .duration(300)
    .attr('x1', function(d) { return xScale(value(d)); })
    .attr('x2', function(d) { return xScale(value(d)); });
```

The transitions aren't just to make the chart look pretty; they allow the user to follow the objects as they change. This is called **object constancy**. If we just move the bars instantly, the user might have difficulty understanding what happened with the old bars or realizing whether the chart changed at all. We will add a button to add items to the dataset in the page as follows:

```
<button id="btn-update">Add data</button>
<div class="chart-example" id="chart"></div>
```

We can use D3 to configure the callback for the click event of the button. The callback function will add 30 new items to the dataset (with 180 seconds between them on an average) and rebind the selection to the updated dataset as follows:

```
d3.select('#btn-update')
    .on('click', function() {
        // Add more random data to the dataset.
        data = addData(data, 30, 3 * 60);
        // Rebind the data-item selection with the updated dataset.
        d3.select('#chart').selectAll('div.data-item')
            .data([data])
            .call(barcode);
    });
```

Fixing the enter and exit transitions

If we click on the button a couple of times, we will see the new bars appear suddenly, and then, the existing bars shifting to the left-hand side. We would expect the new bars to enter by the right-hand side, moving all the bars together to the left-hand side. This can be achieved by adding the new bars using xScale as it was before adding the new elements and then updating the position of all the bars at the same time.

This strategy will work, except that we didn't store the previous state of xScale. We do, however, have access to the data before appending the new elements. We can access the data bounded to the selection of lines as follows:

```
// Select the chart group and the lines in that group
var g = svg.select('g.chart-content'),
    lines = g.selectAll('line');
```

The first time we use the chart, the lines selection will be empty; in this case, we need to use the most recent item of the data array to compute the last date. If the selection isn't empty, we can use the previous most recent date. We can use the selection.empty method to check whether or not the chart contains bars as follows:

```
// Compute the most recent date from the dataset.
var lastDate = d3.max(data, value);

// Replace the lastDate with the most recent date of the
// dataset before the update, if the selection is not empty.
lastDate = lines.empty() ? lastDate : d3.max(lines.data(), value);

// Compute the date of the lastDate minus the time interval.
var firstDate = timeInterval.offset(lastDate, -1);

// Compute the horizontal scale with the new extent.
var xScale = d3.time.scale()
    .domain([firstDate, lastDate])
    .range([0, width - margin.left - margin.right]);
```

We can bind the data now, and we can create the new bars and set their position with the old scale:

```
// Select the lines and bind the new dataset to it.
var bars = g.selectAll('line').data(data, value);

// Create the bars on enter
bars.enter().append('line')
    .attr('x1', function(d) { return xScale(value(d)); })
    // set more attributes ...
    .attr('stroke-opacity', 0.5);
```

Once the new bars were appended, we can update the xScale domain to include the most recent items and update the position of all the bars:

```
// Update the scale with the new dataset.
lastDate = d3.max(data, value);
firstDate = timeInterval.offset(lastDate, -1);
xScale.domain([firstDate, lastDate]);

// Update the position of the bars, with the updated scale.
bars.transition()
    .duration(300)
    .attr('x1', function(d) { return xScale(value(d)); })
    .attr('x2', function(d) { return xScale(value(d)); });
```

The last thing to do is to remove the bars that don't have corresponding data items, fading them by changing their stroke opacity to zero:

```
// Remove the bars that don't have corresponding data items.
bars.exit().transition()
    .duration(300)
    .attr('stroke-opacity', 0)
    .remove();
```

A basic version of the barcode chart is now ready. There are some additional attributes of the chart that we might want to configure; a user might want to change the color of the bars, their opacity, the duration of the transitions, or the color of the background rectangle.

Using the barcode chart

In this section, we will use the barcode chart with a more complex dataset and learn how to use the chart that is integrated within a table. Imagine that we have an application that monitors the mention of stocks on Twitter. One element of this fictional application might be a table that displays the aggregated information about the stock's mentions and the barcode chart with the mentions of the last day. We will assume that the data is already loaded on the page. Each data item will have the name of the stock, an array with mentions, and the average of mentions by hour. Refer to the following code:

```
var data = [
    {name: 'AAPL', mentions: [...], byHour: 34.3},
    {name: 'MSFT', mentions: [...], byHour: 11.1},
    {name: 'GOOG', mentions: [...], byHour: 19.2},
    {name: 'NFLX', mentions: [...], byHour:  6.7}
];
```

The `mentions` array will have objects with the `date` attribute. These items can have other attributes as well. We will create the table structure with D3, binding the rows of the table body to the data array. We create the table by binding the `table` element with a single element array as follows:

```
// Create a table element.
var table = d3.select('#chart').selectAll('table')
    .data([data])
    .enter()
    .append('table')
    .attr('class', 'table table-condensed');
```

We append the table head and body:

```
// Append the table head and body to the table.
var tableHead = table.append('thead'),
    tableBody = table.append('tbody');
```

We add three cells in the row header to display the column headers:

```
// Add the table header content.
tableHead.append('tr').selectAll('th')
    .data(['Name', 'Today Mentions', 'mentions/hour'])
    .enter()
    .append('th')
    .text(function(d) { return d; });
```

We append one row to the table body for each element in the data array:

```
// Add the table body rows.
var rows = tableBody.selectAll('tr')
    .data(data)
    .enter()
    .append('tr');
```

For each row, we need to add three cells, one with the stock name, one with the barcode chart, and the last one with the hourly average of mentions. To add the name, we simply add a cell and set the text:

```
// Add the stock name cell.
rows.append('td')
    .text(function(d) { return d.name; });
```

Now, we add a cell with the chart. The data item bound to the row is not an array with dates, so we can't call the barcode function directly. Using the `datum` method, we can bind the data item to the `td` element. Note that this method does not perform a join, and thus, it doesn't have the `enter` and `exit` selections:

```
// Add the barcode chart.
rows.append('td')
    .datum(function(d) { return d.mentions; })
    .call(barcode);
```

The `datum` method receives a data item directly; it doesn't require an array like the `data` method. Finally, we add the last cell with the hourly average of mentions. The content of this cell is a number, so it must be aligned to the right-hand side:

```
// Add the number of mentions by hour, aligned to the right.
rows.append('td').append('p')
    .attr('class', 'pull-right')
    .html(function(d) { return d.byHour; });
```

The barcode charts are integrated in the table, along with other information about the stock mentions as shown in the following screenshot:

The barcode chart, integrated within a table, displaying fictional Twitter mentions of stocks

We used D3 to create a data-bound table with a chart in each row. We could have created the structure and header of the table in the HTML document and bound the data array to the rows in the table body, but we created the entire table with D3, instead.

If the table will be used in more than one page, we can also think of creating the table as a reusable chart, using the structure presented in the previous section. We could even add an attribute and an accessor to set the charting function and use the table chart with a different chart without having to change the code of the table chart.

Creating a layout algorithm

Every chart makes assumptions about the kind and structure of the data that they can display. A scatter plot needs pairs of quantitative values, a bar chart requires categories with a quantitative dimension, and a tree map needs nested objects. To use a chart, the user will need to group, split, or nest the original dataset to fit the chart requirements. Functions that perform these transformations are called **layout algorithms**. D3 already provides a good set of layouts, from the simple pie layout to the more complex force layout. In this section, we will lean how to implement a layout algorithm, and we will use it to create a simple visualization using the barcode dataset.

The radial layout

The array with dates used in the barcode example can be visualized in several ways. The barcode chart represents every data item as a small bar in a time interval. Another useful way to display a series of events is to group them in intervals. The most common among these kind of visualizations is a bar chart, with one bar for each time interval and the height of each bar representing the number of events that occurred in the corresponding time interval.

A **radial chart** is a circular arrangement of arc segments, each one representing a category. In this chart, each arc has the same angle, and the area of each arc is proportional to the number of items in the category. We will create a radial layout that groups and counts the events in hourly segments and compute the start and end angles for each arc.

The purpose of a layout algorithm is to allow the user to easily transform its dataset to the format required by a chart. The layout usually allows a certain amount of customization. We will implement the layout function as a closure with accessors to configure the layout behavior as follows:

```
var radialLayout = function() {

    // Layout algorithm.
    function layout(data) {
        var grouped = [];
        // Transform and returns the grouped data ...
        return grouped;
    }
    return layout;
};
```

The usage of a layout is similar to the usage of the barcode chart. First, we invoke `RadialLayout` to get the layout function and then call the layout with the dataset as the argument in order to obtain the output dataset. We will generate an array of random dates using the `addData` function from the previous section:

```
// Generate a dataset with random dates.
var data = addData([], 300, 20 * 60);

// Get the layout function.
var layout = radialLayout();

// Compute the ouput data.
var output = layout(data);
```

We need the layout to group and count the data items for each hour and to compute the start and end angles for each arc. To make the counting process easier, we will use a map to temporarily store the output items. D3 includes `d3.map`, a dictionary-like structure that provides key-value storage:

```
function layout(data) {
    // Create a map to store the data for each hour.
    var hours = d3.range(0, 24),
        gmap = d3.map(),
        groups = [];

    // Append a data item for each hour.
    hours.forEach(function(h) {
        gmap.set(h, {hour: h, startAngle: 0, endAngle: 0, count: 0});
    });

    // ...

    // Copy the values of the map and sort the output data array.
    groups = gmap.values();
    groups.sort(function(a, b) { return a.hour > b.hour ? 1 : -1; });
    return groups;
}
```

As the layout must return an array, we will need to transfer the map values to the grouped array and sort it to return it as the output. The output items don't have any useful information yet:

```
[
    {hour:  0, startAngle: 0, endAngle: 0, count: 0},
    ...
    {hour: 23, startAngle: 0, endAngle: 0, count: 0}
]
```

The next thing to do is to count the items that belong to each hour. To do this, we iterate through the input data and compute the hour of the date attribute:

```
// Count the items belonging to each hour
data.forEach(function(d) {
    // Get the hour from the date attribute of each data item.
    var hour = d.date.getHours();

    // Get the output data item corresponding to the item
      hour.
    var val = gmap.get(hour);

    // We increment the count and set the value in the map.
    val.count += 1;
    gmap.set(hour, val);
});
```

At this point, the output contains the count attribute with the correct value. As we did in the barcode chart, we will add a configurable accessor function to retrieve the date attribute:

```
var radialLayout = function() {
    // Default date accessor
    var value = function(d) { return d.date; }

    function layout(data) {
        // Content of the layout function ...
    }

    // Date Accessor Function
    layout.value = function(accessorFunction) {
        if (!arguments.length) { return value; }
        value = accessorFunction;
        return layout;
    };
};
```

In the layout function, we replace the references to `d.date` with invocations to the date accessor method, `value(d)`. The user now can configure the date accessor function with the same syntax as that in the barcode chart:

```
// Create and configure an instance of the layout function.
var layout = radialLayout()
    .value(function(d) { return d.date; });
```

Computing the angles

With the `count` attribute ready, we can proceed to compute the start and end angles for each output item. The angle for each arc will be the the same, so we can compute `itemAngle` and then iterate through the `hours` array as follows:

```
// Compute equal angles for each hour item.
var itemAngle = 2 * Math.PI / 24;

// Adds a data item for each hour.
hours.forEach(function(h) {
    gmap.set(h, {
        hour: h,
        startAngle: h * itemAngle,
        endAngle: (h + 1) * itemAngle,
        count: 0
    });
});
```

The output dataset now has the start and end angles set. Note that each data item has a value that is 1/24th of the circumference:

```
[
    {hour:  0, startAngle: 0,      endAngle: 0.2618, count:  7},
    {hour:  1, startAngle: 0.2618, endAngle: 0.5236, count: 14},
    ...
    {hour: 23, startAngle: 6.0214, endAngle: 6.2832, count: 17}
]
```

Here, we used the entire circumference, but a user might want to use a semicircle or want to start in a different angle. We will add the `startAngle` and `endAngle` attributes and the `angleExtent` accessor method in order to allow the user to set the angle extent of the chart:

```
var radialLayout = function() {

    // Default values for the angle extent.
    var startAngle = 0,
```

```
        endAngle = 2 * Math.PI;

    // Layout function ...

    // Angle Extent
    layout.angleExtent = function(value) {
        if (!arguments.length) { return value; }
        startAngle = value[0];
        endAngle = value[1];
        return layout;
    };
};
```

We need to change the `itemAngle` variable in order to use the new angle range. Also, we add the layout start angle to the start and end angles for each output item:

```
// Angle for each hour item.
var itemAngle = (endAngle - startAngle) / 24;

// Append a data item for each hour.
hours.forEach(function(h) {
    gmap.set(h, {
        hour: h,
        startAngle: startAngle + h * itemAngle,
        endAngle: startAngle + (h + 1) * itemAngle,
        count: 0
    });
});
```

We can configure the start and end angles of the layout to use a fraction of the circumference:

```
// Create and configure the layout function.
var layout = radialLayout()
    .angleExtent([Math.PI / 3, 2 * Math.PI / 3]);
```

In this section, we implemented a simple layout algorithm that counts and groups an array of events in hours and computes the start and end angles to display the returned value as a radial chart. As we did in the barcode chart example, we implemented the layout as a closure with getter and setter methods.

Using the layout

In this section, we will use the radial layout to create a radial chart. To keep the code simple, we will create the visualization without creating a `chart` function. We begin by creating a container for the radial chart:

```
<div class="chart-example" id="radial-chart"></div>
```

We define the visualization variables and append the svg element to the container. We append a group and translate it to the center of the svg element:

```
// Visualization Variables
var width = 400,
    height = 200,
    innerRadius = 30,
    outerRadius = 100;

// Append a svg element to the div and set its size.
var svg = d3.select('#radial-chart').append('svg')
    .attr('width', width)
    .attr('height', height);

// Create the group and translate it to the center.
var g = svg.append('g')
    .attr('transform', 'translate(' + [width / 2, height / 2] + ')');
```

We represent each hour as an arc. To compute the arcs, we need to create a radius scale:

```
// Compute the radius scale.
var rScale = d3.scale.sqrt()
    .domain([0, d3.max(output, function(d) { return d.count; })])
    .range([2, outerRadius - innerRadius]);
```

As we have the angles and the radius, we can configure the d3.svg.arc generator to create the arc paths for us. The arc generator will use the startAngle and endAngle attributes to create the arc path:

```
// Create an arc generator.
var arc = d3.svg.arc()
    .innerRadius(innerRadius)
    .outerRadius(function(d) {
        return innerRadius +    rScale(d.count);
    });
```

The arc function receives objects with `startAngle`, `endAngle`, and `count` attributes and returns the path string that represents the arc. Finally, we select the path objects in the container group, bind the data, and append the paths:

```
// Append the paths to the group.
g.selectAll('path')
    .data(output)
    .enter()
    .append('path')
        .attr('d', function(d) { return arc(d); })
        .attr('fill', 'grey')
        .attr('stroke', 'white')
        .attr('stroke-width', 1);
```

The radial chart represents the number of items in each hour as radial arcs. Refer to the following screenshot:

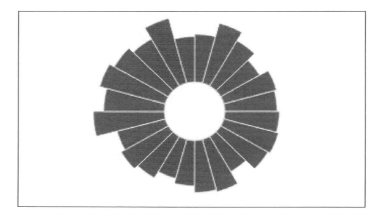

We have shown you how to use the radial layout to create a simple visualization. As we mentioned previously, the layout can be used to create other charts as well. For instance, if we ignore the start and end angles, we can use the radial layout to create a bar chart or even use the output data to create a table with the data aggregated by hour.

Summary

In this chapter, we learned how to create a reusable chart and how to add configuration methods to it so that the chart can be used in several projects without having to change its code in order to use it. We created a barcode chart and used it with data with a different format. We also learned how to create a reusable layout algorithm and how to use it to transform the data source to the format expected by a chart.

In the next chapter, we will learn how to create data visualizations in D3 for browsers without SVG support using canvas and div elements.

3
Creating Visualizations without SVG

Most of the visualizations created with D3 use the SVG element. SVG graphics are resolution independent, which means that they can be scaled without pixelation, and they are relatively easy to create with D3. The SVG elements are also part of the DOM tree and allow us to select and manipulate individual elements of the figures and to change their attributes, triggering an automatic update by the browser.

There are a significant number of users who don't use a browser with SVG support, and sometimes, we can't just forget them. In this chapter, we will examine alternatives that provide visualizations without using SVG. We will create a visualization using only the div elements, discuss libraries that provide SVG support for older browsers, and show an example of integrating D3 and the canvas element.

SVG support in the browser market

The global browser market has a good support for SVG, both in mobile and desktop browsers. There is, however, a significant portion of users who don't enjoy SVG support; the most notable examples are the users of Internet Explorer 8.0 and older as well as users of the stock browser of Android under 3.0.

According to `http://caniuse.com/`, about 86 percent of the global browser market has basic SVG support (as of May 2014). Most of the applications can't afford to leave 14 percent of their users behind. With these users in mind, we will learn how to create data visualizations without using SVG and how to add SVG support to the browser using polyfilling. You can check a more up-to-date version of this and other tables on *Can I use...* (`http://caniuse.com/#feat=svg`).

Visualizations without SVG

In this section, we will create a visualization without using SVG. We will create a bubble chart to show the usage of browser versions in the browser market. A circle will represent each browser version; the area of the circle will be proportional to the global browser usage. Each browser will be assigned a different color. We will use the force layout to group the bubbles on the screen. To follow the examples, open the `chapter03/01-bubble-chart.html` file.

Loading and sorting the data

To make the processing easier, the browser market data was arranged in a JSON file. The main object will have a name that describes the dataset and an array that will contain the data for each browser version. Refer to the following code:

```
{
  "name": "Browser Market",
  "values": [
    {
      "name": "Internet Explorer",
      "version": 8,
      "platform": "desktop",
      "usage": 8.31,
      "current": "false"
    },
    // more items ...
  ]
}
```

We will use the `d3.json` method to load the JSON data. The `d3.json` method creates an asynchronous request to the specified URL and invokes the callback argument when the file is loaded or when the request fails. The callback function receives an error (if any) and the parsed data. There are similar methods to load text, CSV, TSV, XML, and HTML files. Refer to the following code:

```
<script>
    // Load the data asynchronously.
    d3.json('/chapter03/browsers.json', function(error, data) {

    // Handle errors getting or parsing the JSON data.
    if (error) {
        console.error('Error accessing or parsing the JSON file.');
```

```
        return error;
    }

    // visualization code ...

});
</script>
```

Note that the callback function will be invoked only when the data is loaded. This means that the code after the d3.json invocation will be executed while the request is being made, and the data won't be available at this point. The visualization code should go either inside the callback or somewhere else and should use events to notify the charting code that the data is ready. For now, we will add the rendering code inside the callback.

We will create the circles with the div elements. To avoid the smaller elements being hidden by the bigger elements, we will sort the items and create the elements in decreasing usage order, as follows:

```
// Access the data items.
var items = data.values;

// Sort the items by decreasing usage.
items.sort(function(a, b) { return b.usage-a.usage; });
```

The `Array.prototype.sort` instance method sorts the array in place using a comparator function. The comparator should receive two array items: a and b. If a must go before b in the sorted array, the comparator function must return a negative number; if b should go first, the comparator function must return a positive value.

The force layout method

The force layout is a method to distribute elements in a given area, which avoids overlap between the elements and keeps them in the drawing area. The position of the elements is computed based on simple constraints, such as adding a repulsive force between the elements and an attractive force that pulls the elements towards the center of the figure. The force layout is specially useful to create bubble and network charts.

Although the layout doesn't enforce any visual representation, it's commonly used to create network charts, displaying the nodes as circles and the links as lines between the nodes. We will use the force layout to compute the position of the circles, without lines between them, as follows:

```
// Size of the visualization container.
var width = 700,
    height = 200;

// Configure the force layout.
var force = d3.layout.force()
    .nodes(items)
    .links([])
    .size([width, height]);
```

As we don't intend to represent the relationships between the browser versions, we will set the links attribute to an empty array. To start the force computation, we invoke the start method as follows:

```
// Start the force simulation.
force.start();
```

The force layout will append additional properties to our data items. Of these new attributes, we will use only the x and y attributes, which contain the computed position for each node. Note that the original data items shouldn't have names that conflict with these new attributes:

```
{
    "name": "Android Browser",
    "version": 3,
    "platform": "mobile",
    "usage": 0.01,
    "current": "false",
    "index": 0,
    "weight": 0,
    "x": 522.7463498711586,
    "y": 65.54744869936258,
    "px": 522.7463498711586,
    "py": 65.54744869936258
}
```

Having computed the position of the circles, we can proceed to draw them. As we promised not to use SVG, we will need to use other elements to represent our circles. One option is to use the div elements. There are several ways to specify the position of divs, but we will use **absolute positioning**.

A block element styled with absolute positioning can be positioned by setting its `top` and `left` offset properties (the bottom and right offsets can be specified as well). The offsets will be relative to their closest positioned ancestors in the DOM tree. If none of its ancestors are positioned, the offset will be relative to the viewport (or the `body` element, depending on the browser). We will use a positioned container div and then set the position of the divs to `absolute`. The container element will be the div with the `#chart` ID. We will select this to modify its style to use the relative position and set its `width` and `height` to appropriate values, as follows:

```
<!-- Container div -->
<div id="chart"></div>
```

We will also set `padding` to `0` so that we don't have to account for it in the computation of the inner element positions. Note that in order to specify the style attributes that represent length, we need to specify the units, except when the length is zero, as follows:

```
// Select the container div and configure its attributes
var containerDiv = d3.select('#chart')
    .style('position', 'relative')
    .style('width', width + 'px')
    .style('height', height + 'px')
    .style('padding', 0)
    .style('background-color', '#eeeeec');
```

We can now create the inner divs. As usual, we will select the elements to be created, bind the data array to the selection, and append the new elements on enter. We will also set the style attributes to use absolute positioning, and set their offsets and their `width` and `height` to `10px` as follows:

```
// Create a selection for the bubble divs, bind the data
// array and set its attributes.
var bubbleDivs = containerDiv.selectAll('div.bubble')
    .data(items)
    .enter()
    .append('div')
    .attr('class', 'bubble')
    .style('position', 'absolute')
    .style('width', '10px')
    .style('height', '10px')
    .style('background-color', '#222');
```

The force layout will compute the position of the nodes in a series of steps or ticks. We can register a **listener** function to be invoked on each tick event and update the position of the nodes in the listener as follows:

```
// Register a listener function for the force tick event, and
// update the position of each div on tick.
force.on('tick', function() {
    bubbleDiv
        .style('top', function(d) { return (d.y - 5) + 'px'; })
        .style('left', function(d) { return (d.x - 5)+ 'px';
            });
});
```

The divs will move nicely to their positions. Note that we subtract half of the div width and height when setting the offset. The divs will be centered in the position computed by the force layout as shown in the following screenshot:

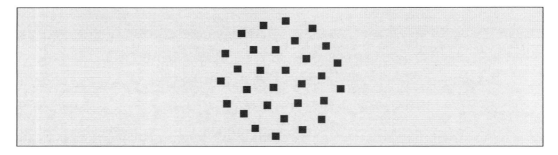

The nodes are nicely positioned, but they all have the same size and color

Setting the color and size

Now that we have our nodes positioned, we can set the color and size of the div elements. To create a color scale for the nodes, we need to get a list with unique browser names. In our dataset, the items are browser versions; therefore, most of the browser names are repeated. We will use the d3.set function to create a set and use it to discard duplicated names, as follows:

```
// Compute unique browser names.
var browserList = items.map(function(d) { return d.name; }),
    browserNames = d3.set(browserList).values();
```

With the browser list ready, we can create a categorical color scale. Categorical scales are used to represent values that are different in kind; in our case, each browser will have a corresponding color:

```
// Create a categorical color scale with 10 levels.
var cScale = d3.scale.category10()
    .domain(browserNames);
```

The default range of `d3.scale.category10` is a set of 10 colors with similar lightness but different hue, specifically designed to represent categorical data. We could use a different set of colors, but the default range is a good starting point. If we had more than 10 browsers, we would need to use a color scale with more colors. We will also set the `border-radius` style attribute to half the `height` (and `width`) of the div in order to give the divs a circular appearance. Note that the `border-radius` attribute is not supported in all the browsers but has better support than SVG. In browsers that don't support this attribute, the divs will be shown as squares:

```
// Create a selection for the bubble divs, bind the data
// array and set its attributes.
var bubbleDivs = containerDiv.selectAll('div.bubble')
    .data(items)
    .enter()
    .append('div')
    // set other attributes ...
    .style('border-radius', '5px')
    .style('background-color', function(d) {
        return cScale(d.name);
    });
```

We can now compute the size of the circles. To provide an accurate visual representation, the area of the circles should be proportional to the quantitative dimensions that they represent, in our case, the market share of each version. As the area of a circle is proportional to the square of the radius, the radius of the circles must be proportional to the square root of the market share. We set the minimum and maximum radius values and use this extent to create the scale:

```
// Minimum and maximum radius
var radiusExtent = [10, 50];

// create the layout ...

// Create the radius scale
var rScale = d3.scale.sqrt()
    .domain(d3.extent(items, function(d) { return d.usage; }))
    .range(radiusExtent);
```

We will use the radius to compute the width, height, position, and border radius of each circle. To avoid calling the `scale` function several times (and to have cleaner code), we will add the radius as a new attribute of our data items:

```
// Add the radius to each item, to compute it only once.
items.forEach(function(d) {
    d.r = rScale(d.usage);
});
```

We can modify the width, height, and border radius of the divs to use the new attribute, as follows:

```
// Create the bubble divs.
var bubbleDivs = containerDiv.selectAll('div.bubble')
    .data(items)
    .enter()
    .append('div')
    // set other attributes ...
    .style('border-radius', function(d) { return d.r + 'px'; })
    .style('width', function(d) { return (2 * d.r) + 'px'; })
    .style('height', function(d) { return (2 * d.r) + 'px'; });
```

We need to update the position of the div elements to account for the new radius:

```
// Update the div position on each tick.
force.on('tick', function() {
    bubbleDiv
        .style('top', function(d) { return (d.y - d.r) + 'px'; })
        .style('left', function(d) { return (d.x - d.r)+ 'px'; });
});
```

The first draft of the visualization is shown in the following screenshot:

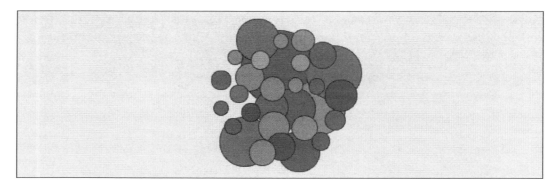

At this point, we have the first draft of our visualization, but there are still some things that need to be improved. The space around each div is the same, regardless of the size of each circle. We expect to have more space around bigger circles and less space around smaller ones. To achieve this, we will modify the `charge` property of the force layout, which controls the strength of repulsion between the nodes.

The `charge` method allows us to set the charge strength of each node. The default value is `-30`; we will use a function to set greater charges for bigger circles. In physical systems, the charge is proportional to the volume of the body; so, we will set the charge to be proportional to the area of each circle as follows:

```
// Configure the force layout.
var force = d3.layout.force()
    .nodes(items)
    .links([])
    .size([width, height])
    .charge(function(d) { return -0.12 * d.r * d.r; })
    .start();
```

We don't know in advance which proportionality constant will give a good layout; we need to tweak this value until we are satisfied with the visual result. Bubbles created with chart with the divs and force layout is shown in the following screenshot:

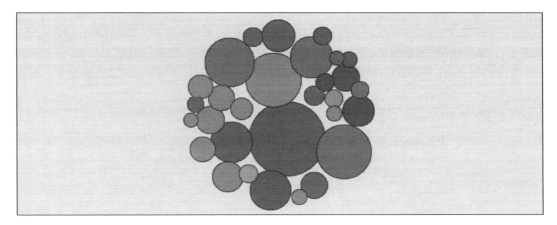

Now that we have a good first version of our visualization, we will adapt the code to use a reusable chart pattern. As you will surely remember, a reusable chart is implemented as a closure with the setter and getter methods as follows:

```
function bubbleChart() {

    // Chart attributes ...

    function chart(selection) {
        selection.each(function(data) {

            // Select the container div and configure its
              attributes.
            var containerDiv = d3.select(this);

            // create the circles ...
        });
    }

    // Accessor methods ...

    return chart;
};
```

The code in the chart function is basically the same code that we have written until now. We also added accessor methods for the color scale, width, height, and radius extent, as well as accessor functions for the value, name, and charge function to allow users to adapt to the repulsion force when using the chart with other datasets. We can create and invoke the charting function in the callback of d3.json as follows:

```
d3.json('../data/browsers.json', function(error, data) {

    // Handle errors getting or parsing the JSON data.
    if (error) { return error; }

    // Create the chart instance.
    var chart = bubbleChart()
        .width(500);

    // Bind the chart div to the data array.
    d3.select('#chart')
        .data([data.values])
        .call(chart);
});
```

The visualization is incomplete without a legend, so we will create a legend now. This time, we will create the legend as a reusable chart from the beginning.

Creating a legend

The legend should display which color represents which browser. It can also have additional information such as the aggregated market share of each browser. We must use the same color code as that used in the visualization:

```
function legendChart() {

// Chart Properties ...

      // Charting function.
    function chart(selection) {
        selection.each(function(data) {

        });
    }

    // Accessor methods ...

    return chart;
};
```

We will implement the legend as a div element that contains paragraphs; each paragraph will have the browser name and a small square painted with the corresponding color. In this case, the data will be a list of browser names. We will add a configurable color scale to make sure that the legend uses the same colors that are used in the bubble chart:

```
function legendChart() {

    // Color Scale
    var cScale = d3.scale.category20();

    // Charting function.
    function chart(selection) {
        // chart content ...
    }

    // Color Scale Accessor
    chart.colorScale = function(value) {
        if (!arguments.length) { return cScale; }
```

```
        cScale = value;
        return chart;
    };

    return chart;
};
```

We can create a div for the legend and put it alongside the chart div as follows:

```
d3.json('/chapter03/browsers.json', function(error, data) {
    // Create an instance of the legend chart.
    var legend = legendChart()
        .colorScale(chart.colorScale());

    // Select the container and invoke the legend.
    var legendDiv = d3.select('#legend')
        .data([chart.colorScale().domain()])
        .call(legend);
});
```

We used the domain of the chart's color scale as the dataset for the legend and set the color scale of the legend with the color scale of the chart. This will ensure that you have the same items and colors in the legend that are in the chart. We also added a `width` attribute and its corresponding accessor. In the legend chart function, we can create the title and the legend items using the data:

```
        // Select the container element and set its attributes.
        var containerDiv = d3.select(this)
            .style('width', width + 'px');

        // Add the label 'Legend' on enter
        containerDiv.selectAll('p.legent-title')
            .data([data])
            .enter().append('p')
            .attr('class', 'legend-title')
            .text('Legend');

        // Add a div for each data item
        var itemDiv = containerDiv.selectAll('div.item')
            .data(data)
            .enter().append('div')
            .attr('class', 'item');
```

We have labels that show up in the legend, but we need to add a marker with the corresponding color. To keep things simple, we will add two points and set them with the same background and text color:

```
itemP.append('span').text('..')
    .style('color', cScale)
    .style('background', cScale);
```

To finish the legend, we will compute the market share of each browser. We will create a map to store each browser name and its aggregated usage, as follows:

```
// Create a map to aggregate the browser usage
var browsers = d3.map();

// Adds up the usage for each browser.
data.values.forEach(function(d) {
    var item = browsers.get(d.name);
    if (item) {
        browsers.set(d.name, {
            name: d.name,
            usage: d.usage + item.usage
        });
    } else {
        browsers.set(d.name, {
            name: d.name,
            usage: d.usage
        });
    }
});
```

The final version of the bubble chart is shown in the following screenshot:

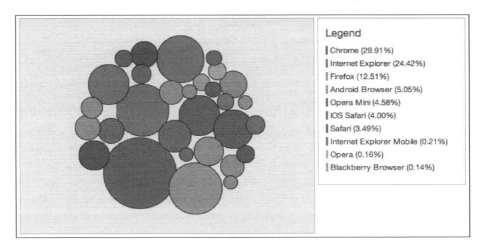

In this example, we created a simple visualization using the div elements and displayed them as circles with the help of the `border-radius` attribute. Using divs with rounded corners is not the only alternative to create this visualization without using SVG; we could have used raster images of circles instead of div elements, using absolute positioning and changing the image width and height.

One great example of a sophisticated visualization made without SVG is the Electoral Map by the New York Times graphic department (`http://elections. nytimes.com/2012/ratings/electoral-map`). In this visualization, the user can create their own scenarios for the presidential elections of 2012 in the United States.

Polyfilling

A **polyfill** is a JavaScript library that replicates an API feature for the browsers that don't have it natively. Usually, a polyfill doesn't add its own API or additional features; it just adds the missing feature.

Polyfills are available for almost every HTML5 and CSS3 feature, but this doesn't mean that we can start adding libraries to provide all the modern features in the web browser. Also, the modern features can conflict with each other, so polyfills must be included carefully. To support SVG in those browsers, the following two polyfills can be used:

- **svgweb**: This provides partial SVG support, falling back to Flash if the browser doesn't support SVG (`https://code.google.com/p/svgweb/`).
- **canvg**: This is an SVG parser written in JavaScript. It parses the SVG element and renders it using a canvas (`https://code.google.com/p/canvg/`).

The first step to use a polyfill is to detect whether a feature is available in the browser or not.

Feature detection

There are several ways to find out whether the browser supports a particular feature. One of them is to get the user agent attribute of the `navigator` global object, but this is highly unreliable because the user can configure the user agent property. Another option is try to use the feature to check whether it has the methods and properties that we expect. However, this method is error prone and depends on the particular feature that we are looking for.

The most reliable way is to use the **Modernizr** library. Despite its name, it doesn't add any modern features to old browsers; it only detects the availability of the HTML5 and CSS3 features. However, it does interact well with the libraries that implement the missing features, providing a script loader to include the libraries in order to fill the gaps. The library can be customized to include the detection of only the features that we need.

The library performs a suite of tests to detect which features are available and which are not, and sets the results of these tests in the Boolean attributes of the global `Modernizr` object, add classes to the HTML object that explains which features are present. The library should be loaded in the header, because the features that we want to add must be available before the `<body>` element:

```
<!-- Include the feature detection library -->
<script src="/assets/js/lib/modernizr-latest.js"></script>
```

To detect the support of SVG in the browser, we can use the `Modernizr.svg` property. We can also use it to properly handle the lack of support:

```
<script>
    // Handle the availability of SVG.
    if (Modernizr.svg) {
        // Create a visualization with SVG.
    } else {
        // Fallback visualization.
    }
</script>
```

The canvg example

We will begin our example by creating an SVG image with D3. In this example, we will create an array of circles in SVG and then display them with canvas using the canvg library. We begin by including the libraries in the header as follows:

```
<!-- Canvg Libraries -->
<script src="/assets/js/lib/rgbcolor.js"></script>
<script src="/assets/js/lib/StackBlur.js"></script>
<script src="/assets/js/lib/canvg.js"></script>
```

For now, we will begin as usual by selecting the container div, appending the SVG element, and setting its width and height:

```
// Set the width and height of the figure.
var width = 600,
    height = 300;

// Select the container div and append the SVG element.
var containerDiv = d3.select('#canvg-demo'),
    svg = containerDiv.append('svg')
        .attr('width', width)
        .attr('height', height);
```

We will generate a data array with one item per circle. We want to have one circle for each 10 pixels. The position of each circle will be given by the x and y attributes. The z attribute will contain a number proportional to both x and y; this number will be used to compute the radius and color scales, as follows:

```
// Generate data for the position and size of the rectangles.
var data = [];
for (var k = 0; k < 60; k += 1) {
    for (var j = 0; j < 30; j += 1) {
        data.push({
            x: 5 + 10 * k,
            y: 5 + 10 * j,
            z: (k - 50) + (20 - j)
        });
    }
}
```

We can create the radius and color scales. Both the scales will use the extent of the z property to set their domains:

```
// Create a radius scale using the z attribute.
var rScale = d3.scale.sqrt()
    .domain(d3.extent(data, function(d) { return d.z; }))
    .range([3, 5]);

// Create a linear color scale using the z attribute.
var cScale = d3.scale.linear()
    .domain(d3.extent(data, function(d) { return d.z; }))
    .range(['#204a87', '#cc0000']);
```

We can now create the circles in the SVG element. We create a selection for the circles to be created, bind the data array, append the circles on enter, and set their attributes:

```
// Select the circle elements, bind the dataset and append
// the circles on enter.
svg.selectAll('circle')
    .data(data)
    .enter()
    .append('circle')
    .attr('cx', function(d) { return d.x; })
    .attr('cy', function(d) { return d.y; })
    .attr('r', function(d) { return rScale(d.z); })
    .attr('fill', function(d) { return cScale(d.z); })
    .attr('fill-opacity', 0.9);
```

Until now, this is a standard D3. In a browser without SVG support, the elements will be created but not rendered. The canvg function interprets the SVG content and draws it with canvas instead. The function receives the canvas target (where we want SVG to be drawn), the SVG string, and an object with options. If it is called without arguments, the function will convert all the SVG elements present on the page. We will use this option as follows:

```
// Replace all the SVG elements by canvas drawings.
canvg();
```

If you inspect the page, you will see that the SVG element is gone, and in its place, there is a canvas element of the same size as the original SVG. The visual result is the same as that without using the canvg polyfill. Note that the event handlers bound to the original SVG elements won't work. For instance, if we added a callback for the click event on the circles, the callback for the event won't be invoked in the canvas version. Using canvg to render an SVG element is shown in the following screenshot:

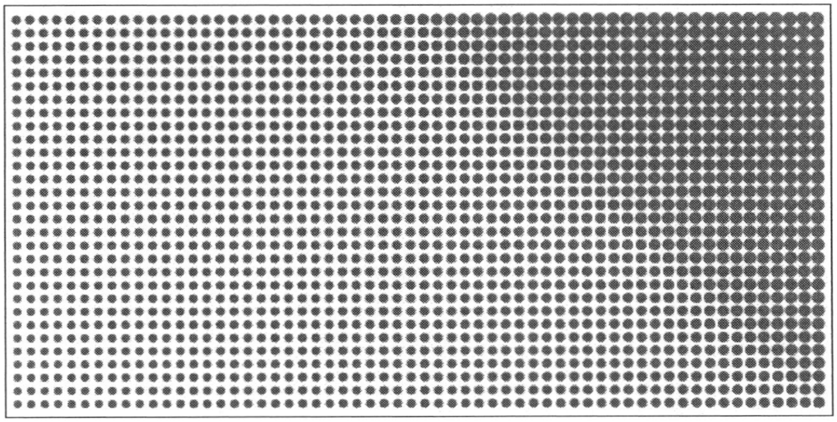

Using canvas and D3

Until now, we have used D3 to create visualizations by manipulating SVG elements and divs. In some cases, it can be more convenient to render the visualizations using the canvas elements, for performance reasons or if we need to transform and render raster images. In this section, we will learn how to create figures with the HTML5 canvas element and how to use D3 to render figures with the canvas element.

Creating figures with canvas

The HTML canvas element allows you to create raster graphics using JavaScript. It was first introduced in HTML5. It enjoys more widespread support than SVG and can be used as a fallback option. Before diving deeper into integrating canvas and D3, we will construct a small example with canvas.

The canvas element should have the `width` and `height` attributes. This alone will create an invisible figure of the specified size:

```
<!- Canvas Element -->
<canvas id="canvas-demo" width="650px" height="60px"></canvas>
```

If the browser supports the canvas element, it will ignore any element inside the canvas tags. On the other hand, if the browser doesn't support the canvas, it will ignore the canvas tags, but it will interpret the content of the element. This behavior provides a quick way to handle the lack of canvas support:

```
<!- Canvas Element -->
<canvas id="canvas-demo" width="650px" height="60px">
<!-- Fallback image -->
<img src="img/fallback-img.png" width="650" height="60"></img>
</canvas>
```

If the browser doesn't support canvas, the fallback image will be displayed. Note that unlike the `<img>` element, the canvas closing tag (`</canvas>`) is mandatory. To create figures with canvas, we don't need special libraries; we can create the shapes using the canvas API:

```
<script>
    // Graphic Variables
    var barw = 65,
        barh = 60;

    // Append a canvas element, set its size and get the node.
```

```
var canvas = document.getElementById('canvas-demo');

// Get the rendering context.
var context = canvas.getContext('2d');

// Array with colors, to have one rectangle of each color.
var color = ['#5c3566', '#6c475b', '#7c584f', '#8c6a44',
    '#9c7c39',
'#ad8d2d', '#bd9f22', '#cdb117', '#ddc20b', '#edd400'];

// Set the fill color and render ten rectangles.
for (var k = 0; k < 10; k += 1) {
    // Set the fill color.
    context.fillStyle = color[k];
    // Create a rectangle in incremental positions.
    context.fillRect(k * barw, 0, barw, barh);
}
</script>
```

We use the DOM API to access the canvas element with the `canvas-demo` ID and to get the **rendering context**. Then, we set the color using the `fillStyle` method and use the `fillRect` canvas method to create a small rectangle. Note that we need to change `fillStyle` every time or all the following shapes will have the same color. The script will render a series of rectangles, each filled with a different color, shown as follows:

A graphic created with canvas

Canvas uses the same coordinate system as SVG, with the origin in the top-left corner, the horizontal axis augmenting to the right, and the vertical axis augmenting to the bottom. Instead of using the DOM API to get the canvas node, we could have used D3 to create the node, set its attributes, and created scales for the color and position of the shapes. Note that the shapes drawn with canvas don't exist in the DOM tree; so, we can't use the usual D3 pattern of creating a selection, binding the data items, and appending the elements if we are using canvas.

Creating shapes

Canvas has fewer primitives than SVG. In fact, almost all the shapes must be drawn with paths, and more steps are needed to create a path. To create a shape, we need to open the path, move the cursor to the desired location, create the shape, and close the path. Then, we can draw the path by filling the shape or rendering the outline. For instance, to draw a red semicircle centered in (325, 30) and with a radius of 20, write the following code:

```
// Create a red semicircle.
context.beginPath();
context.fillStyle = '#ff0000';
context.moveTo(325, 30);
context.arc(325, 30, 20, Math.PI / 2, 3 * Math.PI / 2);
context.fill();
```

The moveTo method is a bit redundant here, because the arc method moves the cursor implicitly. The arguments of the arc method are the x and y coordinates of the arc center, the radius, and the starting and ending angle of the arc. There is also an optional Boolean argument to indicate whether the arc should be drawn counterclockwise. A basic shape created with the canvas API is shown in the following screenshot:

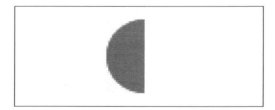

Integrating canvas and D3

We will create a small network chart using the force layout of D3 and canvas instead of SVG. To make the graph look more interesting, we will randomly generate the data. We will generate 250 nodes that are sparsely connected. The nodes and links will be stored as the attributes of the data object:

```
// Number of Nodes
var nNodes = 250,
    createLink = false;

// Dataset Structure
var data = {nodes: [],links: []};
```

We will append nodes and links to our dataset. We will create nodes with a `radius` attribute and randomly assign it a value of either 2 or 4 as follows:

```
// Iterate in the nodes
for (var k = 0; k < nNodes; k += 1) {
    // Create a node with a random radius.
    data.nodes.push({radius: (Math.random() > 0.3) ? 2 : 4});

    // Create random links between the nodes.
}
```

We will create a link with a probability of 0.1 only if the difference between the source and target indexes are less than 8. The idea behind this way to create links is to have only a few connections between the nodes:

```
// Create random links between the nodes.
for (var j = k + 1; j < nNodes; j += 1) {

    // Create a link with probability 0.1
    createLink = (Math.random() < 0.1) && (Math.abs(k - j)
      < 8);

    if (createLink) {
        // Append a link with variable distance between
          the nodes
        data.links.push({
            source: k,
            target: j,
            dist: 2 * Math.abs(k - j) + 10
        });
    }
}
```

We will use the `radius` attribute to set the size of the nodes. The links will contain the distance between the nodes and the indexes of the source and target nodes. We will create variables to set the `width` and `height` of the figure:

```
// Figure width and height
var width = 650,
    height = 300;
```

We can now create and configure the force layout. As we did in the previous section, we will set the charge strength to be proportional to the area of each node. This time we will also set the distance between the links using the `linkDistance` method of the layout:

```
// Create and configure the force layout
var force = d3.layout.force()
    .size([width, height])
    .nodes(data.nodes)
    .links(data.links)
    .charge(function(d) { return -1.2 * d.radius * d.radius; })
    .linkDistance(function(d) { return d.dist; })
    .start();
```

We can create a canvas element now. Note that we should use the `node` method to get the canvas element, because the `append` and `attr` methods will both return a selection, which doesn't have the canvas API methods:

```
// Create a canvas element and set its size.
var canvas = d3.select('div#canvas-force').append('canvas')
    .attr('width', width + 'px')
    .attr('height', height + 'px')
    .node();
```

We get the rendering context. Each canvas element has its own rendering context. We will use the `'2d'` context to draw two-dimensional figures. At the time of writing this, there are some browsers that support the `webgl` context; more details are available at `https://developer.mozilla.org/en-US/docs/Web/WebGL/Getting_started_with_WebGL`. Refer to the following `'2d'` context:

```
// Get the canvas context.
var context = canvas.getContext('2d');
```

We register an event listener for the force layout's tick event. As canvas doesn't remember previously created shapes, we need to clear the figure and redraw all the elements on each tick:

```
force.on('tick', function() {
    // Clear the complete figure.
    context.clearRect(0, 0, width, height);

    // Draw the links ...
    // Draw the nodes ...
});
```

The `clearRect` method cleans the figure under the specified rectangle. In this case, we clean the entire canvas. We can draw the links using the `lineTo` method. We iterate through the links by beginning a new path for each link, by moving the cursor to the position of the source node, and by creating a line towards the target node. We draw the line with the `stroke` method:

```
// Draw the links
data.links.forEach(function(d) {
    // Draw a line from source to target.
    context.beginPath();
    context.moveTo(d.source.x, d.source.y);
    context.lineTo(d.target.x, d.target.y);
    context.stroke();
});
```

We iterate through the nodes and draw each one. We use the arc method to represent each node with a black circle:

```
// Draw the nodes
data.nodes.forEach(function(d, i) {
    // Draws a complete arc for each node.
    context.beginPath();
    context.arc(d.x, d.y, d.radius, 0, 2 * Math.PI, true);
    context.fill();
});
```

We obtain a constellation of disconnected network graphs slowly gravitating towards the center of the figure. Using the force layout and canvas to create a network chart is shown in the following screenshot:

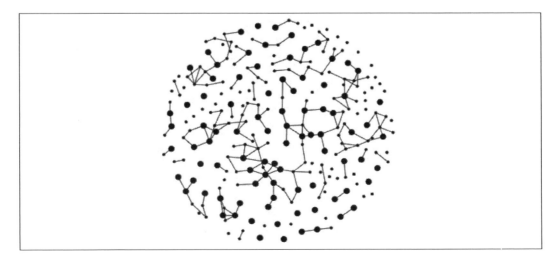

We can think that to erase all the shapes and redraw each shape again and again could have a negative impact on the performance. In fact, sometimes it's faster to draw the figures using canvas, because this way, the browser doesn't have to manage the DOM tree of the SVG elements (but we still have to redraw them if the SVG elements are changed).

Summary

In this chapter, we learned how to handle the lack of SVG support in older browsers. We learned how to create visualizations using only the div elements and how to detect the availability of SVG support. We also discussed how to use polyfills to provide the missing functionality. In particular, we created an example of rendering SVG with canvas using the canvg library.

In the next chapter, we will create a color picker based on the Lab color model. We will learn how to use the drag behavior and use it to create a reusable slider element. Also, we will use the slider to create the color picker.

4
Creating a Color Picker with D3

In this chapter, we will implement a slider and a color picker using D3. We will use the reusable chart pattern to create the slider and the color picker. We will also learn how to compose reusable charts in order to create more complex components.

Creating a slider control

A slider is a control that allows a user to select a value within a given interval without having to type it. It has a handle that can be displaced over a base line; the position of the handler determines the selected value. The value is then used to update other components of the page. In this section, we will create a slider with D3 using the reusable chart pattern. We will include an API to change its visual attributes and modify other elements when the slider value changes. Note that in HTML5, we can create an `input` element of type `range`, which will be displayed as a slider with configurable minimum and maximum steps and values. The type `color` is also available, which allows us to use the native color picker. Native controls include accessibility features and using the keyboard to control the slider. More details on the input element can be found in `https://developer.mozilla.org/en/docs/Web/HTML/Element/Input`. To follow the examples of this section, open the `chapter04/01-slider.html` file.

The final slider component

The drag behavior

We will review how to use the drag behavior with a simple example. We will begin by creating the svg element and put a gray circle in the center:

```
// Width and height of the figure.
var width = 600, height = 150;

// Create the svg element.
var svg = d3.select('#chart').append('svg')
    .attr('width', width)
    .attr('height', height);

// Append a grey circle in the middle.
var circle = svg.append('circle')
    .attr('cx', width / 2)
    .attr('cy', height / 2)
    .attr('r', 30)
    .attr('fill', '#555');
```

This will create the svg and circle elements, but the circle can't be moved yet. D3 allows us to detect gestures on an element by using behaviors, which are functions that create event listeners for gesture events on a container element. To detect the drag gesture, we can use the drag behavior. The drag behavior detects dragging events of three types, `dragstart`, `drag`, and `dragend`. We can create and configure the drag behavior by adding event listeners for one or more drag events; in our case, we will add a listener for the drag event as follows:

```
// Create and configure a drag behavior.
var drag = d3.behavior.drag().on('drag', dragListener);
```

For more details on the D3 drag behavior, consult the D3 wiki page on this subject at `https://github.com/mbostock/d3/wiki/Drag-Behavior`. To add the drag behavior to the circle, we can call the `drag` function, passing the circle selection to it or using the `call` method as follows:

```
// Add dragging handling to the circle.
circle.call(drag);
```

When the user drags the circle, the `dragListener` function will be invoked. The `dragListener` function receives the data item bound to the circle (if any), with the `this` context set to the container element, in our case, the circle element. In the `dragListener` function, we will update the position of the circle. Note that the `cx` and `cy` attributes are returned as strings, and prepending a plus sign will cast these values to numbers. Refer to the following code:

```
// Moves the circle on drag.
function dragListener(d) {
```

```
    // Get the current position of the circle
    var cx = +d3.select(this).attr('cx'),
        cy = +d3.select(this).attr('cy');

    // Set the new position of the circle.
    d3.select(this)
        .attr('cx', cx + d3.event.dx)
        .attr('cy', cy + d3.event.dy);
}
```

The `dragListener` function updates the `cx` and `cy` attributes of the circle, but it can change other attributes as well. It can even change properties of other elements. In the next section, we will use the drag behavior to create a simple SVG slider.

Creating the slider

The slider component will have a configurable width, domain, and a listener function to be called on the slide. To use the slider, attach it to an svg group. As the group can be translated, rotated, and scaled, the same slider can be displayed horizontally, vertically, or even diagonally anywhere inside the SVG element. We will implement the slider using the reusable chart pattern:

```
function sliderControl() {
    // Slider Attributes...

    // Charting function.
    function chart(selection) {
        selection.each(function(data) {
            // Create the slider elements...
        });
    }

    // Accessor Methods...

    return chart;
}
```

We will add attributes for `width` and `domain`, as well as their corresponding accessor methods, `chart.width` and `chart.domain`. Remember that the accessor methods should return the current value if they are invoked without arguments and return the `chart` function if a value is passed as an argument:

```
function chart(selection) {
    selection.each(function(data) {
        // Select the container group.
```

```
        var group = d3.select(this);

        // Create the slider content...
    });
}
```

We will assume that the slider is created within an svg group, but we could have detected the type of the container element and handle each case. If it were a div, for instance, we could append an svg element and then append a group to it. We will work with the group to keep things simple. We will create the base line using the svg line element:

```
// Add a line covering the complete width.
group.selectAll('line')
    .data([data])
    .enter().append('line')
    .call(chart.initLine);
```

We encapsulate the creation of the line in the `chart.initLine` method. This function will receive a selection that contains the created line and sets its position and other attributes:

```
// Set the initial attributes of the line.
chart.initLine = function(selection) {
    selection
        .attr('x1', 2)
        .attr('x2', width - 4)
        .attr('stroke', '#777)
        .attr('stroke-width', 4)
        .attr('stroke-linecap', 'round');
};
```

We set the x1 and x2 coordinates of the line. The default value for the coordinates is zero, so we don't need to define the y1 and y2 coordinates. The `stroke-linecap` attribute will make the ends of the line rounded, but we will need to adjust the x1 and x2 attributes to show the rounded corners. With a stroke width of 4 pixels, the radius of the corner will be 2 pixels, which will be added in each edge of the line. We will create a circle in the group in the same way:

```
// Append a circle as handler.
var handle = group.selectAll('circle')
    .data([data])
    .enter().append('circle')
    .call(chart.initHandle);
```

The `initHandle` method will set the radius, fill color, stroke, and position of the circle. The complete code of the function is available in the example file. We will create a scale to map the value of the slider to the position of the circle:

```
// Set the position scale.
var posScale = d3.scale.linear()
    .domain(domain)
    .range([0, width]);
```

We correct the position of the circle, so its position represents the initial value of the slider:

```
// Set the position of the circle.
handle
    .attr('cx', function(d) { return posScale(d); });
```

We have created the slider base line and handler, but the handle can't be moved yet. We need to add the drag behavior to the circle:

```
// Create and configure the drag behavior.
var drag = d3.behavior.drag().on('drag', moveHandler);

// Adds the drag behavior to the handler.
handler.call(drag);
```

The `moveHandler` listener will update only the horizontal position of the circle, keeping the circle within the slider limits. We need to bind the value that we are selecting to the handle (the circle), but the `cx` attribute will give us the position of the handle in pixels. We will use the `invert` method to compute the selected value and rebind this value to the circle so that it's available in the caller function:

```
function moveHandle(d) {
    // Compute the future position of the handler
    var cx = +d3.select(this).attr('cx') + d3.event.dx;

    // Update the position if it's within its valid range.
    if ((0 < cx) && (cx < width)) {
        // Compute the new value and rebind the data
        d3.select(this).data([posScale.invert(cx)])
            .attr('cx', cx);
    }
}
```

To use the slider, we will append an SVG figure to the container div and set its `width` and `height`:

```
// Figure properties.
var width = 600, height = 60, margin = 20;

// Create the svg element and set its dimensions.
var svg = d3.select('#chart').append('svg')
    .attr('width', width + 2 * margin)
    .attr('height', height + 2 * margin);
```

We can now create the `slider` function, setting its `width` and `domain`:

```
// Valid range and initial value.
var value = 70, domain = [0, 100];

// Create and configure the slider control.
var slider = sliderControl().width(width).domain(domain);
```

We create a selection for the container group, bind the data array that contains the initial value, and append the group on `enter`. We also translate the group to the location where we want the slider and invoke the `slider` function using the `call` method:

```
var gSlider = svg.selectAll('g')
    .data([value])
    .enter().append('g')
    .attr('transform', 'translate(' + [margin, height / 2] + ')')
    .call(slider);
```

We have translated the container group to have a margin, and we have centered it vertically. The slider is now functional, but it doesn't update other components or communicate changes in its value. Refer to the following screenshot:

The slider appended to an SVG group

We will add a user-configurable function that will be invoked when the user moves the handler, along with its corresponding accessor function, so that the user can define what should happen when the slider is changed:

```
function sliderControl() {
    // Slider attributes...

    // Default slider callback.
    var onSlide = function(selection) { };

    // Charting function...
    function chart() {...}

    // Accessor Methods
    // Slide callback function
    chart.onSlide = function(onSlideFunction) {
        if (!arguments.length) { return onSlide; }
        onSlide = onSlideFunction;
        return chart;
    };

    return chart;
}
```

The onSlide function will be called on the drag listener function, passing the handler selection as an argument. This way, the value of the slider will be passed to the onSlide function as the bound data item of the selection argument:

```
function moveHandler(d) {

    // Compute the new position of the handler
    var cx = +d3.select(this).attr('cx') + d3.event.dx;

    // Update the position within its valid range.
    if ((0 < cx) && (cx < width)) {
        // Compute the new value and rebind the data
        d3.select(this).data([posScale.invert(cx)])
            .attr('cx', cx)
            .call(onSlide);
    }
}
```

Remember that the onSlide function should receive a selection, and through the selection, it should receive the value of the slider. We will use the onSlide function to change the color of a rectangle.

Using the slider

We use the slider to change the color of a rectangle. We begin by creating the svg element, setting its `width`, `height`, and `margin`:

```
// Create the svg element
var svg = d3.select('#chart').append('svg')
    .attr('width', width + 2 * margin)
    .attr('height', height + 3 * margin);
```

We create a linear color scale; its range will be the colors yellow and red. The domain of the scale will be the same as that in the slider:

```
// Create a color scale with the same range that the slider
var cScale = d3.scale.linear()
    .domain(domain)
    .range(['#edd400', '#a40000']);
```

We add a rectangle in the svg, reserving some space in its upper side to put the slider on top. We also set its width, height, and fill color:

```
// Add a background to the svg element.
var rectangle = svg.append('rect')
    .attr('x', margin)
    .attr('y', 2 * margin)
    .attr('width', width)
    .attr('height', height)
    .attr('fill', cScale(value));
```

We create the slider control and configure its attributes. The `onSlide` function will change the rectangle fill color using the previously defined scale:

```
// Create and configure the slider control.
var slider = sliderControl()
    .domain(domain)
    .width(width)
    .onSlide(function(selection) {
        selection.each(function(d) {
            rectangle.attr('fill', cScale(d));
        });
    });
```

Finally, we append a group to contain the slider and translate it to put it above the rectangle. We invoke the `slider` function using the `call` method:

```
// Create a group to hold the slider and add the slider to it.
var gSlider = svg.selectAll('g').data([value])
    .enter().append('g')
    .attr('transform', 'translate(' + [margin, margin] + ')')
    .call(slider);
```

Refer to the following screenshot:

The fill color of the rectangle is controlled by the slider

Creating a color picker

We will implement a color picker using the slider from the previous section. A color picker is a UI control that allows the user to select a color. Usually, the color picker is shown as a small, colored rectangle, and when the user clicks on it, a window is opened with controls to change the color. To follow the code snippets, open the `chapter04/02-color-picker.html` file. Refer to the following screenshot:

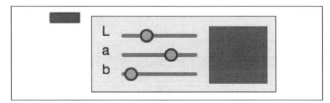

The color picker selector and window that uses the sliders from the previous section

We will implement the color picker using the reusable chart pattern. This will allow us to modularize the components in two parts, the color picker selector and the color picker window. We begin by creating the color picker selector.

The color picker selector

The control element will be shown as a small rectangle. When the user clicks on the rectangle, the color picker will appear, and clicking on the control again will set the value. We will create a color picker using the CIELAB 1976 color model, which is informally known as Lab. In this model, *L* is for lightness, and the *a* and *b* parameters represent colors. This color model aims to be more perceptually uniform than other models, which means that changes in the color value are perceived as changes of about the same visual importance. We create the structure of the color picker using the reusable chart pattern as follows:

```
function labColorPicker() {

    // Selector Attributes

    // Selector shape
    var width = 30,
        height = 10;

    // Default Color
    var color = d3.lab(100, 0, 0);

    // Charting function
    function chart(selection) {
        selection.each(function() {
            // Creation of the color picker...
        });
    }

    // Width and height accessor methods...

    // Color Accessor
    chart.color = function(value) {
        if (!arguments.length) { return color; }
        color = d3.lab(value);
        return chart;
    };

    return chart;
}
```

The `chart.color` method receives a color in any format that can be converted by
`d3.lab` and returns the picker color as a `d3.lab` object with the current color of the
picker. We can also add accessors for the width and height (not shown for brevity).
To use the color picker, we need to create a container group for it and use the `call`
method to create the color selector:

```
// Create the svg figure...

// Create the color picker and set the initial color
var picker = labColorPicker().color('#a40000');

// Create a group for the color picker and translate it.
var grp = svg.append('g')
    .attr('transform', 'translate(' + [offset, offset] + ')')
    .call(picker);
```

We will translate the group to add a margin between the color picker selector and
the surrounding elements. In the charting function, we will create a selection with a
rectangle, bind the current color to that selection, and create the rectangle on `enter`:

```
function chart(selection) {
    selection.each(function() {
        // Create the container group and rectangle
        var group = d3.select(this),
            rect = group.selectAll('rect');

        // Bind the rectangle to the color item and set its
        // initial attributes.
        rect.data([chart.color()])
            .enter().append('rect')
            .attr('width', width)
            .attr('height', height)
            .attr('fill', function(d) { return d; })
            .attr('stroke', '#222')
            .attr('stroke-width', 1);
    });
}
```

This will create the picker rectangle with the initial color.

Adding the color picker window

The color picker window should show up if the color selector is clicked on and hide it if the selector is clicked on a second time. We will use a div element to create the color picker window:

```
// Bind the rectangle to the data
rect.data([chart.color()])
    .enter().append('rect')
    // set more attributes ...
    .on('click', chart.onClick);
```

The openPicker function receives the data item bound to the rectangle. When the user clicks on the rectangle, the openPicker function will be invoked. This method will create the color picker window (a div) or remove it if already exists:

```
var openPicker = function(d) {
    // Select the color picker div and bind the data.
    var div = d3.select('body').selectAll('div.color-picker')
        .data([d]);

    if (div.empty()) {
        // Create the container div, if it doesn't exist.
        div.enter().append('div')
            .attr('class', 'color-picker');
    } else {
        // Remove the color picker div, if it exists.
        d3.select('body').selectAll('div.color-picker')
            .remove();
    }
};
```

Here, we detect whether the element exists using the empty method. If the selection is empty, we create the div and set its attributes. If the selection is not empty, we remove the color picker window. We want the color picker window to appear near the rectangle; we will use the position of the pointer to locate the window to the right-hand side of the selector. To position the color picker window, we need to set its position to absolute, and set its top and left offsets to appropriate values. We also set a provisional width, height, and background color for the div:

```
// Create the container div, if it doesn't exist.
div.enter().append('div')
    .attr('class', 'color-picker')
    .style('position', 'absolute')
    .style('left', (d3.event.pageX + width) + 'px')
    .style('top', d3.event.pageY + 'px')
```

```
        .style('width', '200px')
        .style('height', '100px')
        .style('background-color', '#eee');
```

We now have a div element that is displayed when the user clicks on it and hidden when the user clicks again. Most importantly, the window div is bound to the same data item as the rectangle, and the `this` context in the `onClick` method is the rectangle node. We can now create the color picker window as a reusable chart and bind it to the color picker selector.

The color picker window

Let's review what we have done so far. The color picker has two parts: the color picker selector and the color picker window. The color picker window is a div that appears when the user clicks on the selector and disappears if the user clicks again. We will use the reusable chart pattern to create the color picker window. Refer to the following screenshot:

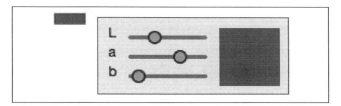

Components of the color picker; we will use the slider from the previous section

We can create the color picker content as an independent chart. For simplicity, this time, we won't add the `width`, `height`, and `margins` as configurable attributes. In this case, there are many elements that need to be created and positioned in the figure; we will only show you the most important ones:

```
function labColorPickerWindow() {

    // Chart Attributes...
    var margin = 10,
        // set more attributes...
        width = 3 * margin + labelWidth + sliderWidth + squareSize,
        height = 2 * margin + squareSize;

    function chart(selection) {
        selection.each(function(data) {
            // Select the container div and set its style
            var divContent = d3.select(this);
```

```
        // set the divContent size and position...

        // Create the SVG Element
        var svg = divContent.selectAll('svg')
            .data([data])
            .enter().append('svg');

        // set the svg width and height...
        // add more elements...
    });
}

return chart;
};
```

Again, we have used the basic structure of a reusable chart. Remember that in the
selection.each function, the data is the color of the selector, and the context is the
container div. We begin by adding the square that will show you the selected color:

```
// Add the color square
var colorSquare = svg.append('rect')
    .attr('x', 2 * margin + sliderWidth + labelWidth)
    .attr('y', margin)
    .attr('width', squareSize)
    .attr('height', squareSize)
    .attr('fill', data);
```

This will put the square to the right-hand side of the window. Next, we will create a
scale to position each slider vertically. The rangePoints method of the scale allows
us to evenly distribute the sliders in the vertical space:

```
// Scale to distribute the sliders vertically
var vScale = d3.scale.ordinal()
    .domain([0, 1, 2])
    .rangePoints([0, squareSize], 1);
```

We will use this scale to set the position of the groups that will contain the slider
elements for each color component. We create a slider for the l component of the color:

```
var sliderL = sliderControl()
    .domain([0, 100])
    .width(sliderWidth);
    .onSlide(function(selection) {
        selection.each(function(d) {
            data.l = d;
            updateColor(data);
        });
    });
```

The l component of the color is updated on the slider, and then the `updateColor` function is invoked, passing the color as the argument. We add a group to display the slider and translate it to the appropriate location. Remember that the data bound to the group is the value that is changed when the user moves the handler:

```
var gSliderL = svg.selectAll('g.slider-l')
    .data([data.l])
    .enter().append('g')
    .attr('transform', function() {
        var dx = margin + labelWidth,
            dy = margin + vScale(0);
        return 'translate(' + [dx, dy] + ')';
    })
    .call(sliderL);
```

This will create the first slider. In a similar way, we add a slider for the a and b color components with its corresponding groups. When the user moves the slider, the square and the rectangle in the selector should get updated. This chart is independent of the color picker selector to which we don't have access to the selector rectangle in this scope. We will add a configurable method that will be invoked on color change, so the user of `labColorWindow` can update other components. The `updateColor` function will update the color of the square and invoke the `onColorChange` function:

```
// Update the color square and invoke onColorChange
function updateColor(color) {
    colorSquare.attr('fill', color);
    divContent.data([color]).call(onColorChange);
}
```

Note that the color is bound to the color picker window div, and `onColorChange` receives the selection that contains the window. We need to add a default function and an accessor to configure this function. The default function will be just an empty function. We can now update the color picker selector, more precisely, the `onClick` method, to create the color picker window as follows:

```
chart.onClick = function(d) {
    // Select the picker rectangle
    var rect = d3.select(this);

    // Select the color picker div and bind the data...
    if (div.empty()) {
        // Create the Color Picker Content
        var content = labColorPickerWindow()
            .onColorChange(function(selection) {
```

```
                selection.each(function(d) {
                    rect.data([d]).attr('fill', d);
                });
            });

        // Create the container div, if it doesn't exist.
        div.enter().append('div')
            .attr('class', 'color-picker')
            // set more attributes....
            .call(content);

        // Bind the data to the rectangle again.
        rect.data([div.datum()]);
    } else {
        // Update the color of the rectangle
        rect.data([div.datum()])
            .attr('fill', function(d) { return d; });

        // Remove the color picker window.
        d3.select('body')
            .selectAll('div.color-picker').remove();
    }
};
```

We can now select a color using the color picker. There is only one thing missing; the user will want to do something with the color once it has been changed. We will add an onChangeColor function and its corresponding accessor to the color picker window and invoke it at the end of the chart.onClick method. With this function, the user will be able to use the color to change other components:

```
chart.onClick = function(d) {
    // ...

    // Invoke the user callback.
    onColorChange(color);
};
```

To use the color picker, we need to attach it to a selection that contains a group and configure the onColorChange function:

```
// Create the color picker
var picker = labColorPicker()
    .color('#fff')
    .onColorChange(function(d) {
```

```
        // Change the background color of the page
        d3.select('body').style('background-color', d);
    });

// Create a group for the color picker and translate it.
var grp = svg.append('g')
    .attr('transform', 'translate(30, 30)')
    .call(picker);
```

This will change the background color of the example page when the user selects a color. In this section, we have used the slider components to create a color picker. The color picker has two independent components: the selector and the color picker window. The color picker selector creates an instance of the color picker window when the user clicks on it and removes the window container when the user clicks on it again.

Summary

In this chapter, we used the drag behavior and the reusable chart pattern to create a slider control. This control can be used to allow users to select values within a range. We used the slider component to create a color picker for the Lab color space. In the implementation of the color picker, we didn't need to know about the internals of the slider; we only used the slider's public interface. The composition between reusable components allows us to create rich components without having to handle the details of their internal elements.

In the next chapter, we will learn how to create tooltips for our charts and how to implement more advanced user interface components. We will also create an area chart that allows us to measure variations between two points in the chart by using brushing.

5
Creating User Interface Elements

In the previous chapter, we learned how to use the drag behavior and SVG elements to create reusable controls and user interface elements. In this chapter, we will learn how to create additional elements to complement our projects. When designing data visualizations, screen real estate is one of the scarcest resources; we need to get the most out of our pixels without cluttering the screen. One of the strategies to solve this problem is to add contextual user interface elements, allowing the user to request any additional information in a quick and nonintrusive way. A **tooltip** does just that: it displays additional information about an item without cluttering the entire visualization.

If the page has a large number of elements, the user can lose track of the important parts of the visualization or have difficulties in tracking individual elements. One solution is to highlight the important elements, so we can guide the users' attention to the most relevant elements in the page.

In this chapter, we will learn how to highlight elements and create reusable tooltips. We will also create a chart with a brushing control, which will allow us to select an interval and display additional information about that interval.

Highlighting chart elements

We will create a simple chart depicting a series of circles that represent fruits and the number of calories we can get from 100 grams of each fruit. To make things easier, we have created a JSON file with information about the fruits. The file structure is as follows:

```
{
    "name": "Fruits",
```

```
    "data": [
      {
        "name": "Apple",
        "description": "The apple is the pomaceous fruit..."
        "amount_grams": 100,
        "calories": 52,
        "color": "#FF5149"
      },
      ...
    ]
}
```

We will represent each fruit with a circle and arrange them horizontally. We will map the area of the circle to the calories by serving, coloring them with the color indicated in the data item. As usual, we will use the reusable chart pattern, creating a closure function with the chart attributes and a charting function that contains the rendering logic, as shown in the following code:

```
function fruitChart() {

    // Chart Attributes
    var width = 600,
        height = 120;

    // Radius Extent
    var radiusExtent = [0, 40];

    // Charting Function
    function chart(selection) {
        selection.each(function(data) {
            // charting function content ...
        });
    }

    // Accessor Methods...

    return chart;
}
```

Although it is unlikely that we will reuse the fruit chart, the reusable chart structure is still useful because it encapsulates the chart variables and we get cleaner code. In the `charting` function, we select the `div` container, create the `svg` element, and set its width and height, as follows:

```
// Charting Function
function chart(selection) {
    selection.each(function(data) {

        // Select the container div and create the svg selection
        var div = d3.select(this),
        svg = div.selectAll('svg').data([data]);

        // Append the svg element on enter
        svg.enter().append('svg');

        // Update the width and height of the SVG element
        svg.attr('width', width).attr('height', height);

        // add more elements...
    });
}
```

We want to have the circles evenly distributed in the horizontal dimension. To achieve this, we will use an ordinal scale to compute the position of each circle, as shown in the following code:

```
// Create a scale for the horizontal position
var xScale = d3.scale.ordinal()
    .domain(d3.range(data.length))
    .rangePoints([0, width], 1);
```

The `rangePoints` method will configure the scale, dividing the `[0,width]` range into the number of elements in the domain. The second argument allows you to add padding, expressed as a multiple of the distance between two items. We will also add a scale for the radius, mapping the number of calories to the area of the circle. As discussed earlier, the area of the circle should be proportional to the quantitative dimensions that we are representing:

```
// Maximum number of calories
var maxCal = d3.max(data, function(d) {
    return d.calories;
});

// Create the radius scale
```

```
var rScale = d3.scale.sqrt()
    .domain([0, maxCal])
    .rangeRound(radiusExtent);
```

We will create groups and translate them to the location where we want the circles and labels. We will append the circles and labels to the groups, as follows:

```
// Create a container group for each circle
var gItems = svg.selectAll('g.fruit-item').data(data)
    .enter()
    .append('g')
    .attr('class', 'fruit-item')
    .attr('transform', function(d, i) {
        return 'translate(' + [xScale(i), height / 2] + ')';
    });
```

We can now append the circle, the label that displays the fruit name, and another label that shows the number of calories per serving. We will set the style of the labels to align them to the center and set the font size for the labels:

```
// Add a circle to the item group
var circles = gItems.append('circle')
    .attr('r', function(d) { return rScale(d.calories); })
    .attr('fill', function(d) { return d.color; });

// Add the fruit name
var labelName = gItems.append('text')
    .attr('text-anchor', 'middle')
    .attr('font-size', '12px')
    .text(function(d) { return d.name; });

// Add the calories label
var  labelKCal = gItems.append('text')
    .attr('text-anchor', 'middle')
    .attr('font-size', '10px')
    .attr('y', 12)
    .text(function(d) { return d.calories + ' kcal'; });
```

We can use the chart at this point. We load the JSON file, create and configure the fruit chart, select the `div` container, and call the chart, passing the selection as an argument, as shown in the following code:

```
// Load and parse the json data
d3.json('/chapter05/fruits.json', function(error, root) {

    // Display the error message
```

```
    if (error) {
        console.error('Error getting or parsing the data.');
        throw error;
    }

    // Create and configure the chart
    var fruits = fruitChart();

    d3.select('div#chart')
        .data([root.data])
        .call(fruits);
});
```

We obtained a series of circles where each one represents a fruit, but without any highlighting yet.

The first draft of the chart, without any highlighting

We will highlight the circles when the pointer moves over the circles by changing the background color to a brighter color of the same hue and by adding a small border, returning the circles to their original state when the mouse leaves the element. The DOM API allows you to bind listeners for events to individual elements, but the `selection.on` method allows you to apply a listener to all the elements in a selection at the same time. As in almost every D3 operator, the `this` context is set to the selected element in the listener function. The `d3.rgb` function constructs a RGB color from the hexadecimal string. The `brighter()` method returns a brighter version of the color. The method receives an optional parameter, `k`, which can be used to specify the increment of brightness. The default value is `1`, and the brightness is increased by multiplying each channel by `0.7^-k`. We will use this method to highlight the circles on a `mouseover` event:

```
// We add listeners to the mouseover and mouseout events
circles
    .on('mouseover', function(d) {
        d3.select(this)
            .attr('stroke-width', 3)
            .attr('fill', d3.rgb(d.color).brighter())
            .attr('stroke', d.color);
    })
```

```
    .on('mouseout', function(d) {
        d3.select(this)
            .attr('stroke-width', 0)
            .attr('fill', d.color);
    });
```

The elements are now highlighted when the user moves the pointer over the circles.

The highlighted element is brighter and has a small border

This is a very simple example, but the method to highlight elements is the same in bigger charts. There are other strategies to highlight elements; for instance, a highlight class can be added or removed when the user moves the cursor over the elements. This strategy is particularly useful when we don't want to hardcode the styles.

Creating tooltips

A **tooltip** is a small element that provides contextual information when the user locates the pointer over an element. This allows you to provide details without cluttering the visualization. In this section, we will create the tooltip as a reusable chart but with a different structure than that in the previous examples. In the previous charts, we bound the data to a selection of containers for the charts; while in this case, the tooltip chart will be bound to the element on which the tooltip should appear. This implies that the selection argument in the `charting` function contains the elements on which the tooltip will appear. In the case of the fruit chart, we will want the tooltip to appear when the user moves the pointer over the circles, follow the pointer as it moves over the circle, and disappear when the pointer leaves the circle. We will create a tooltip as a reusable chart, but instead of invoking the tooltip on a selection of containers, we will invoke the tooltip passing it a selection containing the circle under the cursor. We begin by creating the tooltip chart, bearing in mind these considerations:

```
function tooltipChart() {

    // Tooltip Attributes...

    // Charting function
    function chart(selection) {
```

```
        selection.each(function(d) {
            // Bind the mouse events to the container element
            d3.select(this)
                .on('mouseover', create)
                .on('mousemove', move)
                .on('mouseout', remove);
        });
    }

    // Accessor methods...

    return chart;
}
```

Here, we added listeners for the mouseover, mousemove, and mouseout events on the selection argument. The data bound to each element will be passed on to the create, move, and remove listeners. These functions will create, move, and remove the tooltip, respectively. To create the tooltip, we will create a div container under the body element and set its left and top offsets to the pointer position, plus we add a small offset, as shown in the following code:

```
// Create the tooltip chart
var create = function(data) {

    // Create the tooltip container div
    var tooltipContainer = d3.select('body').append('div')
        .datum(data)
        .attr('class', 'tooltip-container')
        .call(init);

    // Move the tooltip to its initial position
    tooltipContainer
        .style('left', (d3.event.pageX + offset.x) + 'px')
        .style('top', (d3.event.pageY + offset.y) + 'px');
};
```

To locate the tooltip near the pointer, we need to set its position to absolute. The pointer events' style must be set to none so that the tooltip doesn't capture the mouse events. We set the position and other style attributes in an inline style element. We also set the style for the tooltip's title and content, as shown in the following code:

```
<style>
.tooltip-container {
    position: absolute;
    pointer-events: none;
```

```
        padding: 2px 4px 2px 6px;
        background-color: #eee;
        border: solid 1px #aaa;
    }

    .tooltip-title {
        text-align: center;
        font-size: 12px;
        font-weight: bold;
        line-height: 1em;
    }

    .tooltip-content {
        font-size: 11px;
    }
    </style>
```

In the initialization function, we will create the `div` container for the tooltip and add paragraphs for the title and the content. We also added the `title` and `content` methods with their corresponding accessors so that the user can configure the title and content based on the bound data:

```
// Initialize the tooltip
var init = function(selection) {
    selection.each(function(data) {
        // Create and configure the tooltip container
        d3.select(this)
            .attr('class', 'tooltip-container')
            .style('width', width + 'px');

        // Tooltip Title
        d3.select(this).append('p')
            .attr('class', 'tooltip-title')
            .text(title(data));

        // Tooltip Content
        d3.select(this).append('p')
            .attr('class', 'tooltip-content')
            .text(content(data));
    });
};
```

The `chart.move` method will update the position of the tooltip as the pointer moves, changing its left and top offsets. The `chart.remove` method will just remove the tooltip from the document:

```
// Move the tooltip to follow the pointer
var move = function() {
    // Select the tooltip and move it following the pointer
    d3.select('body').select('div.tooltip-container')
        .style('left', (d3.event.pageX + offset.x) + 'px')
        .style('top', (d3.event.pageY + offset.y) + 'px');
};


// Remove the tooltip
var remove = function() {
    d3.select('div.tooltip-container').remove();
};
```

Using the tooltip

We can use the tooltip in the fruit chart, and add tooltips when the user moves the pointer over the circles. We will create and configure the `tooltip` function in the fruit chart closure, as follows:

```
function fruitChart() {

    // Create and configure the tooltip
    var tooltip = tooltipChart()
        .title(function(d) { return d.name; })
        .content(function(d) { return d.description; });

    // Attributes, charting function and accessors...

    return chart;
}
```

In the `charting` function, we can invoke the `tooltip` function by passing the selection of the circles as an argument, as follows:

```
function fruitChart() {

    // Chart attributes...

    // Charting Function
    function chart(selection) {
        selection.each(function(data) {
```

```
        // Charting function content...

        // The event listeners of the tooltip should be
        // namespaced to avoid overwriting the listeners of the
           circles.
        circles
            .on('mouseover', function(d) { ... })
            .on('mouseout', function(d) { ... })
            .call(tooltip);
    });
}


    // Accessor methods....

    return chart;
}
```

 Remember that the circles already have listeners for the mouseover and mouseout events. If we add the tooltip as it is, the first listener will be removed before the new listener is added, disabling the highlighting.

To register multiple listeners for the same event type, we can add an optional namespace to the tooltip-related events, as follows:

```
// Tooltip charting function
function chart(selection) {
    selection.each(function(d) {
        // Bind the mouse events to the container element
        d3.select(this)
            .on('mouseover.tooltip', create)
            .on('mousemove.tooltip', move)
            .on('mouseout.tooltip',  remove);
    });
}
```

Now, we have the tooltips and highlighting enabled in the fruit chart.

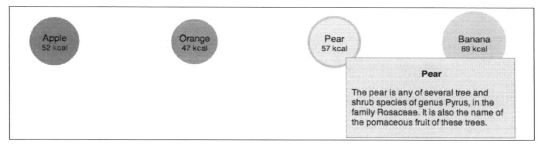

The tooltip and the highlighting listeners are enabled for the fruit chart

Selecting a range with brushing

In this section, we will create an area chart to display stock prices and use brushing to allow the user to select an interval and get additional information about that time interval.

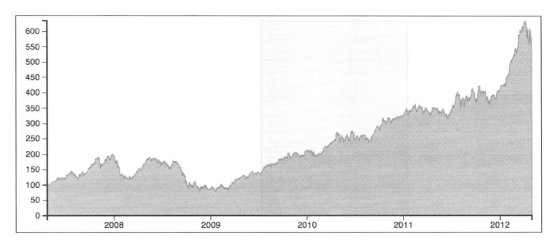

Selecting a time interval with brushing

We will use the time series of the prices of the AAPL stock, available as a TSV file in the D3 examples gallery. The file contains the date and closing price for the date, covering almost 5 years of activity, as shown in the following code:

```
date        close
1-May-12    582.13
30-Apr-12   583.98
27-Apr-12   603.00
26-Apr-12   607.70
...
```

Creating the area chart

We begin by creating the structure of a reusable chart; we will add the width, height, and margin as the chart attributes, and add their corresponding accessors. The complete code is available in the chapter05/02-brushing.html file. In the charting function, we initialize and set the size of the svg element as follows:

```
// Chart Creation
function chart(selection) {
    selection.each(function(data) {

        // Select the container element and create the svg selection
        var div = d3.select(this),
            svg = div.selectAll('svg').data([data]);

        // Initialize the svg element
        svg.enter().append('svg')
            .call(svgInit);

        // Initialize the svg element
        svg.attr('width', width).attr('height', height);

        // Creation of the inner elements...
    });
}
```

The svgInit function will be called only on enter, and it will create groups for the axis and the chart content. We will parse the input data, so we don't have to transform each item later. To parse the date, we will use the d3.time.format D3 method:

```
// Configure the time parser
var parseDate = d3.time.format(timeFormat).parse;

// Parse the data
```

```
data.forEach(function(d) {
    d.date = parseDate(d.date);
    d.close = +d.close;
});
```

The `timeFormat` variable is defined as a chart attribute; we also added an accessor function so that the user can use the chart for other datasets. In this case, the input date format is %d-%b-%y, that is, the day, abbreviated month name, and year. We can now create the *x* and *y* axis:

```
// Create the scales and axis
var xScale = d3.time.scale()
    .domain(d3.extent(data, function(d) { return d.date; }))
    .range([0, width - margin.left - margin.right]);

// Create the x axis
var xAxis = d3.svg.axis()
    .scale(xScale)
    .orient('bottom');

// Invoke the xAxis function on the corresponding group
svg.select('g.xaxis').call(xAxis);
```

We do the same with the *y* axis, but we will use a linear scale instead of the time scale and orient the axis to the left side. We can now create the chart content; we create and configure an area generator that will compute the path and then append the path to the chart group, as follows:

```
// Create and configure the area generator
var area = d3.svg.area()
    .x(function(d) { return xScale(d.date); })
    .y0(height - margin.top - margin.bottom)
    .y1(function(d) { return yScale(d.close); });

// Create the area path
svg.select('g.chart').append("path")
    .datum(data)
    .attr("class", "area")
    .attr("d", area);
```

We will modify the styles for the classes of the axis groups and the area to have a better-looking chart, as follows:

```
<style>
.axis path, line{
    fill: none;
    stroke: #222;
    shape-rendering: crispEdges;
}
.axis text {
    font-size: 11px;
}

.area {
    fill: #ddd;
}
</style>
```

We load the dataset using the d3.tsv function, which retrieves and parses tabular delimited data. Next, we will configure the chart, select the container element, and bind the dataset to the selection as follows:

```
// Load the TSV Stock Data
d3.tsv('/chapter05/aapl.tsv', function(error, data) {

    // Handle errors getting or parsing the data
    if (error) {
        console.error(error);
        throw error;
    }

    // Create and configure the area chart
    var chart = areaChart();

    // Bind the chart to the container div
    d3.select('div#chart')
        .datum(data)
        .call(chart);
});
```

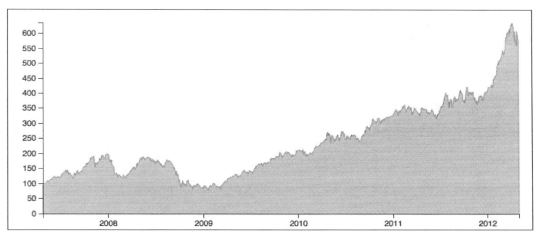

The first version of the area chart

Adding brushing

A brush is a control that allows you to select a range in a chart. D3 provides built-in support for brushing. We will use brushing to select time intervals in our area chart, and use it to show the price and date of the edges of the selected interval. We will also add a label that shows the relative price variation in the interval. We will create an SVG group to contain the brush elements. We will add this group in the svgInit method, as follows:

```
// Create and translate the brush container group
svg.append('g')
    .attr('class', 'brush')
    .attr('transform', function() {
        var dx = margin.left, dy = margin.top;
        return 'translate(' + [dx, dy] + ')';
    });
```

The group should be added at the end of the svg element to avoid getting it hidden by the other elements. With the group created, we can add the brush control in the charting function as follows:

```
function chart(selection) {
    selection.each(function(data) {
        // Charting function contents...

        // Create and  configure the brush
```

```
        var brush = d3.svg.brush()
            .x(xScale)
            .on('brush', brushListener);
    });
}
```

We set the scale of the brush in the horizontal axis, and add a listener for the brush event. The brush can be configured to select a vertical interval by setting the *y* attribute with an appropriate scale and even be used to select areas by setting both the *x* and *y* attributes.

The brushListener function will be invoked if the brush extent changes. The brushstart and brushend events are also available, but we don't need to use them at the moment. In the following code, we apply the brush function to the brush group using the call method of the selection:

```
    var gBrush = svg.select('g.brush').call(brush);
```

When we invoke the brush function in a group, a series of elements are created. A background rectangle will capture the brush events. There will also be a rectangle of the extent class, which will resize as the user changes the brush area. Also, there are two invisible vertical rectangles at the brush edges; so, it's easier for the user to select the brush boundary. The rectangles will initially have zero height; we will set the height to cover the chart area:

```
    // Change the height of the brushing rectangle
    gBrush.selectAll('rect')
        .attr('height', height - margin.top - margin.bottom);
```

We will modify the extent class, so the selected region is visible. We will set its color to gray and set the fill opacity to 0.05.

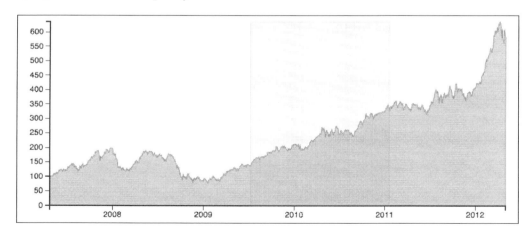

Adding brushing to the chart

The brush listener

We will add lines to mark the prices at the beginning and end of the selected period, and add a label to display the price variation in the interval. We begin by adding the elements in the `chart.svgInit` function and set some of its attributes. We will create groups for the line markers and for the text elements that will display the price and date. We also add a text element for the price variation. We create the `brushListener` function in the charting function scope, as shown in the following code:

```
// Brush Listener function
function brushListener() {
    var s = d3.event.target.extent();

    // Filter the items within the brush extent
    var items = data.filter(function(d) {
        return (s[0] <= d.date) && (d.date<= s[1]);
    });
}
```

When the brush event is triggered, the brush listener will have access to the event attributes through the `d3.event` object. Here, we get the brush extent and use it to filter the dates that lie within the selected interval. Note that the selection is an approximation, because there are a limited number of pixels in the screen. At the beginning of the brush event, the time interval might be too small to contain data items. We will compute the prices only when at least two items have been selected. We then select the first and last elements of the item array, as follows:

```
// Compute the percentual variation of the period
if (items.length > 2) {
    // Get the prices in the period
    priceB = items[0].close;
    priceA = Math.max(items[n - 1].close, 1e-8);

    // Set the lines and text position...
}
```

Having the first and last elements of the selected period, we can compute the relative price variation and set the position of the marker lines and labels. We will also set the color of the variation label to `blue` if the variation is positive and to `red` if it's negative. As the configuration of the positions and labels is rather large, we won't include the code here. However, the code is available in the `chapter05/02-brushing.html` file for reference.

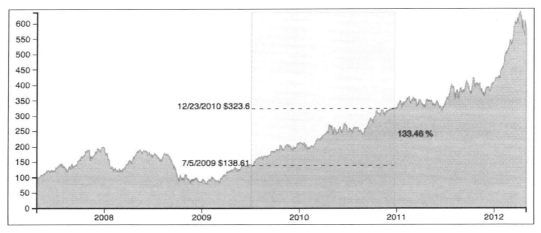

The area chart with brushing and annotations

Summary

In this chapter, we learned how to highlight elements when a user moves the pointer over them, making it easier for the user to spot the elements under the cursor and give hints of which elements can provide additional interactions. We created a reusable tooltip component that can be configured and used in other charts.

We also learned how to use the built-in brush component to create a control in order to select intervals, and used this control to allow the user to select a time interval in an area chart. We used the brush area to further annotate the chart with useful information about variations and the edges of the selected time interval.

In the next chapter, we will learn how to add interaction between chart components and how to integrate D3 and Backbone to create complex applications.

6
Interaction between Charts

Visualization projects are usually implemented as single page applications. Single page applications usually load their code when the browser loads the page and make requests to retrieve additional data when the user interacts with the page, avoiding full page reloads. The application can be used while the request is fulfilled, thereby improving the user experience.

Single page applications generally have a single payload that retrieves the scripts, styles, and markup required to create the interface. When the user interacts with UI components and additional data is required, the client-side code makes asynchronous requests to the server in the background and updates the corresponding elements when the data is ready, allowing the user to continue using the application during the request.

This increase in the complexity of client-side applications has led frontend developers to improve the architecture of client-side components. One of the most successful designs to face these challenges is the **MVC pattern** and its many variations.

In this chapter, we will cover the basics of the Backbone library and use D3 with Backbone to create a stock explorer with several components interacting between them, maintaining a consistent visualization state. We will also learn how to update the application URL to reflect a particular state in the application, allowing users to create bookmarks, navigate, and share the application state.

Learning the basics of Backbone

Backbone is a JavaScript library that helps us structure applications by implementing a version of the **MV* pattern**, which helps us separate different application concerns. The main Backbone components include models, collections, views, and routers; all these components communicate among themselves by triggering and listening to events.

The only hard dependency of Backbone is Underscore, which is a small utility library that provides functional programming support for collections, arrays, functions, and objects. It also provides additional utilities, such as a small template engine, which we will use later. To use the Backbone router and manipulate the DOM, jQuery or Zepto must also be included.

Events

The Events module can be used to extend an object, giving it the ability to listen and trigger custom events, such as listening for key presses, or sending an event when a variable changes. Backbone models, views, collections, and routers have event support. When we include Backbone in a page, the Backbone object will be available, and it can be used to listen or trigger events.

Models

In Backbone, a model is a data container. Model instances can be created, validated, and persisted to a server endpoint. When an attribute of the model is set, the model triggers a change event. The granularity of the change events allows observers to listen for a change in a particular attribute or any attribute in the model.

Besides being data containers, models can validate or convert data from its original format. Models are ignorant of views or external objects observing its changes; a model only communicates when its attributes are changed.

Collections

Collections are ordered sets of models, which are useful in order to manage model instances as a set. If a model instance in the collection is modified (added or removed), the collection will trigger a change event (triggering the add and remove events in each case).

Collections also have a series of enumerable methods that are useful to iterate, find, group, and compute aggregate functions on the collection elements. Of course, collections can be also extended to add new methods. Collections can be synced to the server in order to retrieve records and create new model instances from them and to push model instances created within the application.

Views

The views are components that render one or more attributes of a model in the page. Each view has one DOM element bound to it and a corresponding model (or collection) instance. Usually, the views listen for changes in one or more attributes of a model. Views can be updated from each other independently when a model (or some attributes of a model) changes, updating the view without redrawing the entire page. Note that when using Backbone models and views, the DOM elements in a view don't have references to the corresponding data elements; the view stores references to the DOM elements and the model. In D3, the DOM element contains a reference to the data bound to it.

Views also listen for DOM elements inside the container element. We can bind DOM events in a child element to a view method. For instance, if a view contains a button, we can bind the `click` event of the button with the custom `toggleClicked` method of the view. This is commonly used to update a model attribute.

In most Backbone applications, the views are rendered using templates. In most of the views, we will use D3 to render them instead of templates, but we will also include an example of a view that has been rendered using Underscore templates.

Routers

The Backbone router allows you to connect URLs to the application, allowing the application states to have URLs. This allows the user to navigate between visited application states using the browser's back and forth buttons, save a bookmark, and share specific application states.

Backbone is a subject on its own and we can't cover all its features in one chapter. It's a good idea to invest some time learning Backbone or one of its alternatives.

There are a great number of resources available to help you learn Backbone. The most complete references are the following:

- **Backbone Fundamentals** (`http://addyosmani.github.io/backbone-fundamentals`): This book, written by Addy Osmani, describes the Backbone components in depth and has two complete examples of Backbone-based applications.
- **Backbone** (`http://backbonejs.org`): The official website contains the documentation of the library. The source code of Backbone is also extensively commented on.
- **TodoMVC** (`http://todomvc.com`): As the number of JavaScript MV* frameworks and libraries that allow you to structure an application can be overwhelming, the TodoMVC project contains the same Todo application that was implemented in the most popular MV* JavaScript frameworks available.

The stock explorer application

In this section, we will use D3 and Backbone to create a single page application to display a time series of stock prices. The user will be able to select different stocks and a period of time in order to get a detail view. The page will have several components:

- **Context chart**: This chart will display the complete series of prices that are available for the stock. It will have a brush component that selects a time interval.
- **Detail chart**: This will be a bigger area chart that will show you the stock prices for the time interval selected in the context chart.
- **Control view**: This view will show you a control that selects the stock.
- **Stock title**: This will display the name of the company.

We will display the control and title view on top of the page, a big area with the detail view, and a context area chart at the bottom of the page.

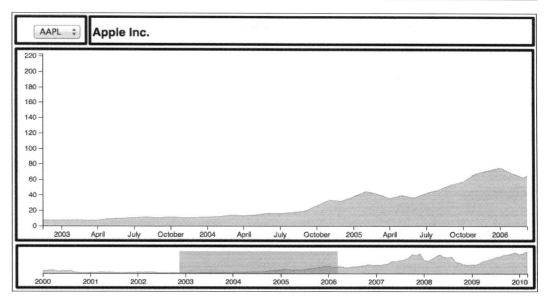

A diagram of the application components

As you can see, there are several components that should be in sync. If we change the stock, the area chart should be updated. If we change the time interval in the context chart, the detail chart must be updated to show you only the selected period. We will use Backbone to structure this application.

The state of our application can be described by the stock and the time interval that we want to examine. We will create a model to store the application state and one view for each component.

The general strategy is that each view will contain an instance of a D3-based chart, which is created following the reusable chart pattern. In the `initialize` method, we will tell the view to listen for changes in the model and invoke the `render` method when one of the model attributes is changed. In the `render` method of the view, we will create a selection for the container element of the view, bind the data corresponding to the selected stock, and invoke the `charting` function using the `selection.call` method. We will begin by creating reusable charts with D3.

Creating the stock charts

In this section, we will implement the charts that will be used by the application. This time, the code of the charts will be in a separated JavaScript file. To follow the examples in this section, open the `chapter06/stocks/js/lib/stockcharts.js` and `chapter06/01-charts.html` files.

We will begin by creating the stock title chart and then implement the stock area chart, which we will be using in the context and detail views. Note that the title chart is not really necessary, but it will be helpful to introduce the pattern that integrates reusable charts and Backbone.

The stock title chart

The stock title chart is a reusable chart that creates a paragraph with the title of the stock. As we mentioned previously, it's probably not a good idea to create a chart just to write a string, but it shows you how to integrate a reusable chart that doesn't involve SVG with Backbone. It has a configurable title accessor function, so the user can define the content of the paragraph using the data that is bound to the container selection. The chart is structured using the reusable chart pattern, as shown in the following code:

```
function stockTitleChart() {
    'use strict';

    // Default title accessor
    var title = function(d) { return d.title; };

    // Charting function
    function chart(selection) {
        selection.each(function(data) {
            // Creation and update of the paragraph...
        });
    }

    // Title function accessor
    chart.title = function(titleAccessor) {
        if (!arguments.length) { return title; }
        title = titleAccessor;
        return chart;
    };

    return chart;
}
```

In the `charting` function, we select the `div` element and create a selection for the paragraph. We add the `stock-title` class to the paragraph in order to allow the user to modify its style, as shown in the following code:

```
// Charting function
function chart(selection) {
    selection.each(function(data) {

        // Create the selection for the title
        var div = d3.select(this),
            par = div.selectAll('p.stock-title').data([data]);

        // Create the paragraph element on enter
        par.enter().append('p')
            .attr('class', 'stock-title'));

        // Update the paragraph content
        par.text(title);
    });
}
```

As usual, we can use the chart by creating and configuring a chart instance, selecting the container element, binding the data, and invoking the chart using the `selection.call` method, as shown in the following code:

```
// Create and configure the title chart
var titleChart = stockTitleChart()
    .title(function(d) { return d.name; });

// Select the container element, bind the data and invoke
// the charting function on the selection
d3.select('div#chart')
    .data([{name: 'Apple Inc.'}])
    .call(titleChart);
```

The stock area chart

The stock area chart will display the time series for the stock price as an area chart. In *Chapter 5, Creating User Interface Elements*, we implemented an area chart that uses the brush behavior to select a time interval and annotate the chart with additional information about the price variation in the period. We will create an improved version of this chart and use it in the stock explorer application.

Besides having the usual width, height, and margin attributes and accessors methods, this chart will have an optional axis, brush behavior, and a configurable brush listener function so that the user can define actions to be performed on the brush. The time extent can be also be configured, allowing the user to show only part of the chart.

We have added all these methods so that we can use two chart instances for different purposes: one to allow the user to select a time interval and another to display the selected time interval in more detail. In the `chapter06/01-charts.html` file, we created one instance in order to select the time interval:

```
var contextAreaChart = stockAreaChart()
    .height(60)
    .value(function(d) { return d.price; })
    .yaxis(false)
    .onBrushListener(function(extent) {
        console.log(extent);
    });
```

We will use the chart accessor methods to set the height, disable the *y* axis, and set the value accessor and the brush listener functions. In this case, the brush listener function will display the time extent in the browser console on brush.

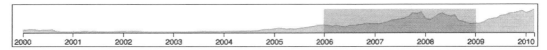

A stock area chart with the brush behavior enabled

We will use a second instance of the same chart to display a specific time interval. In this instance, we will disable the brush control and set the initial time extent, the value, and the date accessors. This chart will display the stock prices between the `from` and `to` dates:

```
// Set the time extent
var from = new Date('2002/01/01'),
    to = new Date('2004/12/31');

// Create and configure the detail area chart
var detailAreaChart = stockAreaChart()
    .value(function(d) { return d.price; })
    .date(function(d) { return new Date(d.date); })
    .timeExtent([from, to])
    .brush(false);
```

As you have probably guessed, the first instance is intended to control the time extent of the second chart instance. We will get to that soon; in the meantime, we will discuss some implications of controlling the time extent of the chart.

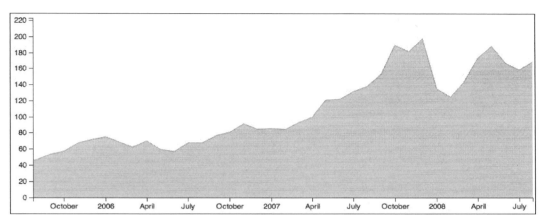

A stock area chart with the y-axis enabled and the brush behavior disabled

If we change the time extent of the chart, we will want the chart to reflect its new state. If the brush is dragged left in the first chart, we will want the area of the second chart to move to the right-hand side until it matches the interval selected in the first chart, and if we shorten the time interval in the first chart, we will want the area of the second chart to compress itself to display the selected interval in the same horizontal space.

The stock area chart will be implemented as a reusable chart. As most of the chart structure is similar to the chart presented in the previous section, we will skip some parts for brevity:

```
function stockAreaChart() {
    'use strict';

    // Chart Attributes
    var width = 700,
        height = 300,
        margin = {top: 20, right: 20, bottom: 20, left: 20};

    // Time Extent
    var timeExtent;

    // The axis and brush are enabled by default
    var yaxis = true,
        xaxis = true,
```

```
            brush = true;

        // Default accessor functions
        var date = function(d) { return new Date(d.date); };
        var value = function(d) { return +d.value; };

        // Default brush listener
        var onBrush = function(extent) {};

        function chart(selection) {
            selection.each(function(data) {
                // Charting function contents...
            });
        }

        var svgInit = function(selection) { ... };

        // Accessor Methods...

        return chart;
    }
```

In order to have the detail chart moving in sync with the context chart, we will
need to draw the complete series in the detail chart but only displaying the interval
selected with the brush in the context chart. To prevent the area chart from being
visible outside the charting area, we will define a clip path, and only the content
inside the clipping path will be visible:

```
var svgInit = function(selection) {
    // Define the clipping path
    selection.append('defs')
        .append('clipPath')
        .attr('id', 'clip')
        .append('rect')
        .attr('width', width - margin.left - margin.right)
        .attr('height', height - margin.top - margin.bottom);

    // Create the chart and axis groups...
};
```

The element that will be clipped should reference the clipping path using the `clip-path` attribute. In the `charting` function, we select the container element and create the SVG element on enter. We also set the SVG element's width and height and translate the axis, chart, and brush groups. We create the scales and axis (if they are enabled) and create and configure the area generator to draw the chart area path:

```
// Charting function...
// Add the axes
if (xaxis) { svg.select('g.xaxis').call(xAxis); }
if (yaxis) { svg.select('g.yaxis').call(yAxis); }

// Area Generator
var area = d3.svg.area()
    .x(function(d) { return xScale(date(d)); })
    .y0(yScale(0))
    .y1(function(d) { return yScale(value(d)); });
```

We create a selection for the path and bind the time series array to the selection. We append the path on enter and set its class to `stock-area`. We set the path data using the area generator and set the `clip-path` attribute using the `clipPath` variable defined previously:

```
// Create the path selection
var path = svg.select('g.chart').selectAll('path')
    .data([data]);

// Append the path element on enter
path.enter().append('path')
    .attr('class', 'stock-area');

// Set the path data string and clip the area
path.attr('d', area)
    .attr('clip-path', 'url(#clip)');
```

We create an envelope brush listener function. In this function, we retrieve the brush extent and invoke the user-configurable `onBrush` function, passing the extent as an argument. We initialize the brush behavior and bind the `brushListener` function to the brush event:

```
// Brush Listener Function
function brushListener() {
    timeExtent = d3.event.target.extent();
    onBrush(timeExtent);
}

// Brush Behavior
```

```
var brushBehavior = d3.svg.brush()
    .x(xScale)
    .on('brush', brushListener);
```

The initial time extent of the chart can be configured. If that's the case, we update the brush behavior extent, so the brush overlay fits the configured time extent:

```
// Set the brush extent to the time extent
if (timeExtent) {
    brushBehavior.extent(timeExtent);
}
```

We call the brush behavior using the `selection.call` method on the brush group and set the overlay height:

```
if (brush) {
    svg.select('g.brush').call(brushBehavior);

    // Change the height of the brushing rectangle
    svg.select('g.brush').selectAll('rect')
        .attr('height', h);
}
```

The preceding charts are implemented following the reusable chart pattern and were created with D3 only. We will use the charts in a Backbone application, but they can be used in other applications as standalone charts.

Preparing the application structure

In Backbone projects, it is a common practice to create directories for the models, views, collections, and routers. In the `Chapter06` directory, we created the `stocks` directory to hold the files for this application:

```
stocks/
    css/
    js/
        views/
        models/
        collections/
        routers/
        lib/
        app.js
    data/
    index.html
```

The models, views, collections, and routers folders contain JavaScript files that contain the Backbone models, views, collections, and routers. We add the D3 charts to the js/lib directory; additional JavaScript libraries would be there too. There is also a data folder with JSON files for the stock data. The index.html file contains the application markup.

The index page

In the header of the page, we include style sheets and JavaScript libraries that we need for our application. To create the page more quickly, we will use a CSS library that will add styles to enable uniform fonts, sizes, and default colors among browsers and define the grid system. A grid system is a set of styles that allows us to define rows and columns of standard column sizes without having to define the styles for each size ourselves. We will use Yahoo's Pure CSS modules to use the grid system, which is a pretty minimal set of CSS modules. These modules are used only in this page; if you are more comfortable with Bootstrap or other libraries, you are free to replace the div classes or define the sizes and behaviors of each container yourself.

We will create a container for the application and add the pure-g-r class, which is a container with responsive behavior enabled. If the viewport is wide, the columns will be shown side by side; if the user has a small screen, the columns will be shown stacked. We will also create two child containers, one for the stock control and title and a second container for the stock area chart, both classed pure-u-1, that is, containers with full width. The pure container uses fractional sizes to define the div width; in order to have a div that covers 80 percent of the parent container width, we can set its class to pure-u-4-5:

```
<div class="pure-g-r" id="stock-app">
  <!-- Stock Selector and Title -->
  <div class="pure-u-1">
    <div id="stock-control"></div>
    <div id="stock-title"></div>
  </div>
  <div class="pure-u-1 charts">
    <div id="stock-detail"></div>
    <div id="stock-context"></div>
  </div>
</div>
```

We include the application files at the end of the page so that the markup is rendered while the remaining assets are loaded:

```
<!-- Application Components -->
<script src="/chapter06/stocks/js/models/app.js"></script>
<script src="/chapter06/stocks/js/models/stock.js"></script>
```

```
<script src="/chapter06/stocks/js/collections/stocks.js"></script>
<script src="/chapter06/stocks/js/views/stocks.js"></script>
<script src="/chapter06/stocks/js/views/app.js"></script>
<script src="/chapter06/stocks/js/routers/router.js"></script>
<script src="/chapter06/stocks/js/app.js"></script>
```

Creating the models and collections

Models contain application data and the logic related to this data. For our application, we will need a model to represent the stock information and the application model, which will store the visualization state. We will also create a collection that holds the available stock instances. To avoid polluting the global namespace, we will encapsulate the application components in the app variable:

```
var app = app || {};
```

Adding this line to all the files in the application will allow us to extend the object with models, collections, and views.

The stock model

The stock model will contain basic information about each stock. It will contain the stock name (Apple Inc.), the symbol (AAPL), and the URL where the time series of prices can be retrieved (aapl.json). Models are created by extending Backbone.Model:

```
// Stock Information Model
app.Stock = Backbone.Model.extend({

    // Default stock symbol, name and url
    defaults: {symbol: null, name: null, url: null},

    // The stock symbol is unique, it can be used as ID
    idAttribute: 'symbol'
});
```

Here, we defined the default values for the model to null. This is not really necessary, but it might be useful to know which properties are expected. We will use the stock symbol as ID. Besides this, we don't need any further initialization code. As stock symbols are unique, we will use the symbol as the ID for easier retrieval later. We can create stock instances by using the constructor and setting the attributes that pass an object:

```
var aapl = new app.Stock({
        symbol: 'AAPL',
```

```
        name: 'Apple',
        url: 'aapl.json'
});
```

We can set or get its attributes using the accessor methods:

```
aapl.set('name', 'Apple Inc.');
aapl.get('name');  // Apple Inc.
```

In this application, we will create and access stock instances using a collection rather than creating individual instances.

The stock collection

To define a collection, we need to specify the model. When defining the collection, we can set the URL of an endpoint where the collection records can be retrieved, which is usually the URL of a REST endpoint. In our case, the URL points towards a static JSON file that contains the stocks records:

```
// Stock Collection
app.StockList = Backbone.Collection.extend({
    model: app.Stock,
    url: '/chapter06/stocks/data/stocks.json'
});
```

Individual stocks can be added to the collection one by one, or they can be fetched from the server using the collection URL. We can also specify the URL when creating the collection instance:

```
// Create a StockList instance
var stockList = new app.StockList({});

// Add one element to the collection
stockList.add({
    symbol: 'AAPL',
    name: 'Apple Inc.',
    url: 'aapl.json'
});
stockList.length; // 1
```

As we defined the stock symbol as idAttribute, individual stock instances can be retrieved using the stock's ID. In this case, the stock symbol is the ID of the stock model, so we can retrieve stock instances using the symbol:

```
var aapl = stockList.get('AAPL');
```

Models use the URL of the collection to construct their own URL. The default URL will have the form `collectionUrl/modelId`. If the server provides a RESTful API, this URL can be used to create, update, and delete records.

The application model

We will create an application model to store and manage the application state.

To define the application model, we extend the `Backbone.Model` object, adding the corresponding default values. The `stock` attribute will contain the current stock symbol (AAPL), and the data will contain the time series for the current stock:

```
// Application Model
app.StockAppModel = Backbone.Model.extend({

    // Model default values
    defaults: {
        stock: null,
        from: null,
        to: null,
        data: []
    },

    initialize: function() {
        this.on('change:stock', this.fetchData);
        this.listenTo(app.Stocks, 'reset', this.fetchData);
    },

    // Additional methods...
    getStock: function() {...},
    fetchData: function() {...}
});
```

We will also set a template for the stock collection data. In this case, the base URL is `chapter06/stocks/data/`. As we mentioned previously, there is a JSON file in the `data` directory with the data of the available stocks:

```
// Compiled template for the stock data url
urlTemplate: _.template('/chapter06/stocks/data/<%= url %>'),
```

We have also added a `fetchData` method in order to retrieve the time series for the corresponding stock. We invoke the template that passes the current stock data and use the parsed URL to retrieve the stock time series. We use the `d3.json` method to get the stock data and set the model data attribute to notify the views that the data is ready:

```
fetchData: function() {
  // Fetch the current stock data
    var that = this,
        stock = this.getStock(),
        url = this.urlTpl(stock.toJSON());

    d3.json(url, function(error, data) {
        if (error) { return error; }
        that.set('data', data.values);
    });
}
```

Implementing the views

To integrate the D3-based charts with Backbone Views, we will use the following strategy:

1. We will create and configure a chart instance as an attribute of the view.
2. In the initialization method, we tell the view to listen for changes on the model application and render the view on model updates.

The views for the page components are in the `chapter06/stocks/js/views/stocks.js` file, and the application view code is in the `chapter06/stocks/js/views/app.js` file.

The title view

This view will simply display the stock symbol and name. It's intended to be used as a title of the visualization. We create and configure an instance of the underlying chart and store a reference to the chart in the `chart` attribute. In the `initialize` method, we tell the view to invoke the render method when the model's `stock` attribute is updated.

In the `render` method, we create a selection that will hold the container element of the view, bind this element to a dataset that contains the current stock, and invoke the chart using `selection.chart`:

```
app.StockTitleView = Backbone.View.extend({

    chart: stockTitleChart()
        .title(function(d) {
            return _.template('<%= symbol %><%= name %>', d);
        }),

    initialize: function() {
        this.listenTo(this.model, 'change:stock', this.render);
        this.render();
    },

    render: function() {
        d3.select(this.el)
            .data([this.model.getStock().toJSON()])
            .call(this.chart);

        return this;
    }
});
```

Changes to the `stock` attribute of the application model will trigger the `change:stock` event, causing the view to invoke its `render` method, updating the D3 chart. In this particular view, using a reusable chart is overkill; for a real-life problem, we could have used a small Backbone View with a template. We did this to have a minimal example of reusable charts working with Backbone Views.

Rendered stock title view

The stock selector view

To add some diversity, we will create the selector without using D3. This view will show you the available stocks as a selection menu, updating the application model's `stock` attribute when the user selects a value. In this view, we will use a template. To create a template, we create a script element of type text/template in the `index.html` file and assign it an ID, in our case, `stock-selector-tpl`:

```
<script type="text/template" id="stock-selector-tpl">
```

```
<select id="stock-selector">
        . . .
</select>
</script>
```

Underscore templates can render variables using `<%= name %>` and execute JavaScript code using `<% var a = 1; %>`. Here, for instance, we evaluate the `callback` function on each element of the `stocks` array:

```
<!-- Create the stocks selector and add its options -->
<% _.each(stocks, function(s) { %>
  <option value="<%= s.symbol %>"><%= s.symbol %></option>
<% }); %>
```

For each one of the elements of the `stocks` array, we add an option with the stock symbol attribute as the value and content of the option element. After rendering the template with the application data, the HTML markup will be as follows:

```
<select id="stock-selector">
  <option value="AAPL">AAPL</option>
  <option value="MSFT">MSFT</option>
  <option value="IBM">IBM</option>
  <option value="AMZN">AMZN</option>
</select>
```

In the Backbone View, we select the content of the script with the `stock-selector-tpl` ID, compile the template to use it later, and store a reference to the compiled template in the template attribute:

```
// Stock Selector View
app.StockSelectorView = Backbone.View.extend({

    // Compiles the view template
    template: _.template($('#stock-selector-tpl').html()),

    // DOM Event Listeners
    events: {
        'change #stock-selector': 'stockSelected'
    },

    // Initialization and render methods...
});
```

We set the `events` attribute, with maps' DOM events of the inner elements of the view, to methods of the view. In this case, we bind changes to the `stock-selector` select element (the user changing the stock) with the `stockSelected` method.

In the `initialize` method, we tell the view to render when the `app.Stocks` collection emits the `reset` event. This event is triggered when new data is fetched (with the `{reset: true}` option) and when an explicit reset is triggered. If a new set of stocks is retrieved, we will want to update the available options. We also listen for changes to the application model's `stock` attribute. The current stock should always be the selected option in the select element:

```
initialize: function() {
    // Listen for changes to the collection and the model
    this.listenTo(app.Stocks, 'reset', this.render);
    this.listenTo(this.model, 'change:stock', this.render);
    this.render();
}
```

In the `render` method, we select the container element and set the element content to the rendered template, writing the necessary markup to display the drop-down control. We pass a JavaScript object with the `stock` attribute set to an array that contains the `app.Stocks` model's data. Finally, we iterate through the options in order to mark the option that matches the current stock symbol as selected:

```
render: function() {
    // Stores a reference to the 'this context'
    var self = this;

    // Render the select element
    this.$el.html(this.template({stocks: app.Stocks.toJSON()}));

    // Update the selected option
    $('#stock-selector option').each(function() {
        this.selected = (this.value === self.model.get('stock'));
    });
}
```

Backbone models and collection instances have the JSON method, which transforms the model or collection attributes to a JavaScript object. This method can be overloaded if we need to add computed properties besides the existing attributes. Note that in the `each` callback, the `this` context is set to the current DOM element, that is, the option element. We store a reference to the `this` context in the `render` function (the self variable) in order to reference it later.

Stock selector view allows selecting a stock by symbol

The stock context view

The context view contains a small area chart that allows the user to select a time interval that can be displayed in the detail view:

We will use the same strategy as the one used in the previous views to create and configure an instance of `stockAreaChart`, and store a reference to it in the `chart` attribute of the view:

```
app.StockContextView = Backbone.View.extend({

    // Initialize the stock area chart
    chart: stockAreaChart()
        .height(60)
        .margin({top: 5, right: 5, bottom: 20, left: 30})
        .date(function(d) { return new Date(d.date); })
        .value(function(d) { return +d.price; })
        .yaxis(false),

    // Render the view on model changes
    initialize: function() { ... },

    render: function(e) { ... }
});
```

In the `initialize` method, we tell the view to listen for changes to the application model and set the chart brush listener to update the `from` and `to` attributes of the model:

```
initialize: function() {

    // Get the width of the container element
    var width = parseInt(d3.select(this.el).style('width'), 10);

    // Bind the brush listener function. The listener will update
    // the model time interval
    var self = this;

    this.chart
        .width(width)
        .brushListener(function(extent) {
            self.model.set({from: extent[0], to: extent[1]});
        });

    // The view will render on changes to the model
    this.listenTo(this.model, 'change', this.render);
},
```

We get the width of the `this.el` container element using D3 and set the chart width. This will make the chart use the full width of the user's viewport.

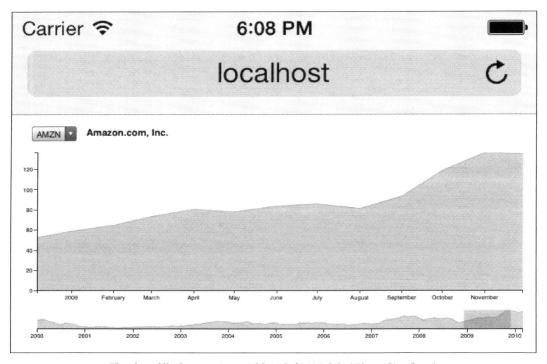

The chart fills the container width in Safari Mobile (iPhone Simulator)

The `render` method will update the chart's time extent, so it reflects the current state of the model, creates a selection that holds the container element of the view, binds the stock data, and invokes the chart using `selection.call`:

```
render: function() {
    // Update the time extent
    this.chart
        .timeExtent([
            this.model.get('from'),
            this.model.get('to')
        ]);

    // Select the container element and call the chart
    d3.select(this.el)
        .data([this.model.get('data')])
        .call(this.chart);

    return this;
}
```

This view is the only component that can change the `from` and `to` attributes of the model.

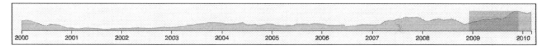

The stock context view uses the brush behavior to set the time interval

The stock detail view

The stock detail view will contain a stock area chart, showing only a given time interval. It's designed to follow the time interval selected in the stock context view.

We create and configure a `stockAreaChart` instance, setting the margin, value, and date accessors and disabling the brushing behavior:

```
// Stock Detail Chart
app.StockDetailView = Backbone.View.extend({

    // Initialize the stock area chart
    chart: stockAreaChart()
        .margin({top: 5, right: 5, bottom: 30, left: 30})
        .value(function(d) { return +d.price; })
        .date(function(d) { return new Date(d.date); })
        .brush(false),

    // Render the view on model changes
    initialize: function() { ... },
    render: function() { ... }
});
```

As we did in the context view, we tell the view to invoke the `render` method on model changes in the `initialize` method:

```
initialize: function() {

    // Get the width of the container element
    var width = parseInt(d3.select(this.el).style('width'), 10);

    // Set the chart width to fill the container
    this.chart.width(width);

    // The view will listen the application model for changes
    this.listenTo(this.model, 'change', this.render);
},
```

In the `render` method, we update the chart time extent, so the visible section of the area chart matches the time interval specified by the application model s `from` and `to` attribute:

```
render: function() {

    // Update the chart time extent
    var from = this.model.get('from'),
        to = this.model.get('to');

    this.chart.timeExtent([from, to]);

    // Select the container element and create the chart
    d3.select(this.el)
        .data([this.model.get('data')])
        .call(this.chart);
}
```

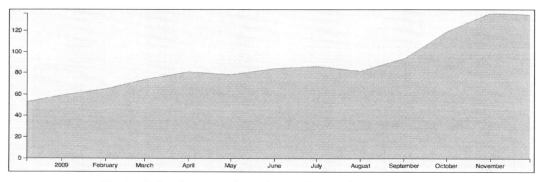

The detail view shows you the stock prices for the selected time interval

Note that when using `object.listenTo(other, 'event', callback)`, the `this` context in the `callback` function will be the object that listens for the events (`object`).

The application view

The application view will be in charge of creating instances of the views for each component of the application.

The `initialize` method binds the reset event of the `app.Stocks` collection and then invokes the collection's `fetch` method, passing the `{reset: true}` option. The collection will request the data to the server using its `url` attribute. When the data is completely loaded, it will trigger the `reset` event, and the application view will invoke its `render` method:

```
// Application View
app.StockAppView = Backbone.View.extend({

    // Listen to the collection reset event
    initialize: function() {
        this.listenTo(app.Stocks, 'reset', this.render);
        app.Stocks.fetch({reset: true});
    },

    render: function() { ... }
});
```

In the `render` method, we create instances of the views that we just created for each component. At this point, the current symbol of the application can be undefined, so we get the first stock in the `app.Stocks` collection and set the `stock` attribute of the model if is not already set.

We proceed to initialize the views for the title, the selector, the context chart, and the detail chart, passing along a reference to the model instance and the DOM element where the views will be rendered:

```
render: function() {

    // Get the first stock in the collection
    var first = app.Stocks.first();

    // Set the stock to the first item in the collection
    if (!this.model.get('stock')) {
        this.model.set('stock', first.get('symbol'));
    }

    // Create and initialize the title view
    var titleView = new app.StockTitleView({
        model: this.model,
        el: 'div#stock-title'
    });

    // Create and initialize the selector view
```

```
var controlView = new app.StockSelectorView({
    model: this.model,
    el: 'div#stock-control'
});

// Create and initialize the context view
var contextView = new app.StockContextView({
    model: this.model,
    el: 'div#stock-context'
});

// Create and initialize the detail view
var detailView = new app.StockDetailView({
    model: this.model,
    el: 'div#stock-detail'
});

// Fetch the stock data.
this.model.fetchData();
return this;
}
```

Finally, we tell the model to fetch the stock data to allow the context and detail chart to be rendered. Remember that when the data is ready, the model will set its data attribute, notifying the charts to update its contents.

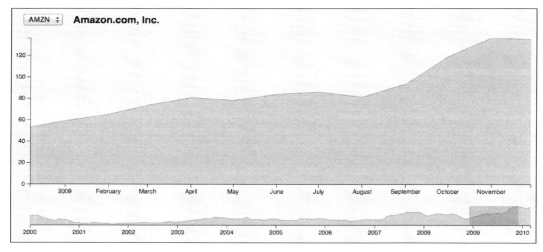

Components of the rendered application

Defining the routes

In our application, the state of the visualization can be described by the stock symbol and the time interval selected in the context chart. In this section, we will connect the URL with the application state, allowing the user to navigate (using the back button of the browser) the bookmark and share a particular state of the application.

We define the routes for our application by assigning callbacks for each hash URL (Backbone provides support for real URLs too). Here, we define two routes, one to set the stock and one to set the complete state of the application. If the user types the #stock/AAPL hash fragment, the setStock method will be invoked, passing the 'AAPL' string as the argument. The second route allows you to navigate to a specific state of the application using a URL fragment of the #stock/AAPL/from/Mon Dec 01 2003/to/Tue Mar 02 2010 form; this will invoke the setState method of the router:

```
app.StockRouter = Backbone.Router.extend({

    // Define the application routes
    routes: {
        'stock/:stock': 'setStock',
        'stock/:stock/from/:from/to/:to': 'setState'
    },

    // Initialize and route callbacks...
});
```

The router also has an initialize method, which will be in charge of synchronizing changes in the application URL with changes in the application model. We will set the model for the router and configure the router to listen for change events of the model. At the beginning, the data might not have been loaded yet (and the from and to attributes might be undefined at this point); in this case, we set the stock symbol only. When the data finishes the loading, the from and to attributes will change and the router will invoke its setState method:

```
    // Listen to model changes to update the url route
    initialize: function(attributes) {
        this.model = attributes.model;
        this.listenTo(this.model, 'change', function(m) {
            if (m.get('from') && m.get('to')) {
                this.setState(m.get('stock'), m.get('from'),
m.get('to'));
            } else {
                this.setStock(m.get('stock'));
            }
        });
    },
```

The `setStock` method updates the `symbol` attribute of the model. The `navigate` method updates the browser URL to reflect the change of stock. Note that we are using the time interval as a variable of the application state. If we select an interval, the back button of the browser will get us to the previously selected time intervals. This might not be desirable in some cases. The choice of which variables should be included in the URL will depend on the application and the behavior that most users will expect. In this case for instance, an alternative approach could be to update the application state on drag start and drag end, not on every change in the interval:

```
// Set the application stock and updates the url
setStock: function(symbol) {
    var urlTpl = _.template('stock/<%= stock %>');

    this.model.set({stock: symbol});
    this.navigate(urlTpl({stock: symbol}), {trigger: true});
},
```

The `setState` method parses the `from` and `to` parameters from the URL as dates and sets the model's `stock`, `from`, and `to` attributes. As we cast the strings to the date, we can use any format recognizable by the date constructor (YYYY-MM-DD, for instance), but this will imply that we format the `from` and `to` attributes to this format when the model changes in order to update the URL. We will use the `toDateString` method to keep things simple. After setting the model state, we construct the URL and invoke the `navigate` method to update the browser URL:

```
// Set the application state and updates the url
setState: function(symbol, from, to) {

    from = new Date(from),
    to = new Date(to);

    this.model.set({stock: symbol, from: from, to: to});

    var urlTpl = _.template('stock/<%= stock %>/from/<%= from
%>/to/<%= to %>'),
        fromString = from.toDateString(),
        toString = to.toDateString();

    this.navigate(urlTpl({stock: symbol, from: fromString,
to: toString}), {trigger: true});
    }
```

The simple addition of a router can make an application way more useful, allowing users to bookmark and share a particular state of the page and navigate back to previous states of the application.

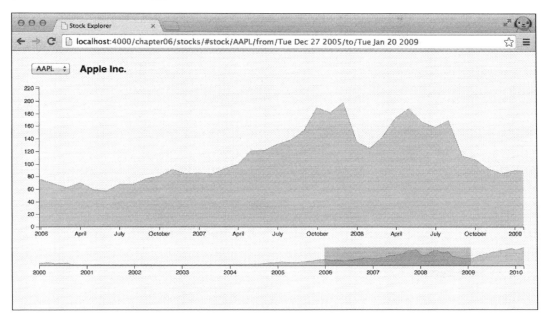

The application state is displayed in the browser URL

Initializing the application

Once we have created the application models, collections, views, and router, we can create the instances for the application model and view. The application initialization code is in the chapter06/stocks/js/app.js file.

We begin by creating an instance of the app.StockList collection:

```
// Create an instance of the stocks collection
app.Stocks = new app.StockList();
```

The collection instances will be retrieved later.

We create an instance of the application model and an instance of the application view. We initialize the application model by indicating the model of the view and the container element ID:

```
// Create the application model instance
app.appModel = new app.StockAppModel();

// Create the application view
app.appView = new app.StockAppView({
    model: app.appModel,
    el: 'div#stock-app'
});
```

Finally, we initialize the router, passing the application model as the first argument, and then we tell Backbone to begin monitoring changes to hashchange events:

```
// Initializes the router
var router = new app.StockRouter({model: app.appModel});
Backbone.history.start();
```

Summary

In this chapter, you learned how to create a single page application that integrates D3 and Backbone. We used the reusable chart pattern and embedded the charts in Backbone Views, allowing us to enjoy the structure of Backbone and keep all the visualization components synchronized.

We created the stock explorer application. This application allows the user to choose and explore the time series of stock prices, allowing the user to select the stock and a time interval in order to have a detail view of the price variations in that period. We used Backbone to store the visualization state and the views in sync.

We used a router to connect the visualization state with the URL, allowing us to share, bookmark, and navigate through visited application states.

In the next chapter, you will learn how to create a charting package, which will contain a layout and a reusable chart. We will also learn how to configure it to make it easier to distribute, install, upgrade, and manage its dependencies on other packages.

7
Creating a Charting Package

Writing good quality software involves several tasks in addition to writing the code. Maintaining a code repository, testing, and writing consistent documentation are some of the tasks that need to be done when working with other people. This is also the case when we write charts and visualizations with D3. If we create a charting package, we would like to make it easy for others to use it and integrate it in their projects. In this chapter, we will describe a workflow and the tools that will help us to create a charting package. In this chapter, we will cover the following tasks:

- **Creating a repository**: A version control system should be used. In some cases, this involves configuring a central repository.

- **Designing the API**: Decide how to organize the code in logic units and how the package functionality will be exposed.

- **Writing the code**: Implement the package components and features.

- **Testing**: The package components should be tested to minimize the risk of introducing unexpected behavior and breaking the existing functionality.

- **Building**: The source code isn't shipped as is to build a package. This implies that at least source files need to be concatenated and a minified version of the distributable files should be created.

- **Hosting the package**: The package should be accessible for others to use, even if it's intended for internal usage.

Also, there are a number of conventions and norms about how these tasks should be performed. There may be protocols for the following:

- **Committing changes**: This is a workflow to know how to merge hot fixes or new features for the next release or the development version of the project. This may include tasks to be done before you push for changes, such as testing the code or having code review sessions.

- **Creating a release**: This is a procedure to create, tag, and release new versions of the software, including how to follow a system to tag releases with version numbers.
- **Writing code**: This is a set of coding practices and conventions agreed upon by the teams.

Most of these tasks and protocols depend on the team and the type of project, but it is almost certain that a number of them will (or should) be in place.

In this chapter, we will create a D3-based charting package. We will use tools to check code conventions, test, and build distributable files for our charting package. Even if the tools that we will use have proven to be successful and are widely used in frontend projects, you may prefer to use different tools for some of the tasks. Feel free to explore and discover a toolset more appropriate for your workflow.

The development workflow

In this section, we will provide an overview of the workflow to create and distribute our charting package. We will also discuss some conventions regarding version numbers and the process of creating a release, introduce tools that will help us to manage the dependences with other projects, run the tests, and automate the package building process.

Writing the code

We begin by creating the project directory and the initial package content. During the development of our charting package, we need to perform the following actions:

- Implement new features or modify the existing code
- Check whether our code follows the coding guidelines
- Implement tests for the new functionality or create additional tests for the existing features
- Run tests to ensure that the modifications don't introduce unexpected behaviors or break the public API
- Concatenate the source files to generate a single JavaScript file that contains the charting package
- Generate a minified file

When implementing new features or fixing bugs, we will modify the code, check for errors, and run the tests. We will repeat the modify-check-test cycle several times until we finish implementing the feature or fix the bug. At this point, we will check and test the code again, build the package, and commit our changes.

As mentioned before, there are many tools that will help us to automate these tasks. There are a great number of tools to make the frontend workflow easier, and every developer has his or her preferences and opinions in this regard. In this chapter, we will use Node.js modules to orchestrate our development tasks. We will use the following tools:

- **Vows**: This is an asynchronous, behavior-driven JavaScript testing framework for Node.js. We will use Vows to test our charting package.

- **Grunt**: This is a task runner for Node.js. We will use Grunt and some plugins to check the source files, concatenate, minify, and test our package.

- **Bower**: This is a frontend package management system. We will configure our package such that users can install our package and its dependencies (D3) easily.

Creating a release

Depending on our development workflow, we may want to create a **release**. A release is a state of our package that we distribute for it to be used. It's usually identified with a version number that indicates how much it has changed from the previous versions.

Semantic Versioning

The version number is especially important in systems with many dependencies. Depending too much on the functionality provided by a specific version of a package can lead to a version lock, that is, the inability to update the package without having to release new versions of our own package. On the other hand, if we update the package assuming that it's compatible with our software, we will eventually find that it is not the case and that the package has made changes to the API that are not compatible with our software.

Semantic Versioning is a useful convention that helps you to know if it's safe to update a package, as long as it follows the Semantic Versioning convention. The complete specification of Semantic Versioning 2.0.0 (yes, the specification itself is versioned) is available at `http://semver.org/`. The key points of the Semantic Versioning convention are as follows.

Each release should be assigned a version number of the form **MAJOR.MINOR. PATCH**, with optional identifiers after a dash (1.0.0-beta, for instance). The version numbers are integers (without leading zeros) and should be incremented when we create a new release by the following rules:

- **MAJOR**: This version is used when you make backward-incompatible changes to the API
- **MINOR**: This version is used when a new functionality is added without breaking the API
- **PATCH**: This version is used for improvements and bug fixes that don't change the public API

When we increment the MAJOR version, MINOR and PATCH are set to zero; increments in MINOR will reset the PATCH number to zero. The content of a release must not be modified; any modification should be released as a new version.

If we follow this convention, users will know that upgrading from 2.1.34 to 2.1.38 is safe and upgrading from 2.1.38 to 2.2.0 is also safe (and it may provide additional backward-compatible features), while upgrading from 2.2.0 to 3.0.1 will require you to check whether the changes in the new version are still compatible with the existing code. In the next sections, we will create the initial content of the package and configure the tools to test and build our package.

Creating the package contents

We will create a small package containing a heat map chart and a layout function. We begin by choosing a name for our project, creating an empty directory, and initializing the repository. The name of our package will be `Windmill`. Once we have created the directory, we can create the initial content. We will organize the code in components and implement the chart and the helper functions in separate files. The source code will be organized in folders, one for each component. Later, we will concatenate the files in the correct order to generate the `windmill.js` file, containing all the components of the package:

```
src/
   chart/
      chart.js
      heatmap.js
   layout/
      layout.js
      matrix.js
   svg/
      svg.js
```

```
    transform.js
  start.js
  end.js
```

We add the `version` attribute and indicate that we will follow the Semantic Version specification:

```
!function() {
    var windmill = {version: '0.1.0'}; // semver
    // Charts
    windmill.chart = {};
    windmill.chart.heatmap = function() {...};
    // Other Components...
}();
```

We can load this file in the browser or using Node.js. In either case, the anonymous function will be invoked, but nothing more will happen. In order to expose the package functionality in Node, we need to load D3 as a Node package in the context of the module and export the contents of the `windmill` object. This will allow other Node modules (our tests, for instance) to load our package as a Node module. If the file is loaded in the browser, we assume that D3 is available and add the `windmill` attribute to the global object and set its value to the package contents. Note that when we run the anonymous function in the global scope, the `this` context is set to the global object:

```
!function() {
    var windmill = {version: '0.1.0'}; // semver

    // Charts
    windmill.chart = {};
    windmill.chart.heatMap = function() {...};

    // Other Components...

    // Expose the package components
    if (typeof module === 'object' && module.exports) {
        // The package is loaded as a node module
        this.d3 = require('d3');
        module.exports = windmill;
    } else {
        // The file is loaded in the browser.
        this.windmill = windmill;
    }
}();
```

To generate this file, we need to concatenate the source files in order. The `src/start.js` file will contain the beginning of the function and the package version, which must be updated in each release:

```
!function() {
    var windmill = {version: '0.1.0'}; // semver
```

Each component will add an attribute to the `windmill` variable. For instance, the `src/chart/chart.js` file will contain the following attribute:

```
// Charts
windmill.chart = {};
```

The `src/chart/heatmap.js` file will add a function to the `chart` attribute:

```
windmill.chart.heatMap = function() {...};
```

The `matrix` layout should be included in the same way. The `src/end.js` file will contain the last part of the consolidated file. If the file is loaded as a Node.js module, the `module.exports` variable will be defined; we import the D3 library and export the windmill package. If the file is loaded in the browser, we assign the `windmill` object to the `window` object, making it available as a global variable:

```
// Expose the package components
if (typeof module === 'object'&& module.exports) {
    // The package is loaded as a node module
    this.d3 = require('d3');
    module.exports = windmill;
} else {
    // The file is loaded in the browser.
    window.windmill = windmill;
}
}();
```

The heat map chart

A heat map is a chart that aims to represent the dependency of one quantitative variable as a function of two ordinal variables.

A heat map is a chart that allows you to visualize the dependency between a variable and two other variables. It resembles a matrix where each cell's color is proportional to the value of the main variable, and the rows and columns represent the other variables. Refer to the following screenshot:

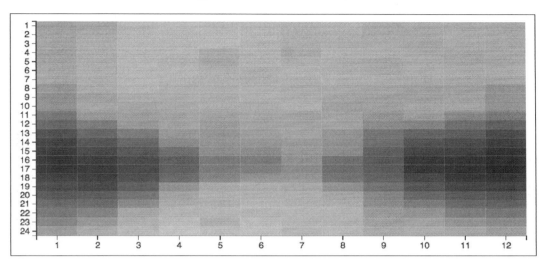

A heat map showing the average wind speeds by hour and month

Heat maps are useful to detect patterns and the dependency between the target variable in the function of the variables represented by the rows and columns. We will put the code for the heat map chart in the src/chart/heatmap.js file. We will implement the heat map chart as a reusable chart, but this time, we will generate the accessor methods automatically to avoid writing similar code for each chart attribute. We begin by adding the heatmap function as an attribute of the windmill.chart object:

```
// HeatMap Chart
windmill.chart.heatmap = function() {
    'use strict';

    function chart(selection) {
        // ...
    }

    return chart;
};
```

Heatmap function usually receives a matrix as data input while heat maps usually receive a matrix as input data. We can represent a matrix as a nested array or use a columnar representation of a matrix, where each cell is represented as an item in a list. Each item has a row, column, and value, indicating the content of each cell in the matrix (this representation is especially useful for sparse matrices). The default input data will be an array of objects with at least three attributes: rows, columns, and values:

```
var data = [
    {row: 1, column: 1, value: 5.5},
    {row: 1, column: 2, value: 2.5},
    // more items...
    {row: 6, column: 4, value: 7.5}
];
```

We will add configurable accessor functions so that the user can configure which attributes will be the rows, columns, and values. As we will generate the accessor methods automatically, we will hold the chart properties in the `attributes` object. This element will be used to generate the accessor methods:

```
// HeatMap Chart
windmill.chart.heatmap = function() {
    'use strict';

    // Default Attribute Container
    var attributes = {
        width: 600,
        height: 300,
        margin: {top: 20, right: 20, bottom: 40, left: 40},
        colorExtent: ['#000', '#aaa'],
        value: function(d) { return d.value; },
        row: function(d) { return d.row; },
        column: function(d) { return d.column; }
    };

    // Charting function...

    return chart;
}
```

We set the default values for the width, height, margin, and color extent. We also define default accessor functions for the rows, columns, and values.

We will generate accessor methods for each attribute. We want the generated accessors to have the same behavior as that of the accessors written explicitly. Also, we want to be able to overwrite accessors if we need to include more logic than to simply get or set a value. Until now, we have written the accessor method for the width attribute as follows:

```
chart.width = function(w) {
    if (!arguments.length) { return width; }
    width = w;
    return chart;
};
```

If no arguments are passed, the chart.width method will return the current value of the width variable. If we pass a value, the width value is updated and we return the chart to allow method chaining. Since our attributes object holds the chart properties, we should update this method:

```
chart['width'] = function(val) {
    if (!arguments.length) { return attributes['width']; }
    attributes['width'] = val;
    return chart;
};
```

Here, we avoided hardcoding the width attribute. This will work, but we still have to write a function that receives a value and modifies the width attribute. We will create a function that returns an accessor function for a specific attribute:

```
// Create an accessor function for the given attribute
function createAccessor(attr) {
    // Accessor function
    function accessor(value) {
        if (!arguments.length) { return attributes[attr]; }
        attributes[attr] = value;
        return chart;
    }
    return accessor;
}
```

We can now assign an accessor function for the width attribute using the following code:

```
// Set the accessor function for the width
chart['width'] = createAccessor('width');
```

This is still not good enough; we should iterate the properties of the attributes object and create one accessor method for each property. First, we should check whether the accessor already exists to avoid overwriting it, and we should verify that the properties are of the attributes object, and not from the higher accessor in the prototype chain:

```
// Create accessors for each element in attributes
for (var attr in attributes) {
    if ((!chart[attr]) && (attributes.hasOwnProperty(attr))) {
        chart[attr] = createAccessor(attr);
    }
}
```

This will generate an accessor for each property in the attributes object. Note that the accessors will just get and set the attributes; there are no validations or logic besides assigning or returning the values. If we need a more complex accessor for an attribute, we can add it and it won't be overwritten.

The charting function will select the div container and create an svg element to contain the chart. As we have done before, we will encapsulate the initialization of the svg element in the chart.svgInit method:

```
// Charting function
function chart(selection) {
    selection.each(function(data) {
        // Initialize the SVG element on enter
        var div = d3.select(this),
            svg = div.selectAll('svg').data([data])
                .enter().append('svg')
                .call(chart.svgInit);
    });
}
```

In the chart.svgInit method, we set the dimensions of the svg element and create groups for the chart and the horizontal and vertical axes:

```
// Initialize the SVG Element
chart.svgInit = function(svg) {

    // Compute the width and height of the charting area
    var margin = chart.margin(),
        width = chart.width() - margin.left - margin.right,
        height = chart.height() - margin.top - margin.bottom,
        translate = windmill.svg.translate;

    // Set the size of the svg element
```

```
svg
    .attr('width', chart.width())
    .attr('height', chart.height());

// Chart Container
svg.append('g')
    .attr('class', 'chart')
    .attr('transform', translate(margin.left, margin.top));

// X Axis Container
svg.append('g')
    .attr('class', 'axis xaxis')
    .attr('transform', translate(margin.left, margin.top +
height));

// Y Axis Container
svg.append('g')
    .attr('class', 'axis yaxis')
    .attr('transform', translate(margin.left, margin.top));
};
```

Here, we used the accessor method generated previously to access the width, height, and margin. We can also access these through the `attributes` object in the charting code, but the attribute won't be accessible for code using the `chart` object. In the charting function, we compute the width and height of the charting area and create shortcuts for the row, column, and value accessors. Without these shortcuts, we would need to invoke the row function either as `attributes.row(d)` or `chart.row()(d)`:

```
// Compute the width and height of the chart area
var margin = chart.margin(),
    width = chart.width() - margin.left - margin.right,
    height = chart.height() - margin.top - margin.bottom;

// Retrieve the accessor functions
var row = chart.row(),
    col = chart.column(),
    val = chart.value();
```

We can create the scales for the position and color of the rectangles. We will use ordinal scales and use the `rangeBands` range. This option allows you to divide an interval into *n* evenly spaced bands, where *n* is the number of unique elements in the domain:

```
// Horizontal Position
var xScale = d3.scale.ordinal()
    .domain(data.map(col))
    .rangeBands([0, width]);

// Vertical Position
var yScale = d3.scale.ordinal()
    .domain(data.map(row))
    .rangeBands([0, height]);

// Color Scale
var cScale = d3.scale.linear()
    .domain(d3.extent(data, val))
    .range(chart.colorExtent());
```

We can create the rectangles on enter as follows:

```
// Create the heatmap rectangles on enter
var rect = gchart.selectAll('rect').data(data)
    .enter().append('rect');
```

We can set the width, height, and position of the rectangles, and set the fill color using the aforementioned scales and accessor functions for the rows, columns, and values. The width and height are set using the width of a band, which is computed by the scale:

```
// Set the attributes of the rectangles
rect.attr('width', xScale.rangeBand())
    .attr('height', yScale.rangeBand())
    .attr('x', function(d) { return xScale(col(d)); })
    .attr('y', function(d) { return yScale(row(d)); })
    .attr('fill', function(d) { return cScale(val(d)); });
```

Finally, we add the axes for the horizontal and vertical axes:

```
// Create the Horizontal Axis
var xAxis = d3.svg.axis()
    .scale(xScale)
    .orient('bottom');
```

```
svg.select('g.xaxis').call(xAxis);

// Create the Vertical Axis
var yAxis = d3.svg.axis()
    .scale(yScale)
    .orient('left');
svg.select('g.yaxis').call(yAxis);
```

We will create an example file for the heat map. In the `examples/heatmap.html` file, we create a container div with the `chart01` ID:

```
<div id="chart01"></div>
```

We will generate a sample data array and create a chart instance, configuring the width, height, and color extent:

```
// Generate a sample data array
var data = [];
for (var k = 0; k < 20; k += 1) {
    for (var j = 0; j < 20; j += 1) {
        data.push({
            row: k,
            column: j,
            value: Math.cos(Math.PI * k * j / 60)
        });
    }
}

// Create and configure the heatmap chart
var heatmap = windmill.chart.heatmap()
    .width(600)
    .height(300)
    .colorExtent(['#555, '#ddd']);
```

Here, the lower values will be **dark gray**, and the higher values will be **blue**. The matrix data contains values for two rows and four columns. We have given a value for each cell; if there were missing items, the cells would just not be drawn. We select the container element, bind the data array, and invoke the heat map using the `selection.call` method:

```
// Create the heatmap chart in the container selection
d3.select('div#chart01').data([data])
    .call(heatmap);
```

The generated heat map will have eight cells; the color of each cell represents the value's magnitude corresponding to each row and column. Refer to the following screenshot:

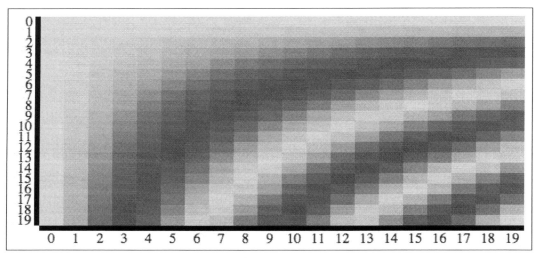

A heat map with the default styles

We will create and include a style sheet file to get a better-looking axis. As the users will need the CSS files to use the chart, we should make the styles available to the users as well. A user could also modify the styles to accommodate the appearance of the chart to the client application. We will add the windmill.css file to the css directory and add the following content:

```css
/* Axis lines */
.axis path, line {
    fill: none;
    stroke: #222222;
    shape-rendering: crispEdges;
}
/* Style for the xaxis */
.xaxis {
    font-size: 12px;
    font-family: sans-serif;
}
/* Style for the yaxis */
.yaxis {
    font-size: 12px;
    font-family: sans-serif
}
```

With these styles, the heat map looks better, which can be seen as follows:

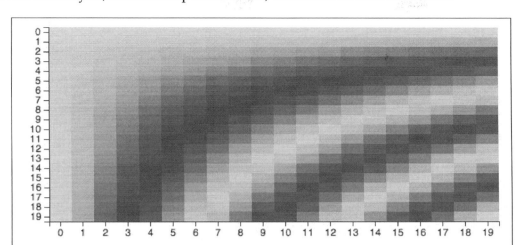

The heat map with improved styles

The matrix layout

In the heat map chart, we assumed that we have unique combinations of the rows and columns in our dataset; having more than one element with the same row and column would cause two overlapping rectangles.

We will create a layout to aggregate the values with the same rows and columns using a configurable aggregation function. For instance, we could have the following dataset:

```
var data = [
    {row: 1, column: 2, value: 5},
    {row: 1, column: 2, value: 4},
    {row: 1, column: 2, value: 9},
    // ...
];
```

The `matrix` layout will allow us to group the values and calculate a single aggregated value, which is usually the sum, count, average, minimum, or maximum value. We will create the `matrix` layout in the `src/layout/matrix.js` file. As in the heat map chart, we begin by adding the `matrix` property to the `layout` object. We will use the reusable chart pattern, except that the charting function is replaced with the `layout` function, which receives the input data and returns the aggregated array:

```
windmill.layout.matrix = function() {
    'use strict';

    function layout(data) {
```

```
        //...
        return groupedData;
    }

    return layout;
};
```

We will use the technique presented in the heat map chart to automatically generate accessor methods. We add the default accessor methods as follows:

```
// Default Accessors
var attributes = {
    row: function(d) { return d.row; },
    column: function(d) { return d.column; },
    value: function(d) { return d.value; },
    aggregate: function(values) {
        var sum = 0;
        values.forEach(function(d) { sum += d; });
        return sum;
    }
};
```

The row, column, and value accessor functions compute the row, column, and value for each input data element. The aggregate function receives an array of values and computes a single aggregated value. The default aggregate function will return the sum of the elements in the input array:

```
// Layout function
function layout(data) {
    // Output data array
    var groupedData = [];

    // Group and aggregate the input values...

    return groupedData;
}
```

We begin by grouping the values for each combination of row and column. We iterate through the input array and compute the item's row, column, and value. The groupedData array will contain elements with the row, col, and values attributes. If the groupedData array contains an element with the same row and column as the current item, we append the value of the item to the values array; if not, we append a new element to the grouped data array:

```
// Group by row and column
data.forEach(function(d) {

    // Compute the row, column, and value

    row = attributes.row(d);
```

```
        col = attributes.column(d);
        val = attributes.value(d);

        // Search corresponding items in groupedData
        found = false;

        groupedData.forEach(function(item, idx) {
            if ((item.row === row) && (item.col === col)) {
                groupedData[idx].values.push(val);
                item.values.push(val);
                found = true;
            }
        });

        // Append the item, if not found
        if (!found) {
            groupedData.push({
                row: row,
                col: col,
                values: [val]
            });
        }
    });
```

We can now aggregate the values using the `aggregate` function. This function receives an array and returns a single value. Finally, we remove the `values` attribute:

```
// Aggregate the values
groupedData.forEach(function(d) {
    // Compute the aggregated value
    d.value = attributes.aggregate(d.values);
    delete d.values;
});
```

We generate accessor methods for the layout automatically, with code that is similar to the code in the heat map chart:

```
// Create accessor functions
function createAccessor(attr) {
    function accessor(value) {
        if (!arguments.length) { return attributes[attr]; }
        attributes[attr] = value;
        return layout;
    }
    return accessor;
```

```
    }

    // Generate automatic accessors for each attribute
    for (var attr in attributes) {
        if ((!layout[attr]) && (attributes.hasOwnProperty(attr))) {
            layout[attr] = createAccessor(attr);
        }
    }
```

We will create an example for the `matrix` layout. In the `examples/layout.html` file, we declare a data array with sample data as follows:

```
// Sample data array
var data = [
    {a: 1, b: 1, c: 10},
    {a: 1, b: 1, c:  5},
    // ...
    {a: 2, b: 2, c:  5}
];
```

Note that for each combination of row and column, we have more than one element in the array. We define the average function, computing the sum of all the elements in the input array and dividing the sum by the array's length:

```
// Define the aggregation function (average of values)
var average = function(values) {
    var sum = 0;
    values.forEach(function(d) { sum += d;});
    return sum / values.length;
}
```

We create and configure a `matrix` layout instance, setting the `row` accessor to be a function that returns the a attribute of each element, the `column` function will return the b attribute, and the value will be the c property. We set the `aggregate` function to use our `average` function:

```
// Create and configure a matrix layout instance
var matrix = windmill.layout.matrix()
    .row(function(d) { return d.a; })
    .column(function(d) { return d.b; })
    .value(function(d) { return d.c; })
    .aggregate(average);
```

We invoke the layout using the sample data array, obtaining an array that groups the values by row and column:

```
var grouped = matrix(data);
```

The value of each element will be the average value for the items with the same combination of row and column:

```
// Output values
grouped = [
    {col: 1, row: 1, value: 7.5},
    // ...
    {col: 2, row: 2, value: 10}
];
```

The `matrix` layout allows us to group and aggregate values, making it easier to format data for the heat map chart. Now that we have the initial content, we will configure the tools to build and distribute the package.

The project setup

In this section, we will install and configure the tools that we will use to build our package. We will assume that you know how to use the command line and you have Node installed on your system. You can install Node by either following the instructions from Node.js's website (`http://nodejs.org/download/`) or using a package manager in Unix-like systems.

Installing the Node modules

The **Node Package Manager** (**npm**) is a program that helps us to manage dependencies between Node projects. As our project could be a dependency of other projects, we need to provide information about our package to **npm**. The `package.json` file is a JSON file that should contain at least the project name, version, and dependencies for use and development. For now, we will add just the name and version:

```
{
  "name": "windmill",
  "version": "0.1.0",
  "dependencies": {},
  "devDependencies": {}
}
```

We will install Grunt, Vows, Bower, and D3 using npm. When installing a package, we can pass an option to save the package that we are installing as a dependency. With the `--save-dev` option, we can specify the development dependencies:

```
$ npm install --save-dev grunt vows bower
```

D3 will be a dependency for our package. If someone needs to use our package, D3 will be needed; the previous packages will be necessary only for development. To install the project dependencies, we can use the `--save` option:

```
$ npm install --save d3
```

A directory named `node_modules` will be created at the topmost level of the project. This directory will contain the installed modules:

```
node_modules/
    bower/
    d3/
    grunt/
    vows/
```

The `package.json` file will be updated with the dependencies as well:

```
{
  "name": "windmill",
  "version": "0.1.0",
  "dependencies": {
    "d3": "~3.4.1"
  },
  "devDependencies": {
    "grunt": "~0.4.2",
    "vows": "~0.7.0"
  }
}
```

Note that the dependencies specify the version of each package. Node.js packages should follow the Semantic Versioning specification. We will include additional modules to perform the building tasks, but we will cover that later.

Building with Grunt

Grunt is a task runner for Node.js. It allows you to define tasks and execute them easily. To use Grunt, we need to have a `package.json` file with the project information and the `Gruntfile.js` file, where we will define and configure our tasks. The `Gruntfile.js` file should have the following structure; all the Grunt tasks and configurations should be in the exported function:

```
module.exports = function(grunt) {
    // Grunt initialization and tasks
};
```

The Grunt tasks may need configuration data, which is usually passed to the `grunt.initConfig` method. Here, we import the package configuration from the `package.json` file. This allows you to use the package configuration values in order to generate banners in target files or to display information in the console when we run tasks:

```
module.exports = function(grunt) {
    // Initialize the Grunt configuration
    grunt.initConfig({
        pkg: grunt.file.readJSON('package.json')
    });
};
```

There are hundreds of Grunt plugins to automate every development task with minimal effort. A complete list of the Grunt plugins is available at `http://gruntjs.com/plugins`.

Concatenating our source files

The `grunt-contrib-concat` plugin will concatenate our source files for us. We can install the plugin as any other Node.js module:

```
$ npm install --save-dev grub-contrib-concat
```

To use the plugin, we should enable it and add its configuration as follows:

```
module.exports = function(grunt) {
    grunt.initConfig({
        pkg: grunt.file.readJSON('package.json'),

        concat: {
            // grunt-contrib-concat configuration...
        }
    });

    // Enable the Grunt plugins
    grunt.loadNpmTasks('grunt-contrib-concat');
};
```

We add the `grunt-contrib-concat` configuration. The `concat` object can contain one or more targets, each containing an array of sources and a destination path for the concatenated file. The files in `src` will be concatenated in order:

```
    // Initialize the Grunt configuration
    grunt.initConfig({

        // Import the package configuration
```

```
        pkg: grunt.file.readJSON('package.json'),

        // Configure the concat task
        concat: {
            js: {
                src: [
                    'src/start.js',
                    'src/svg/svg.js',
                    'src/svg/transform.js',
                    'src/chart/chart.js',
                    'src/chart/heatmap.js',
                    'src/layout/layout.js',
                    'src/layout/matrix.js',
                    'src/end.js'
                ],
                dest: 'windmill.js'
            }
        },
    });
```

There are options to add a banner too, which can be useful to add a comment indicating the package name and version. We can run the concat task from the command line as follows:

```
$ grunt concat
Running "concat:js" (concat) task
File "windmill.js" created.
Done, without errors.
```

If we have several targets, we can build them individually by passing the target after the concat option:

```
$ grunt concat:js
Running "concat:js" (concat) task
File "windmill.js" created.
Done, without errors.
```

The windmill.js file contains the sources of our package concatenated in order, preserving the original spaces and comments.

Minifying the library

It's common practice to distribute two versions of the library: one version with the original format and comments for debugging and another minified version for production. To create the minified version, we will need the `grunt-contrib-uglify` plugin. As we did with the `grunt-contrib-concat` package, we need to install this and enable it in the `Gruntfile.js` file:

```
module.exports = function(grunt) {
    // ...

    // Enable the Grunt plugins
    grunt.loadNpmTasks('grunt-contrib-concat');
    grunt.loadNpmTasks('grunt-contrib-uglify');
};
```

We need to add the `uglify` configuration to the `grunt.initConfig` method as well. In `uglify`, we can have more than one target. The `options` attribute allows us to define the behavior of `uglify`. In this case, we set `mangle` to `false` in order to keep the names of our variables as they are in the original code. If the `mangle` option is set to `true`, the variable names will be replaced with shorter names, as follows:

```
// Uglify Configuration
uglify: {
    options: {
        mangle: false
    },
    js: {
        files: {
            'windmill.min.js': ['windmill.js']
        }
    }
}
```

We can run the minification task in the command line using the same syntax as in the concatenation task:

```
$ grunt uglify
Running "uglify:js" (uglify) task
File windmill.min.js created.
Done, without errors.
```

This will generate the `windmill.min.js` file, which is about half the size of the original version.

Checking our code with JSHint

In JavaScript, it is very easy to write code that doesn't behave as we expect. It could be a missing semicolon or forgetting to declare a variable in a certain scope. A **linter** is a program that helps us to detect potential errors and dangerous constructions by enforcing a series of coding conventions. Of course, a static code analysis tool can't detect these if your program is correct. **JSHint** is a tool that helps us to detect these potential problems by checking the JavaScript code against code conventions. The behavior of JSHint can be configured to match our coding conventions.

 JSHint is a fork of **JSLint**, a tool created by Douglas Crockford to check code against a particular set of coding standards. His choices on coding style are explained in the book *JavaScript: The Good Parts*.

In JSHint, the code conventions can be set by writing a `jshintrc` file, a JSON file containing a series of flags that will define the JSHint behavior. For instance, a configuration file might contain the following flags:

```
{
    "curly": true,
    "eqeqeq": true,
    "undef": true,
    // ...
}
```

The `curly` option will enforce the use of curly braces (`{` and `}`) around conditionals and loops, even if we have only one statement. The `eqeqeq` option enforces the use of `===` and `!==` to compare objects, instead of `==` and `!=`. If you don't have a set of coding conventions already, I would recommend that you read the list of JSHint options available at `http://www.jshint.com/docs/options/` and create a new `.jshintrc` file. Here, the options are listed and explained, so you can make an informed decision about which flags to enable.

Many editors have support for live linting, but even if the text editor checks the code as you write, it is a good practice to check the code before committing your changes. We will enable the `grunt-contrib-jshint` module and configure it so that we can check our code easily. We will enable the plugin as follows:

```
// Enable the Grunt plugins
grunt.loadNpmTasks('grunt-contrib-concat');
grunt.loadNpmTasks('grunt-contrib-uglify');
grunt.loadNpmTasks('grunt-contrib-jshint');
```

Next, we configure the plugin. We will check the `Gruntfile.js` file, our tests, and the code of our chart:

```
jshint: {
    all: [
        'Gruntfile.js',
        'src/svg/*.js',
        'src/chart/*.js',
        'src/layout/*.js',
        'test/*.js',
        'test/*/*.js'
    ]
}
```

We can check our code using the following command lines:

```
$ grunt jshint
Running "jshint:all" (jshint) task
>> 11 files lint free.
Done, without errors.
```

Testing our package

Distributing a software package is a great responsibility. The users of our charting package rely on our code and assume that everything works as expected. Despite our best intentions, we may break the existing functionality when implementing a new feature or fixing a bug. The only way to minimize these errors is to extensively test our code.

The tests should be easy to write and run, allowing us to write the tests as we code new features and to run the tests before committing changes. There are several test suites for JavaScript code. In this section, we will use Vows, an asynchronous behavior-driven test suite for Node.js.

Writing a simple test

In Vows, the largest test unit is a **suite**. We will begin by creating a simple test using JavaScript without any libraries. In the `test` directory, we create the `universe-test.js` file.

We will load the `vows` and `assert` modules and assign them to the local variables:

```
// Load the modules
var vows = require('vows'),
    assert = require('assert');
```

We can create a suite now. The convention is to have one suite per file and to match the suite description with the filename. We create a suite by invoking the vows.describe method:

```
// Create the suite
var suite = vows.describe('Universe');
```

Tests are added to the suite in batches. A suite can have zero or more batches, which will be executed sequentially. The batches are added using the suite.addBatch method. Batches allow you to perform tests in a given order:

```
suite.addBatch({
    //...
});
```

A batch, in turn, contains zero or more **contexts**, which describe the behaviors or states that we want to test. Contexts are run in parallel, and they are asynchronous; the order in which they will be completed can't be predicted. We will add a context to our batch, as follows:

```
suite.addBatch({
    'the answer': {
        //...
    }
});
```

A context contains a topic. The topic is a value or function that returns an element to be tested. The vows are the actual tests. The vows are the functions that make assertions about the topic. We will add a topic to our context as follows:

```
suite.addBatch({
    'the answer': {
        topic: 42,
        //...
    }
});
```

In this case, all our vows in the context the answer will receive the value 42 as the argument. We will add some vows to assert whether the topic is undefined, null, or a number, and finally, whether the topic is equal to 42. Refer to the following code:

```
suite.addBatch({
    'the answer': {
        topic: 42,
        "shouldn't be undefined": function(topic) {
            assert.notEqual(topic, undefined);
        },
```

```
        "shouldn't be null": function(topic) {
            assert.notEqual(topic, null);
        },
        "should be a number": function(topic) {
            assert.isNumber(topic);
        },
        "should be 42": function(topic) {
            assert.equal(topic, 42);
        }
    }
});
```

To execute all the tests in the test directory as a single entity (instead of having to run each one separately), we need to export the suite:

```
suite.export(module);
```

We can run these tests individually by passing the test path as the argument:

```
$ vows test/universe-test.js --spec
◇ Universe


  the answer to the Universe
√ shouldn't be undefined
√ shouldn't be null
√ should be a number
√ should be 42


√ OK » 4 honored (0.007s)
```

We will temporarily modify our topic to introduce an error as follows:

```
suite.addBatch({
    'the answer': {
        topic: 43,
        //...
    }
});
```

The output of the test will show which vows were honored and which failed, displaying additional details for the broken vows. In this case, three vows where honored and one was broken.

```
◇ Universe

  the answer
√ shouldn't be undefined
```

```
√ shouldn't be null
√ should be a number
✗ should be 42
        » expected 42,
    got    43 (==) // universe-test.js:27


✗ Broken » 3 honored · 1 broken (0.564s)
```

This simple example shows you how to create a suite, context, topics, and vows to test a simple feature. We will use the same structure to test our heat map chart.

Testing the heat map chart

The tests for the heat map chart will be more involved than the test from the previous example; for one thing, we need to load D3 and the `windmill` library as Node modules.

D3 is a library that can be used to modify DOM elements based on data. In node applications, we don't have a browser and the DOM doesn't exist. To have a document with a DOM tree, we can use the JSDOM module. When we load D3 as a module, it creates the document and includes JSDOM for us; we don't need to load JSDOM (or create the `document` and `window` objects).

To create a test for the heat map chart, we create the `test/chart/heatmap-test.js` file and load the `vows`, `assert`, and `d3` modules. We also load our charting library as a local file:

```
// Import the required modules
var vows = require("vows"),
    assert = require("assert"),
    d3 = require("d3"),
    windmill = require("../../windmill");
```

We will also add a data array and use it later to create the charts. This array will be accessible for the vows and contexts in the module, but it won't be exported.

```
// Sample Data Array
var data = [
    {row: 1, column: 1, value: 5.5},
    {row: 1, column: 2, value: 2.5},
    // ...
    {row: 2, column: 4, value: 7.5}
];
```

The suite will contain tests for the heat map chart. We will describe the suite. It is not necessary to describe the suite with the path to the method being tested, but it's a good practice and helps you to locate errors when the tests don't pass.

```
// Create a Test Suite for the heatmap chart
var suite = vows.describe("windmill.chart.heatmap");
```

We will add a batch that contains the contexts to be tested. In the first context topic, we will create a div element, create a chart with the default options, bind the data array with the div element, and create a chart in the first context topic:

```
// Append the Batches
suite.addBatch({
    "the default chart svg": {
        topic: function() {


            // Create the chart instance and a sample data array
            var chart = windmill.chart.heatmap();

            // Invoke the chart passing the container div
            d3.select("body").append("div")
                .attr("id", "default")
                .data([data])
                .call(chart);

            // Return the svg element for testing
            return d3.select("div#default").select("svg");
        },

        // Vows...
    }
});
```

We will create vows to assert whether the svg element exists, its width and height match the default values, it contains groups for the chart and axis, and the number of rectangles match the number of elements in the data array:

```
// Append the Batches
suite.addBatch({
    "the default chart svg": {
        topic: function() {...},
        "exists": function(svg) {
            assert.equal(svg.empty(), false);
        },
        "is 600px wide": function(svg) {
```

```
                    assert.equal(svg.attr('width'), '600');
            },
            "is 300px high": function(svg) {
                    assert.equal(svg.attr('height'), '300');
            },
            "has a group for the chart": function(svg) {
                    assert.equal(svg.select("g.chart").empty(), false);
            },
            "has a group for the xaxis": function(svg) {
                    assert.equal(svg.select("g.xaxis").empty(), false);
            },
            "has a group for the yaxis": function(svg) {
                    assert.equal(svg.select("g.yaxis").empty(), false);
            },
            "the group has one rectangle for each data item":
    function(svg) {
                    var rect = svg.select('g').selectAll("rect");
                    assert.equal(rect[0].length, data.length);
            }
        }
    });
```

We can run the test with vows and check whether the default attributes of the chart are correctly set and the structure of the inner elements is organized as it should be:

```
$ vows test/chart/heatmap-test.js  --spec

◇ windmill.chart.heatmap

  the default chart svg
√ exists
√ is 600px wide
√ is 300px high
√ has a group for the chart
√ has a group for the xaxis
√ has a group for the yaxis
√ the group has one rectangle for each data item

√ OK » 7 honored (0.075s)
```

In a real-world application, we would have to add tests for many more configurations.

Testing the matrix layout

The `matrix` layout is simpler to test, because we don't need the DOM or even D3.
We begin by importing the required modules and creating a suite, as follows:

```
// Create the test suite
var suite = vows.describe("windmill.layout.matrix");
```

We add a small data array to test the layout:

```
// Create a sample data array
var data = [
    {a: 1, b: 1, c: 10},
    // ...
    {a: 2, b: 2, c:  5}
];
```

We define an average function, as we did in the example file:

```
var avgerage = function(values) {
    var sum = 0;
    values.forEach(function(d) { sum += d; });
    return sum / values.length;
};
```

We add a batch and a context to check the default layout attributes and generate the
layout in the context's topic:

```
// Add a batch to test the default layout
suite.addBatch({
    "default layout": {
        topic: function() {
        return windmill.layout.matrix();
    },
```

We add vows to test whether the layout is a function and has the `row`, `column`,
and `value` methods:

```
"is a function": function(topic) {
    assert.isFunction(topic);
},
"has a row method": function(topic) {
    assert.isFunction(topic.row);
},
"has a column method": function(topic) {
    assert.isFunction(topic.column);
},
```

```
        "has a value method": function(topic) {
            assert.isFunction(topic.value);
        }
    }
});
```

We can run the tests using `vows test/layout/matrix-test.js --spec`, but we will automate the task of running the tests with Grunt.

Running the tests with Grunt

We will add a test task to the `Gruntfile.js` file in order to automate the execution of tests. We will need to install the `grunt-vows` module:

```
$ npm install --save-dev grunt-vows
```

As usual, we need to enable the `grunt-vows` plugin in the `Gruntfile.js` file:

```
// Enable the Grunt plugins
grunt.loadNpmTasks('grunt-contrib-concat');
// ...
grunt.loadNpmTasks("grunt-vows");
```

We will configure the task to run all the tests in the `test` directory. As we have done when running the tests, we will add the `spec` option to obtain detailed reporting. Removing this option will use the default value, displaying each test as a point in the console:

```
vows: {
    all: {
        options: {reporter: 'spec'},
        src: ['test/*.js', 'test/*/*.js']
    }
},
```

We could create additional targets to test the components individually as we modify them. We can now run the task from the command line:

```
$ grunt vows
Running "vows:all" (vows) task
(additional output not shown)
Done, without errors.
```

Testing the code doesn't guarantee that you will have bug-free code, but it will certainly help you to detect unexpected behaviors. A mature software usually has thousands of tests. At the time of writing, for instance, D3 has about 2,500 tests.

Registering the sequences of tasks

We have created and configured the essential tasks for our project, but we can automate the process further. For instance, while modifying the code, we need to check and test the code, but we won't need a minified version until we are ready to push the changes to the repository. We will register two groups of tasks, test and build. The test task will check the code, concatenate the source files, and run the tests. To register a task, we give the task a name and add a list of the subtasks to be executed:

```
// Test Task
grunt.registerTask('test', ['jshint', 'concat', 'vows']);
```

We can execute the test task in the command line, triggering the jshint, concat, and vows tasks in a sequence:

```
$ grunt test
```

We register the build task in a similar way; this task will run jshint, concat, vows, and uglify in order, generating the files that we want to distribute:

```
// Generate distributable files
grunt.registerTask('build', ['jshint', 'vows', 'concat',
'uglify']);
```

A default task can be added too. We will add a default task that just runs the build task:

```
// Default task
grunt.registerTask('default', ['build']);
```

To run the default task, we invoke Grunt without arguments. There are hundreds of Grunt plugins available; they can be used to automate almost everything. There are plugins to optimize images, copy files, compile the LESS or SASS files to CSS, minify the CSS files, monitor files for changes, and run tasks automatically, among many others. We could automate additional tasks, such as updating the version number in the source files or running tasks automatically when we modify source files.

The objective of automating tasks is not only to save time, but it also makes it easier to actually do the tasks and establish a uniform workflow among peers. It also allows developers to focus on writing code and makes the development process more enjoyable.

Managing the frontend dependencies

If our package is to be used in web applications, we should declare that it depends on D3 and also specify the version of D3 that we need. For many years, projects just declared their dependencies on their web page, leaving the task of downloading and installing the dependencies to the user. Bower is a package manager for web applications (`http://bower.io/`). It makes the process of installing and updating packages easier. Bower is a Node module; it can be installed either locally using `npm`, as we did earlier in the chapter, or globally using `npm install -g bower`:

```
$ npm install --save bower
```

This will install Bower in the `node_modules` directory. We need to create a `bower.json` file containing the package metadata and dependencies. Bower can create this file for us:

```
$ bower init
```

This command will prompt us with questions about our package; we need to define the name, version, main file, and keywords, among other fields. The generated file will contain essential package information, as follows:

```
{
    "name": "windmill",
    "version": "0.1.0",
    "authors": [
        "Pablo Navarro"
    ],
    "description": "Heatmap Charts",
    "main": "windmill.js",
    "keywords": ["chart","heatmap","d3"],
    "ignore": [
        "**/.*","**/.*",
        "node_modules",
        "bower_components",
        "app/_bower_components",
        "test",
        "tests"
    ],
    "dependencies": {}
}
```

Bower has a registry of frontend packages; we can use Bower to search the registry and install our dependencies. For instance, we can search for the D3 package as follows:

```
$ bower search d3
Search results:
    d3 git://github.com/mbostock/d3.git
    nvd3 git://github.com/novus/nvd3
    d3-plugins git://github.com/d3/d3-plugins.git
    ...
```

The results are displayed, showing the package name and its Git endpoint. We can use either the name or the endpoint to install D3:

```
$ bower install --save d3
```

This will create the `bower_components` directory (depending on your global configuration) and update the `bower.json` file, including the D3 library in its most recent release. Note that we included D3 both in our Node dependencies and in the Bower dependencies. We included D3 in the Node dependencies to be able to test our charts (which depend on D3); here, we include D3 as a frontend dependency, so the other packages that use our charting package can download and install D3 using Bower:

```
{
    "name": "windmill",
    "version": "0.1.0",
    ...
    "dependencies": {
        "d3": "~3.4.1"
    }
}
```

We can specify which version of the package we want to include. For instance, we could have installed the release 3.4.0:

```
$ bower install d3#3.4.0
```

We don't need to register the packages to install them with Bower; we can use Bower to install the unregistered packages using their Git endpoint:

```
$ bower install https://github.com/mbostock/d3.git
```

The Git endpoint could also be a local repository, or even a ZIP or TAR file:

```
$bower install /path/to/package.zip
```

Bower will extract and copy each dependency in the bower_components directory. To use the packages, we can use a reference to the bower_components directory, or write a Grunt task to copy the files to another location. We will use the bower_components directory to create example pages for our charts.

Using the package in other projects

In this section, we will create a minimal web page that uses the windmill package. We begin by creating an empty directory, initializing the repository, and creating a README.md file. We create the bower.json file using bower init. We will install bootstrap to use it in our web page:

```
$ bower install --save bootstrap
```

This will download bootstrap and its dependencies to the bower_components directory. We will install the windmill library using the Git endpoint of the repository:

```
$ bower install --save https://github.com/pnavarrc/windmill.git
```

This will download the current version of windmill and the version of D3 on which windmill depends. The contents of the bower_components directory are as follows:

```
bower_components/
    bootstrap/
    d3/
    jquery/
    windmill/
```

In the index page, we will display the average wind speed in a certain city during 2013. We will store the data in the wind.csv file located in the data directory. The CSV file has three columns that display the data (MM/DD/YY), the hour of the measurement, and the average speed in meters per second:

```
Date,Hour,Speed
1/1/13,1,0.2554
1/1/13,2,0.1683
...
```

In the header of the index file, we include D3 and the windmill CSS and
JavaScript files:

```
<link href="/bower_components/windmill/css/windmill.css"
rel="stylesheet">

<script src="/bower_components/d3/d3.min.js" charset="utf-8"></script>
<script src="/bower_components/windmill/windmill.min.js"></script>
```

In the body of the page, we add the title and a container div:

```
<div class="container">
  <h1>Wind Speed</h1>
  <div id="chart01"></div>
</div>
```

We create and configure the chart and layout. We want to display the average wind
speed by month and hour of the day. We set the rows to be the hours, the columns
to return the month number, and the value to return the speed. We will use the
average function to aggregate values with the same hour and month:

```
// Aggregation function (average)
function average(values) {
    var sum = 0;
    values.forEach(function(d) { sum += d; });
    return sum / values.length;
}

// Matrix Layout
var matrix = windmill.layout.matrix()
    .row(function(d) { return +d.Hour; })
    .column(function(d) { return +d.Date.getMonth(); })
    .value(function(d) { return +d.Speed; })
    .aggregate(average);
```

We create and initialize the heat map chart, setting the width, height, and color
extent of the chart:

```
// Create and configure the heatmap chart
var heatmap = windmill.chart.heatmap()
    .column(function(d) { return d.col; })
    .width(700)
    .height(350)
    .colorExtent(['#ccc', '#222']);
```

We load the data using `d3.csv` and parse the dates. We select the container div and bind the grouped data, as follows:

```
// Load the CSV data
d3.csv('/data/wind.csv', function(error, data) {

    // Handle errors getting or parsing the data
    if (error) { return error; }
        // Parse the dates
        data.forEach(function(d) {
            d.Date = new Date(d.Date);
        });

    // Create the heatmap chart in the container selection
    d3.select('div#chart01')
        .data([matrix(data)])
        .call(heatmap);
});
```

The resulting chart will display the variations of wind speed as a function of the hour of the day and the month. We can see that the wind is stronger between 2 pm and 8 pm and that it is weaker between March and September.

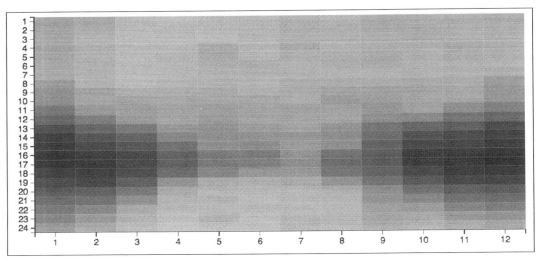

A heat map of the average wind speed by hour and month for 2013

Summary

In this chapter, we created a simple charting package with two components, a layout and a heat map chart. We also discussed the workflow and tasks related to the creation and distribution of a frontend package. We used Grunt with some plugins to concatenate, check the code for errors, test, and minify the assets. We used Vows to create test suites, and Bower to make our package easily installable in third-party frontend projects.

We created a small project with a single web page, which includes the charting package as an external dependency, and used it to visualize the average wind speed by hour and month as a heat map.

In the next chapter, we will learn how to create a data-driven application using third-party data and how to host the application using GitHub pages and Jekyll.

8
Data-driven Applications

In this chapter, we will create a data-driven application using data from the **Human Development Data API** from the United Nations website. We will use D3 to create a reusable chart component, and use Backbone to structure and maintain the application state. We will learn how to use **Jekyll** to create web applications using templates and a simplified markup language. We will also learn how to host our static site both on Amazon Simple Storage Service (S3) and GitHub Pages.

Creating the application

In this section, we will create a data visualization to explore the evolution of the **Human Development Index (HDI)** for different countries, and show the life expectancy, education, and income components of the index. We will create the visualization using D3 and Backbone.

The HDI is a composite statistic of life expectancy, education, and income created to compare and measure the quality of life in different countries. This indicator is used by the United Nations Development Program to measure and report the progress of the ranked countries in these areas.

In this visualization, we want to display how a particular country compares to other ranked countries in the evolution of the index. We will use the Human Development Data API to access the time series of the HDI for the ranked countries and to retrieve information about their main components.

The chart will show the evolution of the HDI for all the ranked countries, highlighting the selected country. In the right-hand side pane, we will display the main components of the HDI: life expectancy at birth, mean and expected years of schooling, and gross national income per capita (GNI). As there are almost two hundred ranked countries, we will add a search form with autocompletion to search among the countries. Selecting a country in the search input field will update the chart and the right-hand side pane.

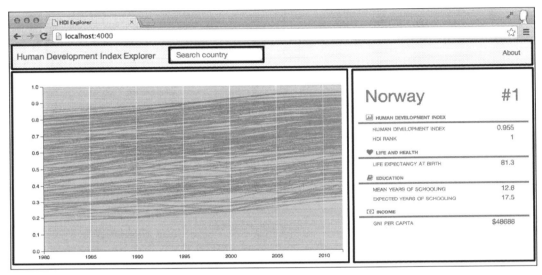

A screenshot of the visualization elements

We will implement our application using D3 and Backbone, following the same pattern as presented in *Chapter 6, Interaction between Charts*. We will also leverage other libraries to provide the design elements and the functionality that we need.

The project setup

When creating software, we are continuously modifying our own work and the work developed for others. The ability to control how those changes are integrated in the project codebase and how to recover the previous versions is the heart of version control systems. As with many other tools, there are plenty of tools available, each with it's own characteristics.

Git is a popular version control system. It's distributed, which means that it's not necessary to have a centralized location as the reference point; each working copy of the repository can be used as a reference. In this section, we will use Git as a version control system. We can't include an introduction to Git in this book; you can learn about Git from its website (http://git-scm.com).

Some content in this chapter is specific to Git and GitHub, a code-hosting repository based on Git, specifically the sections on how to use GitHub Pages to host static pages and the setup of the project. The example application can be implemented even without a version control system or hosting service.

We will begin our application by creating a repository for it in GitHub. To create a repository, go to http://www.github.com, sign in with your account (or create an account), and select **+New repository**. To create a repository, we will need to add a name and description, and optionally, select a license and add a README file. After doing this, the repository URL will be generated; we will use this URL to clone the project and modify it. In our case, the URL of the repository is https://github.com/pnavarrc/hdi-explorer.git. Cloning the repository will create a new directory, containing the initial content set on GitHub, if any:

```
$ git clone https://github.com/pnavarrc/hdi-explorer.git
```

Alternatively, we could have created an empty directory and initialized a Git repository in it to begin working on it right away.

```
$ mkdir hdi-explorer
$ cd hdi-explorer
$ git init
```

If we decide to use GitHub, we can add a remote repository to push our code. Remote repositories are locations on the Internet or in a network to make our code accessible for others. It's customary to set the origin remote to the primary repository for the project. We can set the origin remote and push the initial version of our project by executing the following commands in the console:

```
$ git remote add origin https://github.com/pnavarrc/hdi-explorer.git
$ git push -u origin
```

In either case, we will have a configured repository that is ready to be worked on.

As you may remember, we learned how to use Bower to manage the frontend dependencies in *Chapter 7, Creating a Charting Package*. As we will be using several libraries, we will begin by creating the bower.json file using bower init. We will set the name, version, author, description, and home page of our project. Our bower.json file will contain the basic information of our project as follows:

```
{
  "name": "hdi-explorer"
  "version": "0.1.0"
  "authors": [
    "Pablo Navarro <pnavarrc@gmail.com>"
  ],
  "description": "Human Development Index Explorer"
  "main": "index.html"
  "homepage": "http://pnavarrc.github.io/hdi-explorer"
  "private": true,
  "dependencies": {}
}
```

As mentioned before, we will use D3 and Backbone to create the charts and structure our application. We will install the dependencies in our project:

```
$ bower install --save-dev d3 backbone underscore
```

This will create the bower_components directory and download the packages for us. We will also need *Bootstrap* and *Font Awesome* to include the HDI component icons. We will install these packages as well. As jQuery is a dependency of Bootstrap, Bower will install it automatically:

```
$ bower install --save-dev bootstrap font-awesome typeahead.js
```

We will use the Typeahead library from Twitter to add autocompletion to our search form. Installing packages with the --save-dev option will update our bower.json file, adding the packages to the development dependencies. These libraries would normally be regular dependencies; we are including them as development dependencies because we will later create a file with all the dependencies in that file.

```
{
  "name": "hdi-explorer"
  // ...
  "devDependencies": {
    "d3": "~3.4.1"
    "bootstrap": "~3.1.0"
    "backbone": "~1.1.0"
    "underscore": "~1.5.2"
```

```
    "font-awesome": "~4.0.3"
    "typeahead.js": "~0.10.0"
  }
}
```

Using Bower will help us to manage our dependencies and update the packages without breaking our application. Bower requires its packages to adhere to semantic version numbering, and it's smart enough to update only the nonbackwards-incompatible releases.

Generating a static site with Jekyll

In the previous chapters, we covered how to create data-driven applications and how to use tools to make this task easier. In this section, we will cover how to generate websites using Jekyll and host web applications using Jekyll and GitHub Pages.

Jekyll is a simple, blog-aware, static site generator written in Ruby. This means that we can create a website or blog without having to install and configure web servers or databases to create our content. To create pages, we can write them in a simple markup language and compile them in HTML. Jekyll also supports the use of templates and partial HTML code to create the pages.

In Linux and OS X, we can install Jekyll from the command line. Remember that in order to use Jekyll, Ruby and RubyGems should be installed. To install Jekyll, run the following command in the console:

```
$ gem install jekyll
```

For other platforms and more installation options, refer to the documentation available at http://jekyllrb.com/docs/installation/. Jekyll includes a generator that configures and creates the project boilerplate with sample content and templates (see jekyll new --help), but this time, we will create the templates, content, and configuration from scratch. We will begin by creating the subdirectories and files needed for the Jekyll components:

```
hdi-explorer/
   _includes/
      navbar.html
   _layouts/
      main.html
   _data/
   _drafts/
   _posts/
   index.md
   _config.yml
```

The `_config.yml` file is a configuration file written in YAML, a serialization standard similar to JSON but with additional types, support for comments, and which uses indentation instead of brackets to indicate nesting (for more information, see `http://www.yaml.org/`). The content in this file defines how Jekyll will generate the content and defines some site-wide variables. For our project, the `_config.yml` file defines some Jekyll options and the name, base URL, and repository of our site:

```yaml
# Jekyll Configuration
safe: true
markdown: rdiscount
permalink: pretty

# Site
name: Human Development Index Explorer
baseurl: http://pnavarrc.github.io/hdi-explorer
github: http://github.com/pnavarrc/hdi-explorer.git
```

The `safe` option disables all the Jekyll plugins, the `markdown` option sets the markdown language that we will use, and the `permalink` option defines which kind of URL we want to generate. There are additional options to set the time zone and excluded files, among others.

The `_layouts` directory will contain page templates with placeholders to be replaced by content. On each page, we can declare which layout we will use in a special area called the YAML front matter, which we will describe later. The templates can have variables, such as the `{{ content }}` tag, and include the `{% include navbar. html %}` tag. The content of the variables is defined either in the front matter or in the `_config.yml` file. The `include` tags replace the block with the content of the corresponding file in the `_includes` directory. For instance, our `main.html` template contains the following base page structure:

```html
<!DOCTYPE html>
<html lang="en">
<head>
  <meta charset="utf-8">
  <title>{{ page.title }}</title>
  <link href="{{ site.baseurl }}/hdi.css" rel="stylesheet">
</head>
<body>
  <!-- Navigation Bar -->
  {% include navbar.html %}

  <!-- Content -->
```

```
    <div class="container-fluid">
      {{ content }}
    </div>
  </body>
</html>
```

The value of the {{ site.baseurl }} variable is set in the _config.yml file, the {{ page.title }} variable will use the value of the font matter of the pages using the template, and the {{ content }} variable will be replaced with the content of the files that use the template. In the _config.yml file, we defined the baseurl variable to http://pnavarrc.github.io/hdi-explorer. When Jekyll uses this template to generate content, it will replace the {{ site.baseurl }} variable with http://pnavarrc.github.io/hdi-explorer, and the generated page will have the complete URL for the CSS style, http://pnavarrc.github.io/hdi-explorer/hdi.css. A complete reference to the Liquid Templating language is available at http://liquidmarkup.org/.

The _includes directory contains the HTML fragments to be included in other pages. This is useful to modularize some parts of our page, such as to separate the footer, header, or navigation bar. Here, we created the navbar.html file with the content of our navigation bar:

```
<!-- Navigation Bar -->
<nav class="navbar navbar-default" role="navigation">
  <div class="container-fluid">
    <!-- ... more elements -->
    <a class="navbar-brand" href="#">{{ site.name }}</a>
    <!-- ... -->
  </div>
</nav>
```

The content of the navbar.html file will replace the {% include navbar.html %} liquid tag in the templates. The files in the _includes directory can also contain liquid tags, which will be replaced properly.

The _posts directory contains blog posts. Each blog post should be a file with a name in the YEAR-MONTH-DAY-title.MARKDOWN form. Jekyll will use the filename to compute the date and URL of each post. The _data directory contains additional site-wide variables, and the _draft directory contains posts that we will want to publish later. In this project, we won't create posts or drafts.

The `index.md` file contains content to be rendered using some of the layouts in the project. The beginning of the file contains the YAML front matter, that is, the lines between three dashes. This fragment of the file is interpreted as YAML code and is used to render the templates. For instance, in the main template, we had the `{{ page.title }}` placeholder. When rendering the page, Jekyll will replace this with the `title` variable in the page's front matter. The content after the front matter will replace the `{{ content }}` tag in the template.

```
---
layout: main
title: HDI Explorer
---


<!-- Content -->
Hello World
```

We can add any number of variables to the front matter, but the `layout` variable is mandatory; so, Jekyll knows which layout should be used to render the page. In this case, we will use the `main.html` layout and set the title of the page to `HDI Explorer`. The content of the page can be written in HTML or in text-to-HTML languages, such as *Markdown* or *Textile*. Once we have created the layouts and initial content, we can use Jekyll to generate the site.

```
$ jekyll build
```

This will create the `_site` directory, which contains all the content of the directory except the Jekyll-related directories such as `_layouts` and `_includes`. In our case, it will generate a directory containing an `index.html` file. This file is the result of injecting the contents of the `index.md`, `navbar.html`, and `_config.yml` files in the `main.html` layout. The generated file will look as follows:

```
<!DOCTYPE html>
<html lang="en">
<head>
  <meta charset="utf-8">
  <title>HDI Explorer</title>
  <link href="http://pnavarrc.github.io/hdi-explorer/hdi.css"
rel="stylesheet">
</head>
<body>
  <!-- Navigation Bar -->
  <nav class="navbar navbar-default" role="navigation">
    <div class="container-fluid">
      <!-- ... more elements -->
      <a class="navbar-brand" href="#">
```

```
        Human Development Index Explorer
      </a>
      <!-- ... -->
    </div>
  </nav>

  <!-- Content -->
  <div class="content">
    <!-- Content -->
    <p>Hello World</p>
  </div>
  </body>
</html>
```

We can see that the generated file is pure HTML. Using Jekyll allows us to modularize the page, separate its components, and allows us to focus on writing the actual content of each page.

Jekyll also allows us to serve the generated pages locally, watching for changes in the project files. To do this, we need to overwrite the baseurl variable in order to use the localhost address instead of the value defined in the configuration file. As the addresses will be relative to the project directory, we can set the base URL to an empty string:

$ jekyll serve --watch --baseurl=

We can now access our site by pointing the browser to http://localhost:4000 and use our site. In the next section, we will create the contents of our application using D3 and Backbone, integrating the JavaScript files, styles, and markup with the Jekyll templates and pages created in this section.

Creating the application components

We will separate the Backbone application components from the chart; we will put the models, collections, views, and setup in the js/app directory:

```
js/
  app/
    models/
      app.js
      country.js
    collections/
      countries.js
```

```
views/
  country.js
  countries.js
app.js
setup.js
```

In the `app.js` file, we just define a variable that will have the components of our application:

```
// Application container
var app = {};
```

The `setup.js` file contains the creation of the model, collection, and view instances; the binding of the events; and the callbacks of different components. We will review the models, collections, and views in detail later.

Creating the models and collections

The application model will reflect the application state. In our application, the selected country defines the state of the application; we will use three-letter country codes as the only attribute of the application model:

```
// Application Model
app.ApplicationModel = Backbone.Model.extend({
    // Code of the Selected Country
    defaults: {
        code: ''
    }
});
```

We will have two additional models: the `CountryInformation` model will represent information about the current HDI value and its main components, and the `CountryTrend` model will contain information about the country and time series of HDI measurements.

The data source for these models will be an endpoint of the Human Development Data API. The API allows us to retrieve data about poverty, education, health, social integration, and migrations, among many others. A complete list of the API endpoints and some examples of queries are available at the Human Development Data API website (`http://hdr.undp.org/en/data/api`). The API exposes the data in several formats and receives parameters to filter the data.

The `CountryInformation` model will retrieve information about the **Human Development Index and its Components** endpoint. For instance, we can access this endpoint by passing `name=Germany` as the parameter of the request. The request to `http://data.undp.org/resource/wxub-qc5k.json?name=Germany` will return a JSON file with the main components of the HDI:

```
[
  {
    "_2011_expected_years_of_schooling_note" :"e",
    "_2012_life_expectancy_at_birth" :"80.6",
    "_2012_gni_per_capita_rank_minus_hdi_rank" :"10",
    "_2012_hdi_value" :"0.920",
    "type" : "Ranked Country",
    "abbreviation" : "DEU",
    "_2010_mean_years_of_schooling" :"12.2",
    "_2011_expected_years_of_schooling" :"16.4",
    "name" : "Germany",
    "_2012_hdi_rank" :"5",
    "_2012_gross_national_income_gni_per_capita" :"35431",
    "_2012_nonincome_hdi_value" :"0.948"
  }
]
```

We will define the model such that it has the `name` and `code` attributes and some of the information provided by the JSON file. We will add the `url`, `baseurl`, and `urltpl` attributes to construct the URL for each country, as follows:

```
// Country Information Model
app.CountryInformation = Backbone.Model.extend({

    // Default attributes, the name and code of the country
    defaults: {
        code: '',
        name: ''
    },

    // URL to fetch the model data
    url: '',

    // Base URL
    baseurl: 'http://data.undp.org/resource/wxub-qc5k.json',

    // URL Template
    urltpl: _.template('<%= baseurl %>?Abbreviation=<%= code %>')
});
```

Each country has the `abbreviation` field; this field contains the code for the country. We will use this code as the ID of the country. The names of the attributes of the JSON object contain data; for instance, the `_2012_life_expectancy_at_birth` attribute contains the year of the measurement. If we create an instance of the model and invoke its `fetch` method, it will retrieve the data from the JSON endpoint and add attributes to each attribute of the retrieved object. This will be a problem because the endpoint returns an array and not all the countries have up-to-date measurements. In the case of Germany, the only object in the array has the `_2012_life_expectancy_at_birth` attribute, but in the case of other countries, the most recent measurements could be from 2010.

To have a uniform representation of the data, we can strip the year out of the attribute names before we set the attributes for the model. We can do this by setting the `parse` method, which is invoked when the data is fetched from the server. In this method, we will get the first element of the retrieved array and strip the first part of the attributes beginning with `_` to only have attributes of the form `life_expectancy_at_birth`:

```
// Parse the response and set the model contents
parse: function(response) {

    // Get the first item of the response
    var item = response.pop(),
        data = {
            code: item.abbreviation,
            name: item.name
        };

    // Parse each attribute
    for (var attr in item) {
        if (attr[0] === '_') {
            // Extract the attribute name after the year
            data[attr.slice(6)] = item[attr];
        }
    }

    // Return the parsed data
    return data;
}
```

We will also add a method to update the model with the selected country in the application. The `setState` method will receive the application model and use its code attribute to construct the URL for the selected country and to fetch the new information, as follows:

```
setState: function(state) {
    // Construct the URL and fetch the data
    this.url = this.urltpl({
        baseurl: this.baseurl,
        code: state.get('code')
    });
    this.fetch({reset: true});
}
```

We will create the `CountryTrend` model to store the trends of the HDI for each country, and the `Countries` collection to store the `CountryTrend` instances. The `CountryTrend` model will hold the country code and name, a flag to indicate whether the country has been selected or not, and a series of HDI measurements for different years. We will use the code of the country as an ID attribute:

```
// Country Trend Model
app.CountryTrend = Backbone.Model.extend({

    // Default values for the Country Trend Model
    defaults: {
        name: '',
        code: '',
        selected: false,
        hdiSeries: []
    },

    // The country code identifies uniquely the model
    idAttribute: 'code'
});
```

The `Countries` collection will contain a set of the `CountryTrend` instances. The collection will have an endpoint to retrieve the information for the model instances. We will need to define the `parse` method in the `CountryTrend` model, which will be invoked automatically before new `CountryTrend` instances are generated. In the `parse` method, we construct an object with the attributes of the new model instance. The data retrieved for the collection will have the following structure:

```
{
  _1990_hdi: "0.852"
  _1980_hdi: "0.804"
  _2000_hdi: "0.922"
  // ...
  _2012_hdi: "0.955"
}
```

Here, the year of the HDI measurement is contained in the key of the object. There are other attributes also, which we will ignore. We will split the attribute name using the _ character to extract the year:

```
// Parse the country fields before instantiating the model
parse: function(response) {

    var data = {
        code: response.country_code,
        name: response.country_name,
        selected: false,
        hdiSeries: []
    };

    // Compute the HDI Series
    for (var attr in response) {
        var part = attr.split('_'),
            series = [];

        if ((part.length === 3) && (part[2] === 'hdi')) {
            data.hdiSeries.push({
                year: parseInt(part[1], 10),
                hdi: parseFloat(response[attr])
            });
        }
    }

    // Sort the data items
    data.hdiSeries.sort(function(a, b) {
        return b.year - a.year;
    });

    return data;
}
```

The data object will contain the country's code, name, the selected flag, and the array of hdiSeries, which will contain objects that have the year and HDI value. The Countries collection will contain the CountryTrend instances for each country. The data will be retrieved from the **Human Development Index Trends** endpoint. We set the collection model, the endpoint URL, and a parse method, which will filter the items that have a country code (there are items for groups of countries). We will also add a method to set a selected item in order to ensure that there is only one selected item:

```
// Countries Collection
app.Countries = Backbone.Collection.extend({

    // Model
    model: app.CountryTrend,

    // JSON Endpoint URL
    url: 'http://data.undp.org/resource/efc4-gjvq.json',

    // Remove non-country items
    parse: function(response) {
        return response.filter(function(d) {
            return d.country_code;
        });
    },

    // Set the selected country
    setSelected: function(code) {

        var selected = this.findWhere({selected: true});

        if (selected) {
            selected.set('selected', false);
        }

        // Set the new selected item
        selected = this.findWhere({code: code});
        if (selected) {
            selected.set('selected', true);
        }
    }
});
```

We will proceed to create the views for the models.

Creating the views

The application will have three views: the chart with the trends of HDI values for the ranked countries, the information view at the right-hand side, and the search form.

CountriesTrendView is a view of the Countries collection, which displays the evolution of the HDI for the ranked countries. As we did in *Chapter 6, Interaction between Charts*, we will create a Backbone View that will contain an instance of a D3-based chart:

```
// Countries Trend View
app.CountriesTrendView = Backbone.View.extend({

    // Initialization and render
    initialize: function() {
        this.listenTo(this.collection, 'reset', this.render);
        this.listenTo(this.collection, 'change:selected', this.
render);
    }
});
```

In the initialize method, we start listening for the reset event of the collection and the change:selected event, which are triggered when an element of the collection is selected. In both cases, we will render the view. We will add and configure an instance of the D3-based chart, hdi.chart.trends:

```
app.CountriesTrendView = Backbone.View.extend({

    // Initalization and render...

    // Initialize the trend chart
    chart: hdi.chart.trend()
        .series(function(d) { return d.hdiSeries; })
        .x(function(d) { return d.year; })
        .y(function(d) { return d.hdi; }),

    // Initialize and render methods...
});
```

We will skip the description of the hdi.chart.trend chart for brevity, but as usual, the chart is implemented using the reusable chart pattern and has accessor methods to configure its behavior. The chart displays the time series of HDI measurements for all the ranked countries, highlighting the line bound to a data item with the selected attribute set to true.

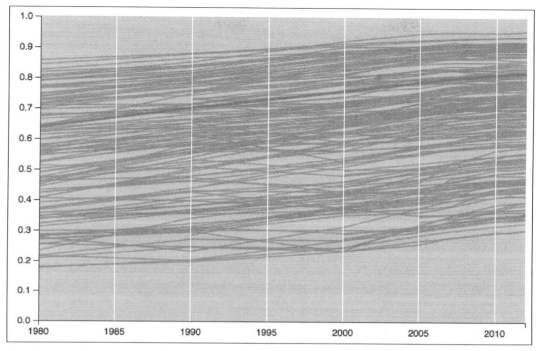

The HDI trend chart

In the `render` method, we get the width of the container element of the view and update the width of the chart using this value. We select the container element, bind the collection data to the selection, and invoke the chart:

```
// Update the chart width and bind the updated data
render: function() {
    // Update the width of the chart
    this.chart.width(this.$el.width());


    // Rebind and render the chart
    d3.select(this.el)
        .data([this.collection.toJSON()])
        .call(this.chart);
},
```

We will also add the `setState` method to change the selected country of the underlying collection. This method will help us to update the selected item of the collection when the application model changes the selected country. We will do this later in the application setup:

```
// Update the state of the application model
setState: function(state) {
    this.collection.setSelected(state.get('code'));
}
```

The search form will allow the user to search among the ranked countries to select one of them. We will use the **Typeahead jQuery plugin** from Twitter (`http://twitter.github.io/typeahead.js/`) to provide autocompletion, and we will populate the suggestion list with the items in the `Countries` collection. The `Typeahead` plugin contains two components: `Bloodhound`, the autocompletion engine, and `Typeahead`, the plugin that adds autocompletion capabilities to an input field.

In the `initialize` method, we bind the `reset` event of the collection to the `render` method in order to update the view when the list of country trends is retrieved:

```
// Search Form View
app.CountriesSearchView = Backbone.View.extend({

    // Initialize
    initialize: function() {
        this.listenTo(this.collection, 'reset', this.render);
    },

    // Events and render methods...
});
```

The DOM element associated with this view will be a div containing the search form, which is located in the navigation bar. We assign an ID to the div and to the input field:

```
<div class="form-group" id="search-country">
  <input type="text" class="form-control typeahead"
         placeholder="Search country"id="search-country-input">
</div>
```

To provide autocompletion, we need to initialize the autocompletion engine and add the autocompletion features to the search input item:

```
// Render the component
render: function() {
    // Initialize the autocompletion engine
    // Add autocompletion to the input field
},
```

We initialize the `Typeahead` autocompletion engine; setting the `datumTokenizer` option is a function that, given a data element, returns a list of strings that should be associated with the element. In our case, we want to match the country names; so, we use the whitespace tokenizer and return the country name split by whitespace characters. The input of the search field will be split using whitespace characters too. We add the list of elements among which we want to search, which in our case are the elements in the collection:

```
// Render the component
render: function() {
    // Initialize the autocompletion engine
    this.engine = new Bloodhound({
        datumTokenizer: function(d) {
            return Bloodhound.tokenizers.whitespace(d.name);
        },
        queryTokenizer: Bloodhound.tokenizers.whitespace,
        local: this.collection.toJSON()
    });
    this.engine.initialize();

    // Add autocompletion to the input field...
},
```

To add the autocompletion features to the search form, we select the input element of the view and configure the `typeahead` options. In our case, we just want to show the name of the country and use the engine dataset as the source for the autocompletion:

```
// Render the element
this.$el.children('#search-country-input')
    .typeahead(null, {
        displayKey: 'name',
        source: this.engine.ttAdapter()
    });
```

When the user begins to type in the input field, the options that match the input will be displayed. When the user selects an option, the `typeahead:selected` event will be triggered by the input element. We will add this to the event's hash of the view, binding the event to the `setSelected` callback:

```
events: {
    'typeahead:selected input[type=text]': 'setSelected'
},
```

Note that the `typeahead:selected` event is a jQuery event. The callback will receive the event and the data item selected by the user, and it will update the selected item in the collection, as follows:

```
//  Update the selected item in the collection
setSelected: function(event, datum) {
    this.collection.setSelected(datum.code);
}
```

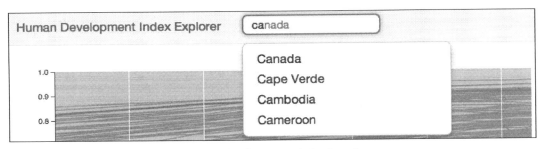

The Typeahead autocompletion in action

The last view will be `CountryInformationView`. This view is a visual representation of the `CountryInformation` model. For this view, we will add the `_includes/country-information.html` file with the contents of the template and include it in the `index.md` file:

```
---
layout: main
title: HDI Explorer
---

{% include country-information.html %}

<!-- More content... -->
```

The template will contain several internal div elements; we will show only a part of the template here:

```
<!-- Country Information Template -->
<script type="text/template" id="country-summary-template">

<!-- Country Name and Rank -->
<div class="row country-summary-title">
  <div class="col-xs-8"><%= name %></div>
```

```
    <div class="col-xs-4 text-right">#<%= hdi_rank %></div>
  </div>

  <!-- HDI Value and Rank of the Country -->
  <div class="row country-summary-box">
    <!-- Header -->
    <div class="col-xs-12 country-summary-box-header">
      <i class="fa fa-bar-chart-o fa-fw"></i>
      human development index
    </div>
    <!-- HDI Index -->
    <div class="col-xs-12">
      <div class="col-xs-9">human development index</div>
      <div class="col-xs-3 text-right"><%= hdi_value %></div>
    </div>
    <!-- Country Rank -->
    <div class="col-xs-12">
      <div class="col-xs-9">hdi rank</div>
      <div class="col-xs-3 text-right"><%= hdi_rank %></div>
    </div>
  </div>

  <!-- More divs with additional information... -->
</script>
```

Here, we create the structure of the bar on the right-hand side, which will contain the Human Development Index, rank, life expectancy, education statistics, and income for the selected country. We will use the Underscore templates to render this view. The view structure is simpler in this case; we just compile the template, listen to the changes of country name in the model, and render the template with the model data:

```
// Country Information View
app.CountryInformationView = Backbone.View.extend({
    // View template
    template: _.template($('#country-summary-template').html()),

    initialize: function() {
        // Update the view on name changes
        this.listenTo(this.model, 'change:name', this.render);
    },

    render: function() {
```

```
    // Render the template
    this.$el.html(this.template(this.model.toJSON()));
  }
});
```

The rendered view will display the current values for the HDI components

The application setup

With the models, collections, and views created, we can create the respective instances and bind events to callbacks in order to keep the views in sync. We begin by creating an instance of the application model and the collection of country HDI trends. In the js/app/setup.js file, we create and configure the model, collection, and view instances:

```
// Application Model
app.state = new app.ApplicationModel();

// HDI Country Trends Collection
app.countries = new app.Countries();
```

After the application's state changes, we will have to update the selected item in the
Countries collection. We bind the change:code event of the application model to
the callback that will update the selected item in the collection:

```
// Update the selected item in the countries collection
app.countries.listenTo(app.state, 'change:code', function(state){
    this.setSelected(state.get('code'));
});
```

We need to update the application state when the Countries collection is populated
for the first time. We will set the application state's code attribute to the code of the
first element in the collection of countries. We also bind the change:selected event
of the collection to update the application model:

```
app.countries.on({
    'reset': function() {
        app.state.set('code', this.first().get('code'));
    },

    'change:selected': function() {
        var selected = this.findWhere({selected: true});
        if (selected) {
            app.state.set('code', selected.get('code'));
        }
    }
});
```

Note that when we are selecting an item, we are also deselecting another item. Both
the items will trigger the change:selected event, but the application should change
its state only when an item is selected. We can now fetch the countries data, passing
the reset flag to ensure that any existing data is overwritten:

```
app.countries.fetch({reset: true});
```

We create an instance of the CountryInformation model and bind the changes to the
code attribute of the application to the changes of the state in the model. The setState
method will fetch the information for the code given by the application state:

```
// HDI Information
app.country = new app.CountryInformation();
app.country.listenTo(app.state, 'change:code', app.country.setState);
```

We can now create instances of the views. We will create an instance of the
CountriesTrendView. This view will be rendered in the div element with
the #chart ID:

```
// Countries Trend View
app.trendView = new app.CountriesTrendView({
    el: $('div#chart'),
    collection: app.countries
});
```

We create an instance and configure the CountriesSearchView. This view will be
rendered in the navigation bar:

```
app.searchView = new app.CountriesSearchView({
    el: $('#search-country'),
    collection: app.countries
});
```

We also create a CountryInformationView instance, which will be rendered in the
right-hand side of the page:

```
app.infoView = new app.CountryInformationView({
    el: $('div#table'),
    model: app.country
});
```

In the index.md file, we create the elements where the views will be rendered and
include the application files. In the main.html layout, we include the CSS styles of
the application, Bootstrap and Font Awesome:

```
---
layout: main
title: HDI Explorer
---

{% include country-information.html %}

<div class="container-fluid">
  <div class="row">
    <div class="col-md-8" id="chart"></div>
    <div class="col-md-4 country-summary" id="table"></div>
```

```
    </div>
</div>

<scriptsrc="{{ site.baseurl }}/dependencies.min.js"></script>
<scriptsrc="{{ site.baseurl }}/hdi.min.js"></script>
```

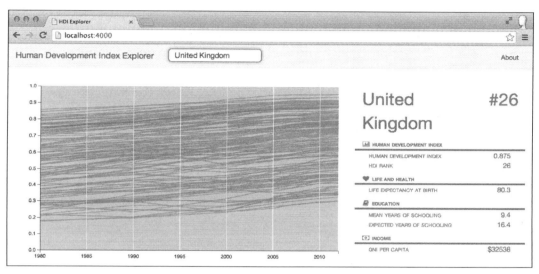

The application served by Jekyll on a localhost

Here, we consolidated jQuery, Bootstrap, Underscore, Backbone, Typeahead, and D3 in the `dependencies.min.js` file and the application models, collections, views, and chart in the `hdi.min.js` file. To create these consolidated files, we created a Gruntfile and configured concatenation and minification tasks as we did in *Chapter 7, Creating a Charting Package*. As the configuration of the tasks is similar to the configuration presented in the previous chapter, we will skip its description.

It is also worth mentioning that in general, it is not a good practice to include complete libraries. For instance, we included the complete Bootstrap styles and JavaScript components, but in the application, we used only a small part of the features.

Bootstrap allows you to include the components individually, reducing the payload of the page and improving the performance. We also included the Font Awesome fonts and styles only to include four icons. In a project where performance is crucial, we will probably include only the components that we really need.

Hosting the visualization with GitHub Pages

In the previous section, we created a web application using Jekyll, Backbone, and D3. With Jekyll, we created a template for the main page and included the minified JavaScript libraries and styles. With Jekyll, we can compile the markup files to generate a static website or serve the site without generating a static version using `jekyll serve`. In this section, we will publish our site using GitHub Pages, a hosting service for personal and project sites.

GitHub Pages is a service from GitHub that provides hosting for static websites created in Jekyll or HTML. To publish our Jekyll site, we need to create a branch named `gh-pages` and push the branch to GitHub. If this branch is a Jekyll project or contains an `index.html` file, GitHub will serve the content of this branch as a static site. We can create the branch from the master branch:

```
$ git checkout -b gh-pages
```

Next, push the branch to our origin, the GitHub endpoint:

```
$ git push -u origin gh-pages
```

This will push the `gh-pages` branch to GitHub, and GitHub Pages will generate the site in a few minutes. The application will be published and will be accessible through an URL of the form `http://user.github.io/project-name`, in our case, `http://pnavarrc.github.io/hdi-explorer`. It's important to remember that the base URL for the project will be `http://user.github.io/project-name`. Set the `baseurl` variable in the `_config.yml` file correctly to avoid path problems with the styles and JavaScript files.

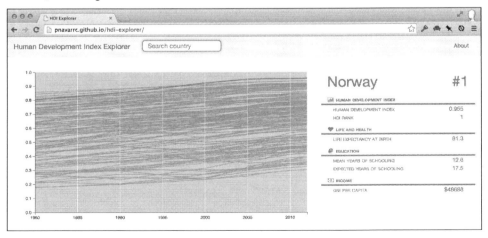

The published version of the HDI Explorer application

We can create personal pages as well, but in this case, we would need to create a repository with a name of the form `user.github.io`, and the site will be a server from the `http://user.github.io` URL. GitHub Pages also allows you to use custom domains and plain HTML instead of Jekyll. More information about GitHub Pages can be found in the project site at `http://pages.github.com/`.

Hosting the visualization in Amazon S3

As an alternative to publishing our pages using GitHub Pages, we can also serve static sites using Amazon S2. Amazon S3 is a data storage service provided by Amazon. It can be used to store files of any kind, and in particular, to store and serve static websites. Amazon S3 stores data with 99.99 percent availability and scales well in terms of storage capacity, number of requests, and users. It also provides fine-grained control access, allowing you to store sensible data.

The pricing depends on how much data you store and how many access requests are made, but it starts at less than 0.1 USD per GB per month, and there is a free tier available to use the platform at no charge to store up to 5 GB (and 20,000 requests per month). In this section, we will assume that you have an Amazon Web Services account. If you don't, you can sign up at `http://aws.amazon.com/` and create an account.

In Amazon S3, the files are stored in **buckets**. A bucket is a container for objects. Buckets are stored in one of several regions; the region is usually chosen to optimize the latency or to minimize costs. The name of the bucket needs to be unique among the buckets in Amazon.

To host our site, we will create a bucket. To create the bucket, we need to go to the Amazon S3 console at `https://console.aws.amazon.com` and select **Create Bucket**. Here, we need to name our bucket and assign it a region. We will name it `hdi-explorer` and select the default region. When the bucket is created, we select the bucket and go to **Properties**. In the **Static Website Hosting** section, we can enable the hosting and retrieve the URL of our bucket. We will use this URL as the base URL of the site.

Configuring Jekyll to deploy files to S3

To deploy static content to Amazon S3, we need to generate a version of the site with the `baseurl` variable set to the Amazon S3 endpoint. We will create an alternate Jekyll configuration file and use it to generate the S3 version of the site. In this case, we only need to update the base URL of the site, but this new file can have different configuration values. We will create the `_s3.yml` file with the following options:

```
# Jekyll Configuration
safe: true
markdown: rdiscount
permalink: pretty
destination: _s3
exclude:
    - bower_components
    - node_modules
    - Gruntfile.js
    - bower.json
    - package.json
    - README.md
# Site
name: Human Development Index Explorer
baseurl: http://hdi-explorer.s3-website-us-east-1.amazonaws.com
```

We set the `destination` folder to `_s3`. This will generate the files that we need to deploy to Amazon in the `_s3` directory. We have also excluded the files that are not needed to serve the page. We can now use this configuration to build the D3 version of the site:

```
$ jekyll build --config _s3.yml
```

We can check whether the links in the generated files point towards the S3 endpoint.

Uploading the site to the S3 bucket

We can upload the files using the web interface in the Amazon AWS console; however, the interface doesn't allow you to upload complete directories. Instead, we will use `s3cmd`, a command-line tool that helps to upload, download, and sync directories with S3 Buckets. To download and install `s3cmd`, follow the instructions available on the project website (`http://s3tools.org/s3cmd`).

Before uploading the files, we need to configure s3cmd to provide the Amazon security credentials. To generate new access keys, go to your account, then go to security credentials, and then select **Access Keys**. You can generate a new pair of access key ID and secret. These strings allow you to authenticate applications to access your S3 Buckets.

With the access key and secret, we can configure s3cmd to use it to upload our files:

```
$ s3cmd --configure
```

This command will request for our access key ID and secret. We can now upload the files. As we just want to upload our files, we can simply use the following command:

```
$ s3cmd sync _s3/ s3://bucket-name
```

The first time, this will upload the files to your bucket. Once you have the content in S3, it will keep the bucket synchronized with the _s3 directory and upload only the files that have changed.

Finally, we need to make our files public so that everyone with the URL can access the application. To do this, go to the bucket page in the browser, select all the files, and select **Make Public** in the **Actions** menu. The site will now be available at the bucket endpoint URL.

Summary

In this chapter, we learned how to create static sites with Jekyll and how to integrate third-party data sources using API endpoints. We used the Human Development Data API from the United Nations to visualize the evolution of the HDI of the ranked countries, displaying the main components of this indicator as a table.

To create the application, we used several JavaScript and CSS libraries, and we used Grunt to concatenate and minify the project assets before publishing the site. We also learned how to publish sites created with Jekyll using GitHub Pages for projects or personal pages, and how to configure and use Amazon S3 to host static websites.

In the next chapter, we will learn how to create data visualization dashboards and how to make our visualizations responsive.

9
Creating a Dashboard

Dashboards are a special kind of data visualization. They are widely used to monitor website analytics, business intelligence metrics, and brand presence in social media, among many other things. Dashboards are especially difficult to design, because a great amount of information should be displayed in a limited amount of space.

In this chapter, we will define what a dashboard is and discuss some of the strategies and design patterns that can help us design an effective dashboard. We will design and create a dashboard to monitor the performance of students in a class.

Defining a dashboard

Before we create our dashboard, it will be useful to clarify what a dashboard is. A quick search on Google Images will reveal that there isn't any consistent definition of what a dashboard is. Most of the results are a collection of charts, tables, gauges, and indicators that seem intended to monitor business performance, website analytics, and presence of a brand in social media, among many other things. Stephen Few, a specialist in business intelligence and information design, provides a great definition of dashboards:

> *A dashboard is a visual display of the most important information needed to achieve one or more objectives, which is consolidated and arranged on a single screen so the information can be monitored at a glance.*

This definition has several implications. First, dashboards are visual displays of information. A dashboard can contain text elements, but it's mainly a visual display. Well-designed graphics and charts are a highly effective medium to communicate quantitative information. Suppose we have a list with the monthly sales of a person in value and units sold. We can display this information in a table, as follows:

Name		Jan	Feb	Mar	Apr	May	Jun	Jul	Aug	Sep	Oct	Nov	Dec
John Doe	Value	$123	$112	$98	$82	$93	$87	$103	$125	$129	$143	$163	$153
	Units	244	214	193	174	155	144	127	138	139	152	171	155

Series of sales shown as a table

We can also create a line chart with the same information. The following image displays the same data in a visual form. We have two lines and their corresponding axes, one for the units sold and another for the value of the monthly sales.

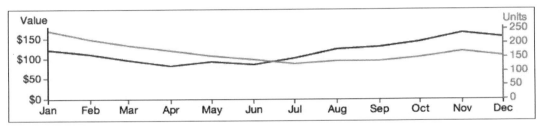

Series of sales, this time as a line chart

In the line chart, we can easily spot seasonal changes in the sales, find the minimum or maximum value, and identify patterns and changes in sales. Of course, if we need precision, we will need the table, but if we need to detect changes quickly, the chart is a better choice.

Dashboards should be designed with a purpose in mind. If our dashboard shows general information, it won't be useful. We should know what kind of decisions will be made, which problems need to be detected, and what information will help the dashboard users make decisions and take action.

The dashboard should display the most important information that is needed to achieve its purpose. This means that it should gather all the relevant data, perhaps from different sources, to help decision makers detect problems.

> The previous definition of dashboards states that the information in a dashboard should be arranged in a single screen, or more generally, the dashboard should fit in the eye span of the user. This is important in order to provide an overall view. The information should be visible at all times, and the user shouldn't have to scroll the page to view a chart or click on something to have a modal window with additional information.

In the next section, we will design and create a dashboard to monitor the performance of students in a class. We will state the purpose of our dashboard, list the relevant information that we need, organize this information in sections, and create charts for each section in order to finally organize our information to help the user detect problems and take actions to solve them.

Good practices in dashboard design

When designing a dashboard, we need to get the most out of each section of the screen so that we can design our graphics to maximize the absorption of information. Some visual attributes are more easily perceived than others, and some of them can communicate effectively without having to pay full attention to them. These attributes are called **preattentive attributes of visual perception**. We will discuss some of them in the context of dashboard design:

- **Color**: There are several ways to describe color. One of the color models is called the **HSL model**, which is better for humans to understand. In this model, the color is described by three attributes, hue (what we usually call color), saturation (intensity of a color), and lightness or brightness. The perception of color depends on the context. A light color will draw attention if it's surrounded by dark colors; a highly saturated blue will be flashy if the background is a pale color. The dashboard should guide the viewer's attention to issues that require action. To achieve this, we need to choose the colors wisely, reserving colors with high contrast to elements and areas that deserve special attention.

- **Form**: Length, width, and size can encode quantitative dimensions effectively, with different degrees of precision. We can quickly determine whether a line is twice the length of another, but it can be more difficult to determine this with the width or the size of circles. Items of different shapes are perceived as belonging to different categories or kinds of elements.

- **Position**: The position of items plays an important role in the communication of information. Scatter plots encode pairs of values with two-dimensional positions; we are inclined to think that items that are close are related. Position can also encode hierarchy. Higher items are considered better or more important than items below them, and items located on the left-hand side will be seen first if the viewer's language is written from left to right.

We can use all these elements to design the components of our dashboard so the viewer's attention is directed to the issues that require action. As dashboards usually contain a huge amount of information, every inch of the screen counts. In desktop environments, the horizontal space is usually enough, but the vertical space is scarce. In mobile environments, there is usually more vertical space, but the overall available space is more challenging.

To use the available space efficiently, we need to select the information that really counts, and prefer compact charts and graphics. It is essential to use charts and graphics that are clear and direct, reducing explicit decoding to the absolute minimum.

The dashboard should be well organized in order to allow the user to quickly locate each piece of information. We will use the aforementioned visual attributes to establish a clear hierarchy between elements and clearly define sections dedicated to displaying information about the students, courses, and the entire class.

These are just a few guidelines that should be considered when creating a dashboard; for more in-depth treatment, please refer to *Information Dashboard Design* by Stephen Few (see the reference in *Chapter 1, Data Visualization*).

Making a dashboard

As we mentioned previously, designing an effective dashboard is a challenging task. The first step to create a useful dashboard is to determine which questions need to be answered by the dashboard, which problems need to be detected on time, and why a dashboard is required.

Once we have determined the purpose of the dashboard, we can begin to gather all the data that can help us answer the questions and understand the issues stated in the dashboard purpose. The data can be originated from several sources.

We will then need to organize the information in meaningful sections in order to help the user easily navigate the dashboard and find the required information.

We will also need to choose the visual displays for each piece of data that we want to put in the dashboard. We need to choose compact displays that are familiar to the user in order to minimize the amount of effort taken in decoding the information.

In this section, we will design and implement a dashboard to monitor the performance of students in a class. We will define the purpose of the dashboard, gather the necessary datasets, choose the charts and graphics that we will use, and organize the information in sections dedicated to the students, courses, and the entire class.

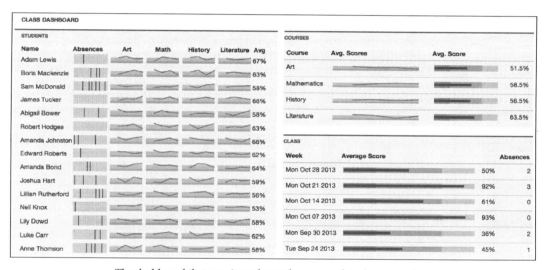

The dashboard that monitors the performance of students in a class

As the main topic in this section is the design of dashboards and we have created several charts previously, we won't include the code for the examples. The code for the charts, each section, and the complete dashboard is available in the `chapter09` directory of the code bundle.

Defining the purpose of the dashboard

The dashboard should be an overall view of the performance of the students in a class. If the scores of all the students in a given course are declining, there might be a problem with the methodology chosen by the teacher; if the scores of just one of the students are dropping, that student might be having personal issues that are interfering with his/her learning. The aim of the dashboard is to display all the information in order to easily detect problems and make decisions to help the students or teachers improve the learning process.

A teacher will want to detect drops in performance at three levels: an individual student, the students in a course, or the students in all the courses at the same time. Besides detecting learning problems, it would be useful to have information that helps identify possible causes of bad performance. The specific objectives of our dashboard will be as follows:

- Assess the performance of each student in a course. The most obvious way to do this is to display the scores of the students in each class. We might want to identify possible causes of bad performance, such as repeated absences.

- Monitor the aggregated performance of the students in each course. This will allow us to take action if a great number of students are having issues with a particular subject.

- Get an overall measure of the performance of the complete class. This will help us detect problems that could affect the class as a group.

We will need to gather the students' data and decide which information is relevant in order to achieve these objectives.

Obtaining the data

As we mentioned earlier, we need to monitor the performance of the students, courses, and the entire class. For this example, the data will be generated with a script. We will need the absences and scores of the students for each course. We will assume that we have a JSON endpoint that provides us with the students' data in the following format:

```
[
  {
    id: 369
    name: 'Adam Lewis',
    absences: [ ... ],
    courses: [ ... ],
    avgScore: 58.84
  },
  {
    id: 372
    name: 'Abigail Bower',
    absences: [ ... ],
    courses: [ ... ],
    avgScore: 67.78
  },
  ...
]
```

For each student, we will have the `name` and `id` attributes. We will also have an `absences` attribute, which will contain just a list of dates on which the student didn't show up to class:

```
{
  name: 'Adam Lewis',
  absences: [
    '2013-09-06',
    '2013-10-04',
    ...
  ],
  ...
}
```

We will also need the scores of the students in their courses. The `courses` field will contain a list of the students' courses, and each course will have the course's name and a list of the scores obtained by the student in the assignments or assessments. For convenience, we will also add the average score of the students for the current period:

```
{
  name: 'Adam Lewis',
  absences: [ ... ],
  courses: [
    {
      name: 'Mathematics',
      scores: [
        {date: '2013-09-23', score: 78},
        {date: '2013-10-04', score: 54},
        ...
      ]
    },
    {
      name: 'Art',
      scores: [...]
    }
  ],
  avgScore: 58.84
}
```

We will also need information about the courses of the students. We will assume that there is a JSON endpoint that provides us with information about the courses:

```
[
  {
    name: 'Mathematics',
    avgScores: [
```

```
        {date: '2013-09-18', score: 72.34},
        {date: '2013-10-07', score: 64.45},
        ...
      ],
      avgScore: 63.21
    },
    {
      name: 'Arts',
      avgScores: [
        {date: '2013-09-16', score: 76.62},
        {date: '2013-10-01', score: 58.53},
        ...
      ],
      avgScore: 63.21
      }
    ]
```

The avgScores attribute will contain a list with the dates of assessment and the average score obtained by the students. The avgScore attribute will contain the average of the scores for all the assessments in the current period.

Organizing the information

The next step is to organize the information in logical units. Each section of the dashboard should help us detect the issues that require attention.

In our example, the organization of the information is fairly direct; there will be sections for the students, courses, and the complete class.

The students section will help us detect the performance drop of individual students. We will consider that absences can be an explanatory factor in individual changes in the assessment scores.

The course section will help us monitor scores, thereby aggregating the scores of all the students at the same time. Drops in the scores of all the students at the same time could mean that the cause is a particular subject in the course or the teaching methodology.

The class section will allow us to monitor the average scores of the entire class, thereby averaging scores in each course for all the students. Here, the number of absences will be considered an important factor as well.

Creating the dashboard sections

In this section, we will discuss each dashboard section separately, explaining what information will be present in each section. We will also choose charts to represent these pieces of information. Later, we will decide how to organize the sections in the dashboard to make good use of the space and reflect the hierarchy of the information presented in each area.

The students section

The students section of the dashboard will display the students in a table, displaying information about each student in rows. The most relevant information will be the scores, but we will also include the absences from class, because this could be a possible explanation of changes in performance.

The absences will be displayed using a barcode chart that is similar to the one presented in *Chapter 2, Reusable Charts*. This version will be smaller and have a background. This chart will help teachers know how many students didn't show up in class and when, whether the absences are concentrated in a certain period, or whether they are evenly distributed.

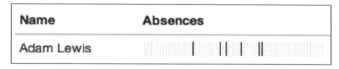

Absences for given students, displayed as a barcode chart

We will add a column for each course and display the scores of the students in the course assignments as a line chart. The scales of the chart will be implicit; they will always cover from 0 to 100 percent in the y axis and the current period in the x axis. The background of the chart will highlight score ranges that are considered important; the area below 25 percent has a different background, and the area between 25 percent and 75 percent has a different background.

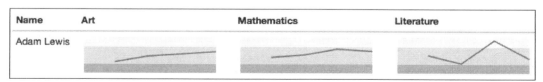

Scores of a student in different classes. The background of the chart highlights areas of poor and high performance.

Finally, we will include the average score of the students in the current period. The complete students section will gather all these elements.

Name	Absences	Art	Math	History	Literature	Avg
Adam Lewis	‖ ‖					60%
Boris Mackenzie	‖					62%
Sam McDonald	‖ ‖					61%
James Tucker	‖ ‖‖					60%
Abigail Bower	‖‖					61%
Robert Hodges	‖ ‖					54%
Amanda Johnston	‖ ‖					55%
Edward Roberts	‖					55%
Amanda Bond	‖					60%
Joshua Hart	‖					55%
Lillian Rutherford	‖ ‖ ‖ ‖					54%
Neil Knox	‖ ‖					59%
Lily Dowd	‖ ‖					59%
Luke Carr	‖ ‖					61%
Anne Thomson	‖					60%

Students section of the dashboard

The courses section

Monitoring the performance of the courses is as important as monitoring the scores of individual students. Small drops in the scores for a class could simply mean that the concepts being taught are a little more difficult than usual, but an important drop in the average score can have several causes that are worth investigating. For instance, it could be interesting to know whether there are other courses with similar behavior, as they could be interfering with each other due to difficult assignments on the same dates, for instance.

The courses section of the dashboard will show the user the evolution of the scores of each course and the average score of each course. To display the average score, we will use bullet charts, which are a compact display that shows us how actual measures compare with target values. Bullet charts are used to show us the value of an indicator, adding backgrounds to give context to the indicator's value. In this case, we will define regions of poor, regular, and good performance, and use the bullet chart to know the average score of each class based on these regions. The following figure illustrates a bullet chart:

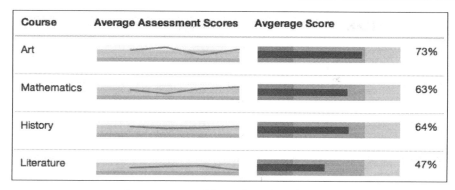

Course	Average Assessment Scores	Avgerage Score	
Art			73%
Mathematics			63%
History			64%
Literature			47%

Average scores of the students in each course

The class section

In the class context, we need to know whether there are relevant changes in average scores of the entire class. We will monitor weekly performance metrics so the teachers can detect problems before they become too difficult to solve.

We will display the average score of the students in all the courses. The absences for each week will also be included in the dashboard, so the user can quickly work out whether scores and absences are related for a particular student. We will list the date of the Monday of each week, displaying the average score for that week as a bullet chart. We will also include the average score as a number and the number of absences in the week as well.

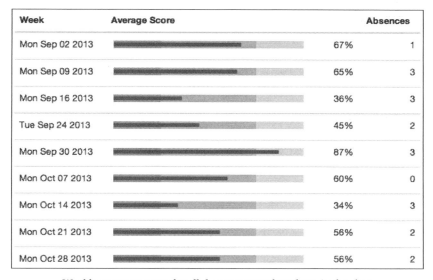

Week	Average Score		Absences
Mon Sep 02 2013		67%	1
Mon Sep 09 2013		65%	3
Mon Sep 16 2013		36%	3
Tue Sep 24 2013		45%	2
Mon Sep 30 2013		87%	3
Mon Oct 07 2013		60%	0
Mon Oct 14 2013		34%	3
Mon Oct 21 2013		56%	2
Mon Oct 28 2013		56%	2

Weekly average scores for all the courses and students in the class

Gathering the dashboard sections

The last step is to gather all the sections in one screen. The final layout of the dashboard will depend on the relative importance of the sections. In this case, we will organize them from the most granular to the more general, giving more space to the students section. The rationale behind this is that most of the time, the performance problems will be at an individual level and less frequently at the level of a course or class.

We will render each section inside a `div` element and assign it the `section` class. We will add styles to help us differentiate the sections and make logical groups more evident. We will add a light grey background and add a small border on top of each section. We also added a small title to give it an additional context.

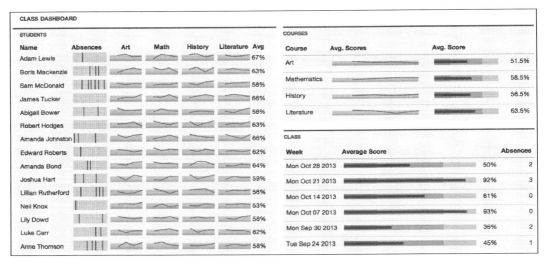

The completed dashboard. The sections are delimited with a light grey background.

In this example, the title of the dashboard is neither useful nor informative. In a real-world dashboard, the area of the title would be a good place to add navigation menus and links to other dashboard sections.

Summary

In this chapter, we described the characteristics of good dashboards and discussed the process behind the design and implementation of dashboards. We learned good practices to create effective dashboards. We also created an example dashboard to monitor the performance of the students in a class, including sections to assess the scores of individual students, courses, and classes.

In the next chapter, we will learn how to use GeoJSON and TopoJSON files to create maps with D3. We will learn about projections, how to use maps to display data, and how to integrate D3 with Mapbox.

10
Creating Maps

Maps are a 2D representation of the relevant features of places. Which features are relevant will depend on the purpose of the map; a map for a zoo will show the entrances, thematic areas, gift store, and where each animal is. In this case, there is no need for the sizes and distances to be precise. In a geologic map, we will need accurate distances and representations of the rock units and geologic strata.

Positions on the surface of the earth are described by two coordinates, longitude and latitude. The longitude of a point is the angle between the point and the Greenwich meridian, and the latitude is the angle between the point and the equator. The latitude and longitude are the angles measured with respect to the equator and the Greenwich meridian, as shown in the following diagram:

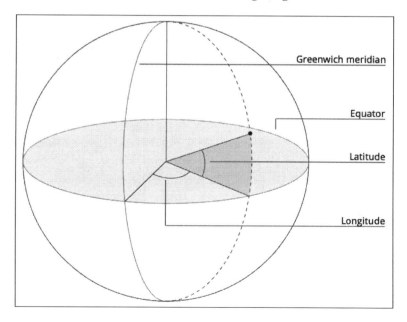

The longitude can take values between -180 and 180, while the latitude can have values between 90 (the North Pole) and -90 (the South Pole).

Shapes on the earth can be described by listing the coordinates of the points in their boundary in order. We can, for instance, describe an island by listing the coordinates of points on the coastline separated by one kilometer in a clockwise order. This representation won't be perfectly accurate, because it will not represent the irregularities in the coastline that are smaller than one kilometer in size, but this will be useful if we only need to have an idea of the shape of the island.

To create a map of a feature, we need to translate the coordinates that describe the feature to points in a 2D surface. The functions that perform this translation are called **projections**. As projections intend to represent a 3D surface in a 2D medium, distortions will be introduced as follows:

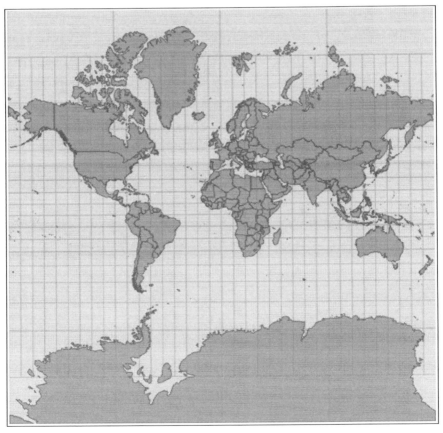

The Mercator projection severely distorts the areas near the poles

Each projection has been created in order to minimize distortions of some kind. Some projections will represent relative directions accurately but not the area of certain regions; others will do the exact opposite. When using maps, it's important to know what kinds of distortions are acceptable in each case.

In this chapter, we will learn how to create map-based charts with D3. We will learn how to obtain, transform, and use geographic data in GeoJSON and TopoJSON formats to create SVG-based maps. We will create a map to visualize the distortions introduced by the Mercator projection, coloring each country by its area. Maps in which regions are colored by a characteristic of the regions (population, income, and so on) are called **choropleths**. In this section, we will implement a choropleth map using D3 and GeoJSON. We will also learn how to use TopoJSON to create maps with more compact geographic data files, and how to use TopoJSON to display topologic information, such as the connection between features and boundaries. Lastly, we will learn how to integrate D3 with Mapbox, an excellent map provider.

Obtaining geographic data

To create a map, we will need files that describe the coordinates of the features that we intend to include in our map. One of the most reliable sources for medium-scale geographic data is Natural Earth (http://www.naturalearthdata.com), a collaborative effort to curate and organize geographic datasets.

The geographic datasets available at Natural Earth are in the public domain and are available at 1:10,000, 1:50,000, and 1:110,0000 scales. There are vector and raster datasets, and the map files are classified in three categories:

- **Cultural**: This contains countries, administrative divisions, states and provinces, populated places, roads, urban areas, and parks
- **Physical**: This describes coastlines, land, islands, oceans, rivers, lakes, and glaciated areas among others
- **Raster**: This contains images, depicting the relief as shades and with colors based on climate

The files are in the **ESRI shapefile** format, the de facto standard for geographic data. ESRIshape files represent the geometry of features as sets of points, lines, and polygons. The files might also contain additional attributes about the features, such as the name of the place, population in the last census, or the average income of the population living in that area. A shapefile is a set of several files, which must include the following three files:

- `.shp`: Shape format, the geometry of the feature
- `.shx`: An index to locate the features in the `.shp` file
- `.dbf`: The feature attributes in the dBase IV format

The shapefile set can also contain optional files, such as the `.prj` file, which contains information of the coordinate system and projection in which the vector data is stored.

Shapefiles are widely used in geographic information systems; however, the format is not suited for its use in web platforms. We will transform the shapefiles to JSON-based formats and use D3 to create maps from them.

Understanding the GeoJSON and TopoJSON formats

The most widely used formats to create maps with D3 are the GeoJSON and TopoJSON formats. In this section, we will describe both the formats briefly and learn how to transform ESRIshapefiles to GeoJSON or TopoJSON.

The **GeoJSON** format encodes geometries, features, or collections of features using the JSON format. We will describe the central aspects of the GeoJSON format; the complete specification is available at `http://geojson.org/`.

A GeoJSON file always contains one top-level object. The GeoJSON object must have a `type` attribute; for geometries, the type can be `Point`, `MultiPoint`, `LineString`, `MultiLineString`, `Polygon`, or `MultiPolygon`. For a collection of geometries, features, and collections of features, the type will be `GeometryCollection`, `Feature`, or `FeatureCollection`, respectively. One GeoJSON file can contain a small island or a collection of countries nested in the top-level object.

The GeoJSON objects that represent geometries must have a `coordinates` attribute, whose contents will depend on the type of geometry. For a `Point` attribute, the `coordinates` attribute will be an array of two elements, representing a position:

```
{"type": "Point", "coordinates": [10.0, 10.0]}
```

A `LineString` object represents a line, and its coordinates array contains a pair of locations (the longitude and latitude of a place):

```
{
  "type": "LineString",
  "coordinates": [[10.0, 10.0], [10.0, 0.0]]
}
```

A `Polygon` object is more complex. It's intended to represent a polygon that can have holes on it. Polygons are represented by first describing the exterior boundary and then the boundaries of the holes on it. A `Polygon` object with one hole could be described with the following GeoJSON object:

```
{
  "type": "Polygon",
  "coordinates": [
    [[0, 0], [0, 10], [10, 10], [0, 10], [10, 0]],
    [[2, 2], [8, 2], [8, 8], [8, 2], [2, 2]]
  ]
}
```

Here, the exterior ring describes a square of size 10, and the hole on it is a centered square of size 6. Also, there are geometries to describe the collections of the mentioned geometries; a `MultiPoint` object will contain an array of points, a `MultiLineString` object will contain an array with pairs of points, and a `MultiPolygon` object will contain an array of polygons.

A Feature object must have a geometry attribute that will contain a geometry object, usually `Polygon` or `MultiPolygon`. It may have a properties member that can be used to store nongeographic data about the features, such as the name of the place, population, or average income. For instance, the following feature object describes the country of Aruba; it contains about a dozen properties, and the polygon contains 26 points:

```
{
  "type": "Feature",
  "properties": {
    ...
    "type": "Country",
    "admin": "Aruba",
    "adm0_a3": "ABW",
    ...
  },
  "geometry": {
    "type": "Polygon",
```

```
      "coordinates": [
        [
          [-69.899121, 12.452001],
          [-69.895703, 12.422998],
          ...
        ]
      ]
    }
  }
```

A `FeatureCollection` object will contain a features array, which will contain feature objects.

As mentioned earlier, GeoJSON files describe features in terms of their geometry, and in some cases, they are highly redundant. If two features share a boundary, the common boundary coordinates will appear twice, once for each feature. Moreover, the description of the boundary might not match exactly, generating artificial gaps between the shapes. These shortcomings are addressed by the TopoJSON format created by Mike Bostock, the creator of D3.

TopoJSON objects encode topologies instead of geometries, that is, describing the relationship between points, lines, and shapes. In a TopoJSON object, shapes are described as sequences of **arcs**, which are essentially boundary segments. Each arc is defined once, but it can be referenced several times by the shapes that share that arc. This removes redundancy, making TopoJSON lighter than their GeoJSON counterparts. The coordinates in TopoJSON files are encoded in a more efficient way, making TopoJSON even more compact.

The following TopoJSON object represents the country of Aruba. The object contains an array of `arcs`, a `transform` attribute with information on how to decode the coordinates of the arcs to longitude and latitude, and the `objects` member, which contains the description of the features:

```
{
  "type": "Topology",
  "objects": {
    "aruba": {
      "type": "GeometryCollection",
      "geometries": [
        {
```

```
          "type": "Polygon",
          "arcs": [[0]]
        }
      ]
    }
  },
  "arcs": [
    [
      [9798,    1517],
      [ 201, -1517],
      [-2728,    812],
      ...
    ]
  ],
  "transform": {
    "scale": [
      0.00001704271989698,
      0.00001911323944894461
    ],
    "translate": [
      -70.06611328125,
      12.422998046874994
    ]
  }
}
```

The `objects` member can contain one or more objects describing geometry, but instead of listing the coordinates of the geometry object, the `arcs` array contains a list of references to the arcs defined at the top level of the TopoJSON object. If several features share a boundary, they will reference the same arc.

Besides the TopoJSON format, Mike Bostock created utilities to manipulate TopoJSON and GeoJSON files. The TopoJSON program has two components: the command-line program and the client-side library. The command-line program allows you to convert shapefiles, CSV or GeoJSON formats, to TopoJSON. It has options to simplify the features, combine several files in one output, and add or remove properties from the original features. The JavaScript library allows you to parse the TopoJSON files and construct Feature objects. The complete specification of the format and the programs is available at `https://github.com/mbostock/topojson`.

Transforming and manipulating the files

We might need to manipulate the geographic data files in several ways. We might want to reduce the level of detail of our features to have smaller files and simpler features, include additional metadata not present in the original files, or even filter some features.

To convert the files from one format to another, we will need to install the **Geospatial Data Abstraction Library (GDAL)**. GDAL provides command-line tools to manipulate and convert geographic data between different formats, shapefiles and GeoJSON among them. There are binaries available for Windows, Mac, and Linux systems on their site, http://www.gdal.org/.

Depending on how we want our files, our workflow will include several steps that we might need to redo later. It's a good idea to automate this process in a way that allows us to understand why and how we transformed the files. One way to do this is to use the **make** program or a similar system. We will use *make* to download and transform the geographic datasets that we need for this chapter.

For the first chart, we will need to download the cultural vectors from Natural Earth. In a world map, we don't need the most detailed level; we will download medium-scale data. Then, we will uncompress the shapefiles and use the **ogr2ogr** program to transform the shapefiles to GeoJSON.

We will implement these transformations using make. The `Makefile` is in the `chapter10/data` directory of the code bundle. Each step can be done individually in a terminal provided that it is performed in the correct order. In a `Makefile`, we describe each step in the transformation process as a target, which can have zero or more **dependencies**. To generate the target file from the dependencies, we need to perform one or more commands. For instance, to generate the `ne_50m_admin_0_countries.shp` target file, we need to uncompress the `ne_50m_admin_0_countries.zip` file. This file is a dependency of the target file, because the target can't be generated if the ZIP file doesn't exist. The command to generate the shapefile is `unzip ne_50m_admin_0_countries.zip`. The following `Makefile` will generate a GeoJSON file that contains all the countries:

```
# Variables
ADMIN0_URL = http://.../ne_50m_admin_0_countries.zip


# Targets

# Download the Compressed Shapefiles
ne_50m_admin_0_countries.zip:
```

```
    curl -LO $(ADMIN0_URL)

# Uncompress the Shapefiles
ne_50m_admin_0_countries.shp: ne_50m_admin_0_countries.zip
    unzip ne_50m_admin_0_countries.zip
    touch ne_50m_admin_0_countries.shp

# Convert the shapefiles to GeoJSON
countries.geojson: ne_50m_admin_0_countries.shp
    ogr2ogr -f GeoJSONcountries.geojso nne_50m_admin_0_countries.shp
```

The `Makefiles` manage the dependencies between targets; building the `countries.geojson` file will check the dependency chain and run the target commands in the correct order. To generate the GeoJSON file in one step, run the following command:

```
$ make countries.geojson
```

It will download, uncompress, and transform the shapefiles to GeoJSON. It will only perform the commands to generate the files that are not present in the current directory; it won't download the ZIP file again if the file is already present.

We can use the GeoJSON file to create a TopoJSON version of the same file. By default, `topojson` will strip all the properties of the original file. We can preserve the properties by using the `-p` name option:

```
$ topojson -o countries.topojson -p admin -p continent
  countries.geojson
```

Note that the file size of the GeoJSON file is about 4.4 M; the TopoJSON file is only 580 K. We will begin by using the `countries.geojson` file to create our first maps, and then learn how to use the TopoJSON files to create maps. We will also include this command in the `Makefile` to be able to replicate this conversion easily.

Creating maps with D3

In this section, we will create map-charts based on SVG. We will use the GeoJSON file with the countries to create a choropleth map that shows the distortions introduced by the Mercator projection.

We will also create maps using the more compact format, TopoJSON, and use topologic information contained in the file to find the neighbors and specific frontiers between countries.

Creating a choropleth map

In this section, we will create a choropleth map to compare the areas of different countries. We will paint each country according to its area; countries with greater areas will be colored with darker colors. In general, the Mercator projection is not suitable to create choropleth maps showing large areas, as this projection shows the regions near the poles bigger than they really are. For instance, Antarctica is smaller than Russia, but using the Mercator projection, it seems bigger. Brazil has a greater area than Greenland, but with this projection, it looks smaller.

In this example, we will use the Mercator projection to show this effect. Our choropleth map will allow us to compare the size of the countries. We will use the GeoJSON file, chapter10/data/countries.geojson, available in the code bundle. The chapter10/01-countries-geojson.html file displays the contents of the file for a more convenient inspection of the features and their attributes.

We will begin by reading the contents of the GeoJSON file and creating the SVG element to display the map. GeoJSON is encoded in the JSON format, so we can use the d3.json method to retrieve and parse the content from GeoJSON:

```
d3.json(geoJsonUrl, function(error, data) {

    // Handle errors getting or parsing the GeoJSON file
    if (error) { return error; }

    // Create the SVG container selection
    var div = d3.select('#map01'),
        svg = div.selectAll('svg').data([data]);

    // Create the SVG element on enter
    svg.enter().append('svg')
        .attr('width', width)
        .attr('height', height);
});
```

The data variable contains the GeoJSON object. In this case, the GeoJSON object contains a FeatureCollection object, and the features array contains Feature objects, one for each country.

To map the feature coordinates, we will need a projection function. D3 includes about a dozen of the most used projections, and there are even more available as plugins (see https://github.com/d3/d3-geo-projection for the complete list). We will create an instance of the Mercator projection and translate it so that the point with the coordinates [0, 0] lies in the center of the SVG figure:

```
// Create an instance of the Mercator projection
var projection = d3.geo.mercator()
    .translate([width / 2, height / 2]);
```

With this function, we can compute the SVG coordinates of any point on earth. For instance, we can compute the SVG coordinates of a point in the coast of Aruba by invoking the projection function with the [longitude, latitude] array as an argument:

```
projection([-69.899121, 12.452001])
// [17.004529145013294, 167.1410458329102]
```

We have the geometric description of each feature; the geometries contain arrays of coordinates. We could use these arrays to compute the projection of each point and draw the shapes using the d3.svg.path generator, but this will involve interpreting the geometries of the features. Fortunately, D3 includes a geographic path generator that does the work for us:

```
// Create the path generator and configure its projection
var pathGenerator = d3.geo.path()
    .projection(projection);
```

The d3.geo.path generator needs the projection to compute the paths. Now, we can create the path objects that will represent our features:

```
// Create a selection for the countries
var features = svg.selectAll('path.feature')
    .data(data.features);

// Append the paths on enter
features.enter().append('path')
    .attr('class', 'feature');

// Set the path of the countries
features.attr('d', pathGenerator);
```

We have added the class feature to each path in order to configure its style using CSS. After including the `chapter10/map.css` style sheet file, our map will look similar what is shown in to the following figure:

A map of the world countries, using the Mercator projection with the default scale

We can see that the features are correctly drawn, but we would like to add colors for the ocean and scale the map to show all the countries. Projections have a scale method that allows you to set the projection's scale. Note that different projections interpret the scale in different ways. In the case of the Mercator projection, we can map the entire world by setting the scale as the ratio between the figure width and the complete angle, in radians:

```
// The width will cover the complete circumference
var scale = width / (2 * Math.PI);

// Create and center the projection
var projection = d3.geo.mercator()
    .scale(scale)
    .translate([width / 2, height / 2]);
```

We will also want to add a background to represent the oceans. We could simply add a SVG rectangle before inserting the features; instead, we will create a feature object that spans the globe and uses the path generator to create an SVG path. This is a better approach because if we change the projection later, the background will still cover the complete globe. Note that we need to close the polygon by adding the first point in the last position:

```
var globeFeature = {
    type: 'Feature',
    geometry: {
        type: 'Polygon',
        coordinates: [
            [
                [-179.999,  89.999],
                [ 179.999,  89.999],
                [ 179.999, -89.999],
                [-179.999, -89.999],
                [-179.999,  89.999]
            ]
        ]
    }
};
```

To avoid overlapping, the rectangle defined by the coordinates doesn't completely cover the globe. We can now create the path for the globe and add a style to it, as we did for the rest of the features:

```
// Create a selection for the globe
var globe = svg.selectAll('path.globe')
    .data([globeFeature]);

// Append the graticule paths on enter
globe.enter().append('path')
    .attr('class', 'globe');

// Set the path data using the path generator
globe.attr('d', pathGenerator);
```

We will also add reference lines for the meridians and parallels. These lines are called as graticules, and D3 includes a generator that returns a MultiLineString object with the description of the lines:

```
// Create the graticule feature generator
var graticule = d3.geo.graticule();

// Create a selection for the graticule
```

```
var grid = svg.selectAll('path.graticule')
    .data([graticule()])

// Append the graticule paths on enter
grid.enter().append('path')
    .attr('class', 'graticule');

// Set the path attribute for the graticule
grid.attr('d', pathGenerator);
```

We have also added a class to the graticule lines to apply styles using CSS. The map now looks better:

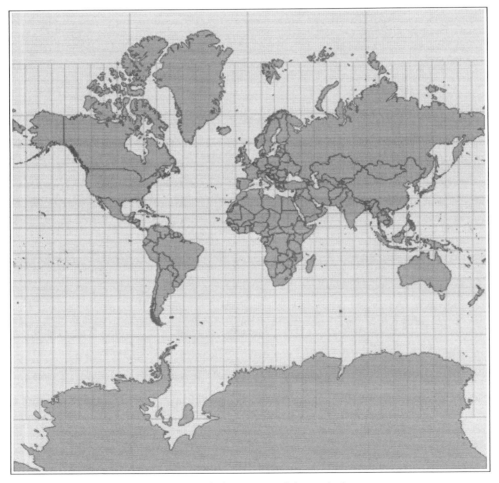

The map with the oceans and the graticule

When creating a choropleth map, one of the most important choices to be made is the color scale to be used. Color Brewer (http://colorbrewer2.org/) is an online tool that helps developers and designers to choose good color scales for their maps. There are color scales for qualitative dimensions as well as for sequential and diverging quantitative dimensions. The colors of each palette have been carefully chosen so that there is a good contrast between the colors and they look good on the screen.

For a map that shows a qualitative dimension, the color scale should be composed of colors that differ primarily in hue but have a similar brightness and saturation. An example of this could be a map showing which languages are spoken in each country, as shown in the following figure:

A qualitative color scale doesn't suggest order between the items

For quantitative variables that are sequential, that is, ranging from less to more in one dimension, a color scale with increasing darkness will be a good choice. For instance, to display differences in income or housing costs, a sequential scale would be a good fit, as shown in the following figure:

A sequential color scale is a good choice for ordinal variables

For a quantitative variable that covers two extremes, the color palette should emphasize the extremes with dark colors of different hue and show the critical mid-range values with lighter colors. An example of this could be a map that shows the average winter temperatures, showing the countries with temperatures below zero in blue, temperatures above zero in red, and the zero value in white, as shown in the following figure:

A diverging color scale is useful to show variables that cover extremes

In our case, we will use a sequential scale because our quantitative variable is the area of each country. Countries with a bigger surface will be shown in a darker color. We will use Color Brewer to generate a sequential palette:

```
var colorRange = [
    '#f7fcfd',
    '#e0ecf4',
    '#bfd3e6',
    '#9ebcda',
    '#8c96c6',
    '#8c6bb1',
    '#88419d',
    '#6e016b'];
```

This color palette has eight levels, ranging from almost white to dark purple. The d3.geo.area method computes the area of a feature in steradians, which is the measurement unit for solid angles. We will use the d3.scale.quantize scale to assign the area of each feature to one of the colors of our palette:

```
// Create the color scale for the area of the features
var colorScale = d3.scale.quantize()
    .domain(d3.extent(data.features, d3.geo.area))
    .range(colorRange);
```

We use the d3.geo.area method to compute the area of each feature and to compute the fill color using the color scale:

```
// Set the path of the countries
features.attr('d', pathGenerator)
    .attr('fill', function(d) {
        return colorScale(d3.geo.area(d));
    });
```

We obtain a map with each country colored according to its area, as shown in the following figure:

The choropleth that shows the area of each country

When we take a look at the choropleth, we can see several inconsistencies between the size and the colors. Greenland, for instance, looks twice as big as Brazil, but it's actually smaller than Brazil, Australia, and the United States.

Mapping topology

As mentioned in the previous section, TopoJSON files are more compact than their GeoJSON counterparts, but the real power of TopoJSON is that it encodes topology, that is, information about connectedness and the boundaries of the geometries it describes. Topology gives us access to more information than just the shapes of each feature; we can identify the neighbors and boundaries between geometries.

In this section, we will use the `countries.topojson` file to create a world map, replacing GeoJSON from the previous section. We will also identify and map the neighboring countries of Bolivia and identify a particular frontier using the TopoJSON library. As we did in the previous section, we have created the `chapter10/03-countries-topojson.html` file to display the contents of the TopoJSON file for easier inspection.

To create a world map with TopoJSON, we need to create the SVG container and the projection in the same way that we did with the GeoJSON file. The geographic path generator expects GeoJSON objects, but at this point, we have a TopoJSON object that encodes the geometry of our features. The `topojson.feature` object computes the GeoJSON `Feature` or `FeatureCollection` object, corresponding to the object given as the second argument. Remember that the object attribute contains the TopoJSON geometry objects, which have an array of references to the arcs defined at the top level of the TopoJSON object. In this case, the `geodata` variable stores a `FeatureCollection` object, which we can use to generate the shapes using the same code as that used earlier:

```
d3.json(url, function(error, data) {

    // Create the SVG container...

    // Construct the Feature Collection
    var geodata = topojson.feature(data,data.objects.countries);

    // Render the features
});
```

The `geodata` object is a `FeatureCollection` object, and we can use the same projection and path generator that we used in the last section to generate the world map:

```
// Create a selection for the countries and bind the feature data
var features = svg.selectAll('path.feature')
    .data(geodata.features)
    .enter()
    .append('path')
    .attr('class', 'feature')
    .attr('d', pathGenerator);
```

This allows us to replace the GeoJSON file that we used in the previous section with the TopoJSON file, which is about one-eight the size of the `countries.geojson` file and obtains the same result, as shown in the following figure:

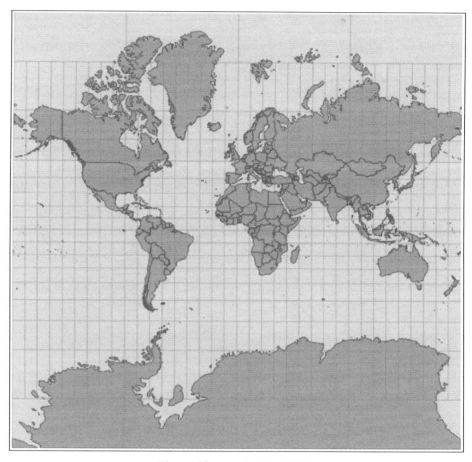

The world map using TopoJSON

As TopoJSON files describe geometries by listing references to the arcs, we can verify that two geometries are neighbors by checking whether they have arcs in common. The `topojson.neighbors` method does exactly this, given an array of geometries; it returns an array with the indices of the neighbors of each geometry object.

To illustrate this point, we will create a map that highlights the countries that share a boundary with Bolivia. We will begin by scaling and centering the map to display South America. We begin by filtering the countries that belong to South America and creating a `FeatureCollection` object for them:

```
// Construct the FeatureCollection object
var geodata = topojson.feature(data, data.objects.countries);

// Filter the countries in South America
var southAmerica = geodata.features.filter(function(d) {
        return (d.properties.continent === 'South America');
    });

// Create a feature collection for South America
var southAmericaFeature = {
        type: 'FeatureCollection',
        features: southAmerica
    };
```

We would like to adapt the scale and translation of the projection to just display South America. D3 provides tools to compute the bounding box and centroid of a feature:

```
// Compute the bounds, centroid, and extent of South America
// to configure the projection
var bounds = d3.geo.bounds(southAmericaFeature),
    center = d3.geo.centroid(southAmericaFeature);
```

The d3.geo.bounds method returns the bottom-left and top-right corners of the feature's bounding box in geographic coordinates. The d3.geo.centroid method returns an array with the longitude and latitude of the centroid of the feature.

To compute a scale factor that displays our feature object properly, we need to know the angular distance between the two corners of our bounding box. We could also use another characteristic distance of the feature, such as the distance from the centroid to one of the bounding box corners:

```
// Compute the angular distance between bound corners
var distance = d3.geo.distance(bounds[0], bounds[1]);
```

The d3.geo.distance method takes two locations and returns the angular distance between the points (in radians). For the Mercator projection, we can compute the scale as the ratio between the desired screen size and the angular span of our feature. We can recompute the scale with the angular distance between the corners of the bounding box:

```
// The width will cover the complete circumference
var scale = width / distance;
```

We can now center and scale our projection. This will show our feature centered in the screen and at a better scale:

```
// Create and scale the projection
var projection = d3.geo.mercator()
    .scale(scale)
    .translate([width / 2, height / 2])
    .center(center);
```

Note that this way of computing the scale will only work with the Mercator projection. The scales are not consistent among projections, as shown in the following figure:

Centering and scaling a map around a feature

Having centered and scaled the South American continent properly, we can proceed to compute the neighbors of Bolivia. We begin by obtaining the neighbors of each country in our dataset:

```
// Compute the neighbors of each geometry object.
var neighbors =
    topojson.neighbors(data.objects.countries.geometries);
```

This will return an array with as many elements as the input array. Each element will be an array with the indices of the neighbor geometries of each object. The geometry of Bolivia is described by the thirtieth element in the `data.objects.countries. geometries` array. The contents of `neighbors[30]` is the `[8, 31, 39, 169, 177]` array; each element is the index of the geometry element of each neighboring country. To find Bolivia's neighbors, we need to know the index of Bolivia, so, we will search for it in the geometries array:

```
// Find the index of Bolivia in the geometries array
var countryIndex = 0;
data.objects.countries.geometries.forEach(function(d, i) {
    if (d.properties.admin === 'Bolivia') {
        countryIndex = i;
    }
});
```

The `neighbors[countryIndex]` array will contain the indices of the neighbors of Bolivia. To display the neighbor's features in the map, we need to compute a feature that contains their geometries. We can create a `GeometryCollection` object in order to use the `topojson.feature` method to construct the `FeatureCollection` object with the neighbors:

```
// Construct a Geometry Collection with the neighbors
var geomCollection = {
    type: 'GeometryCollection',
    geometries: []
};

// Add the neighbor's geometry object to the geometry collection
neighbors[countryIndex].forEach(function(i) {
    var geom = data.objects.countries.geometries[i];
    geomCollection.geometries.push(geom);
});
```

The geometry collection object we just created contains the geometries of the countries that share boundaries with Bolivia. We will create a feature collection object for these geometries in order to add them to the map:

```
// Construct a Feature object for the neighbors
var neighborFeature = topojson.feature(data, geomCollection);
```

We can now create the path for the feature containing the neighbors, and add a class to the path to set its style with CSS:

```
// Add paths for the neighbor countries
var neighborPaths = svg.selectAll('path.neighbor')
    .data([neighborFeature])
    .enter()
    .append('path')
    .attr('class', 'neighbor')
    .attr('d', pathGenerator);
```

The countries that share a boundary with Bolivia are highlighted in the following figure:

The TopoJSON file gives us more information. Let's say that we need to show the frontier between Bolivia and Brazil. We know that this frontier is identifiable, because we could inspect the geometries for both countries and select the arcs that are common to both geometries, but there is an easier way. The `topojson.mesh` method returns a GeoJSON `MultiLineString` geometry that represents the mesh for a given object and geometry. It has an optional argument to filter the arcs that meet a condition. We will use this method to generate a `MultiLineString` object, representing the boundary between Brazil and Bolivia:

```
// Compute the mesh of the boundary between Brazil and Bolivia
var frontier = topojson.mesh(data, data.objects.countries, function(a,
b) {
    return ((a.properties.admin === 'Brazil') && (b.properties.admin
=== 'Bolivia')) ||
            ((a.properties.admin === 'Bolivia') && (b.properties.admin
=== 'Brazil'));
});
```

Note that the optional filter receives two TopoJSON geometries, not GeoJSON features. To obtain the frontier between Brazil and Bolivia, we need to select the arcs that are shared by both the countries. We can now create a path for the frontier and add it to our map:

```
// Add the frontier to the SVG element
var frontierPath = svg.selectAll('path.frontier')
    .data([frontier])
    .enter()
    .append('path')
    .attr('class', 'frontier')
    .attr('d', pathGenerator);
```

The boundary between the two countries is highlighted in the following updated map:

Note that the `topojson.mesh` method can be used to identify frontiers of any kind. In other datasets, this can be useful to show or hide internal frontiers or frontiers with countries that meet certain conditions.

In this section, we learned how to use GeoJSON to create SVG-based maps. We have also learned how to use TopoJSON files to reconstruct GeoJSON objects and create a map. We've also learned how to create maps that highlight topologic relations between places, such as highlighting countries that are connected to each other and show specific boundaries between features.

Using Mapbox and D3

SVG-based maps are great for data visualization projects, but sometimes, we will need more advanced features in our maps, such as a feature that allows us to search for an address or location, get information at the street level, or show satellite images. The most convenient way to provide these features is to integrate our visualization with map providers such as Google Maps, Yahoo! Maps, or Mapbox. In this section, we will learn how to integrate D3 with Mapbox, an excellent map provider.

Mapbox is an online platform used to create custom-designed maps for web and mobile applications. It provides street maps and terrain and satellite view tiles. The street maps from Mapbox use data from OpenStreetMap, a community-powered open data repository with frequent updates and accurate information.

A distinctive feature of Mapbox is that it allows customization of the map views. Users can customize the visual aspects of every feature in their maps. The web platform has tools to customize the maps, and the desktop tool, TileMill, makes this customization even easier.

To follow the examples in this section, you will need a Mapbox account. The free plan allows you to create maps, add markers and features, and get up to 3,000 views per month. To create a Mapbox account, visit `https://www.mapbox.com`.

Mapbox counts the views to your map, and each plan has a limit on the number of views per month. If you create a visualization using Mapbox and it becomes popular (I hope so!), you might want to upgrade your account. In any case, you will be notified if you are about to spend your monthly quota.

The Mapbox JavaScript API is implemented as a Leaflet plugin and includes a release of Leaflet, an open source library to create interactive map applications. Leaflet provides an API that allows you to create layers, interactive elements (such as zooming and panning), add custom markets, and many others. We will use the Mapbox and Leaflet APIs to create maps and integrate the maps with D3.

Creating a Mapbox project

We will begin by pointing the browser to `https://www.mapbox.com/projects/` and create a new project. In Mapbox, a project is a map that we can customize according to our needs. By clicking on **Create a Project**, we can access the map editor, where we can customize the colors of land, buildings, and other features; select the base layer (street, terrain, or satellite); and select the primary language for the features and locations in the map. We can also add markers and polygons and export them to KML or GeoJSON in order to use them in other projects. You can also set the map as private or public, remove geocoding, or remove sharing buttons.

Once we save the map, it will be given a map ID. This ID is necessary to load the map using the JavaScript API, view the tiles, or embed the map in a page. The ID is composed of the username and a map handle. To use the JavaScript API, we need to include the `Mapbox.js` library and styles. These files can also be downloaded and installed locally with Bower (`bower install --save-devmapbox.js`):

```
<script src='https://api.tiles.mapbox.com/mapbox.js/
  v1.6.2/mapbox.js'></script>
<link href='https://api.tiles.mapbox.com/mapbox.js/
  v1.6.2/mapbox.css'rel='stylesheet' />
```

To include the map in our page, we need to create a container div and set its position to absolute. We will also create a container for this div element in order to give the map container a positioning context:

```
<div class="map-container">
  <div id="map"></div>
</div>
```

The top and left offsets of the map container will be governed by the parent element. For this example, we will add the styles at the top of our page:

```
<style>
.map-container {
    position: relative;
    width: 600px;
    height: 400px;
}

#map {
    position: absolute;
    top: 0;
    bottom: 0;
    width: 100%;
}
</style>
```

The next step is to create an instance of the map. We can set the view's center and zoom level by chaining the `setView` method:

```
<script>
var mapID = 'username.xxxxxxxx', // replace with your map ID
    center = [12.526, -69.997],
    zoomLevel = 11;

var map = L.mapbox.map('map', mapID)
    .setView(center, zoomLevel);
</script>
```

The map of Aruba created by Mapbox is shown in the following figure:

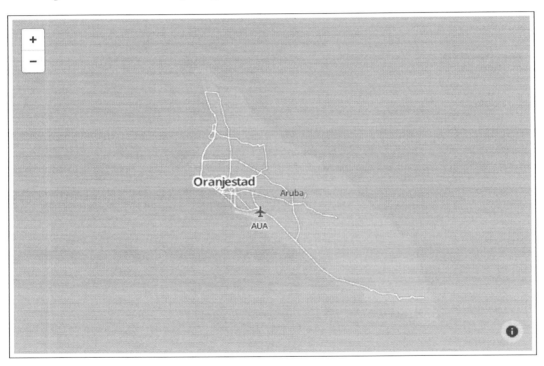

The map will be rendered in the container div. Note that the maps support all the interactions that we expect; we can zoom in or out and drag the map to explore the surrounding areas.

Integrating Mapbox and D3

In this example, we will create a bubble plot map to show the population of the main cities in Aruba. We have created a JSON file with the necessary information. The JSON file has the following structure:

```
{
  "country": "Aruba",
  "description": "Population of the main cities in Aruba",
  "cities": [
    {
      "name": "Oranjestad",
      "population": 28294,
      "coordinates": [12.519, -70.037]
    },
    ...
  ]
}
```

To create the bubbles, we will create a **layer**. Layers are objects attached to a particular location, such as markers or tiles. Most Leaflet objects are created by extending the L.Class object, which implements simple classical inheritance and several utility methods. We will create a D3 layer class by extending the L.Class object. Layers must at least have an initialize and the onAdd methods. We will also include the onRemove method to remove the bubbles if the layer is removed. A basic layer will have the following structure:

```
var D3Layer = L.Class.extend({

    initialize: function(arguments...) {
        // Initialization code
    },

    onAdd: function(map) {
        // Create and update the bubbles
    },

    onRemove: function(map) {
        // Clean the map
    }
});
```

The `initialize` method will be invoked when the layer instance is created. The `onAdd` method is invoked when the layer is added to the map. It receives the map object as an argument, which gives us access to the panes, zoom level, and other properties of the map. The `onRemove` method is invoked when the layer is removed from the map, and it also receives the map as an argument.

Whenever the user interacts with the map by dragging or zooming, the map triggers the `viewreset` event. This method notifies that the layers need to be repositioned. The `latLngToLayerPoint` method can be used to set the new position of the objects, given their geographic coordinates.

In our case, the `initialize` method will receive a single data argument, which will contain the array with the cities of Aruba. We will store the data array as an attribute of the layer:

```
initialize: function(data) {
    this._data = data;
},
```

The data array will be accessible from each method of the layer. In the `onAdd` method, we will select a pane from the map and append the bubbles to it. The container div for our bubbles will be the overlay pane of the map, which is a pane designed to contain custom objects. The overlay pane gets repositioned automatically each time the user pans the map.

One strategy is to create a single svg container to hold our bubbles and to resize it each time the user zooms in or out. Another strategy we will use is to create one svg element for each bubble and position it absolutely using the projection of the coordinates of each feature. We will create a selection for the svg elements and bind the data to the selection:

```
onAdd: function(map) {

    // Create SVG elements under the overlay pane
    var div = d3.select(map.getPanes().overlayPane),
        svg = div.selectAll('svg.point').data(this._data);

    // Create the bubbles...
},
```

To position the SVG elements, we need to project the latitude and longitude of each point and use these coordinates to set the offsets of our svg containers. We will add the `L.LatLng` objects with the coordinates of each city to each data item:

```
// Stores the latitude and longitude of each city
this._data.forEach(function(d) {
```

```
        d.LatLng = new L.LatLng(d.coordinates[0],
  d.coordinates[1]);
        });
```

We will use this attribute in just a few moments. The svg elements will be created to contain just one bubble, so they don't overlap other areas of the map. Before setting the size of the svg elements, we need to compute the radius scale. The area of the bubbles should be proportional to the population of the city:

```
// Create a scale for the population
var rScale = d3.scale.sqrt()
    .domain([0, d3.max(this._data, function(d) {
        return d.population;
    })])
    .range([0, 35]);
```

We can now create the svg elements and set their size and position. Note that the svg element's width and height are twice as big as the radius of the bubble:

```
svg.enter().append('svg')
    .attr('width', function(d) {
        return 2 * rScale(d.population);
    })
    .attr('height', function(d) {
        return 2 * rScale(d.population);
    })
    .attr('class', 'point leaflet-zoom-hide')
    .style('position', 'absolute');
```

We have added the leaflet-zoom-hide class to each svg element so that they are hidden when the map is being zoomed in or out by the user. We also set the position of the svg container to absolute. We can finally add the bubbles as usual, appending a circle to each svg container:

```
svg.append('circle')
    .attr('cx', function(d) { return rScale(d.population); })
    .attr('cy', function(d) { return rScale(d.population); })
    .attr('r', function(d) { return rScale(d.population); })
    .attr('class', 'city')
    .on('mouseover', function(d) {
        d3.select(this).classed('highlight', true);
    })
    .on('mouseout', function(d) {
        d3.select(this).classed('highlight', false);
    });
```

We added event listeners for the `mouseover` and `mouseout` events. In these events, we add the `highlight` class to the circles, which will increase the opacity of the circles.

When the user drags the map, the overlay pane will be moved as well and the bubbles will be well positioned. When the user zooms in/out of the map, the `viewreset` event will be triggered, and we must reposition the svg containers. We will create an `updateBubbles` function to update the position of the bubbles on zoom, and invoke this function on `viewreset`:

```
// Update the position of the bubbles on zoom
map.on('viewreset', updateBubbles);
```

When the callback of the `viewreset` event is invoked, the `map.latLngToLayerPoint` projection method is updated with the new zoom level and position. So, we can use it to set the offsets of the svg elements:

```
function updateBubbles() {
    svg
        .style('left', function(d) {
            var dx = map.latLngToLayerPoint(d.LatLng).x;
            return (dx - rScale(d.population)) + 'px';
        })
        .style('top', function(d) {
            var dy = map.latLngToLayerPoint(d.LatLng).y;
            return (dy - rScale(d.population)) + 'px';
        });
}
```

Finally, we invoke the `updateBubbles` method to render the bubbles:

```
// Render the bubbles on add
updateBubbles();
```

The `onRemove` method is simpler; we just select the overlay pane and remove all the svg elements from it:

```
onRemove: function(map) {
    var div = d3.select(map.getPanes().overlayPane);
    div.selectAll('svg.point').remove();
}
```

Having created our layer, we can retrieve the JSON file and append it to the map:

```
// Retrieve the dataset of cities of Aruba
d3.json('/chapter10/data/aruba-cities.json', function(error, data) {

    // Handle errors getting or parsing the data
    if (error) { return error; }

    // Create a layer with the cities data
    map.addLayer(new D3Layer(data.cities));
});
```

Our following map shows the bubbles that represent the population of the cities of Aruba:

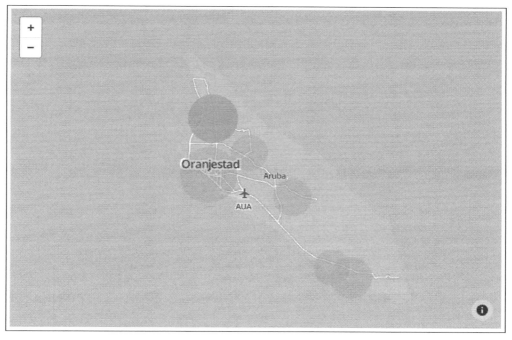

A bubble plot map with D3 and Mapbox

Summary

In this chapter, we learned how to obtain and transform geographic datasets using open source tools. We learned how to use and interpret two popular formats for mapping information for the Web, GeoJSON, and TopoJSON.

We also learned how to create simple charts based on SVG, rendering the geographic features as svg paths. We created a choropleth map using the Mercator projection and used TopoJSON to obtain information about topology, allowing us to identify neighbors and frontiers between countries.

Finally, we learned how to use Mapbox and D3 to create data visualizations for applications that require street-level detail.

In the next chapter, we will learn how to use other projections to create 3D-like views of our maps and how to project raster images in our maps.

11
Creating Advanced Maps

In the last chapter, we learned how to use the GeoJSON and TopoJSON formats to create map-based charts using SVG. In this chapter, we will explore different cartographic projections and learn how to use the Orthographic and Stereographic projections to create 3D-like renderings of our maps.

We will add interaction to our maps by adding drag and zoom behavior, allowing the user to rotate and zoom the map views. We will use the Orthographic projection to create a rotating view of the Earth, and we will create a star map using the Orthographic projection.

We will also learn how to project raster images of the Earth using canvas and D3 projections in order to have realistic renderings of it.

Using cartographic projections

As we mentioned in the previous chapter, cartographic projections are functions that map positions on the Earth to points on a flat surface. The d3.geo module of D3 implements about a dozen of the most used cartographic projections, and there are even more cartographic projections available in the extended geographic projections plugin at https://github.com/d3/d3-geo-projection/.

There are a great number of projections because none of them are appropriate for every application. The Mercator projection, for instance, was created as a navigation tool. Straight lines on the Mercator projection are rhumb lines, which are lines of constant compass bearing. This projection is very useful for navigation, but the areas near the poles are extremely distorted. The poles, which are points on the surface of the Earth, are represented as lines that are as long as the equator. The Orthographic projection, on the other hand, is closer to what we would see from space, creating a more accurate mental image of how the Earth really is, but it's probably not very useful to navigate by sea.

In this section, we will learn how to use more projections and discuss some of their properties. The examples in this section are in the `chapter11/01-projections` file in the code bundle. For the examples in this section, we will use a TopoJSON file that contains land features, which are generated from the medium-scale shapefiles from Natural Earth. The `Makefile` in the `chapter11/data` folder will download and transform the necessary files for us.

Using the Equirectangular projection

The **Equirectangular** projection linearly maps longitude to a horizontal position and latitude to a vertical position using the same scale. As there are 180 degrees from pole to pole, and the circumference of the earth covers 360 degrees, the width of a world map created with this projection will be twice its height. It's mathematical simplicity is about its only useful property.

To create a world map, we begin by loading the TopoJSON file and using the `topojson.feature` method to compute the GeoJSON object, representing the shapes described in the `ne_50m_land` object:

```
d3.json('/chapter11/data/land.json', function(error, data) {

    // Notifies about errors getting or parsing the data
    if (error) { console.error(error); }

    // Construct the GeoJSON features
    var geojson = topojson.feature(data,
      data.objects.ne_50m_land);

    // Create the projection and draw the features...
});
```

As usual, we set the width and height of the svg container of the map. We select the container div for the map and append the svg element, setting its width and height:

```
    // Set the width and height of the svg element
    var width = 600,
        height = 300;

    // Append the svg container and set its size
    var div = d3.select('#map-equirectangular'),
        svg = div.append('svg')
            .attr('width', width)
            .attr('height', height);
```

We create an instance of the `d3.geo.equirectangular` projection and configure its scale and translation by chaining the corresponding methods. Note that scales are not consistent among projections. In this case, in order to show the world map, we can set the scale either to `height / Math.PI` or `width / (2 * Math.PI)`. In both cases, the result will be the same:

```
// Create an instance of the Equirectangular projection
var equirectangular = d3.geo.equirectangular()
    .scale(width / (2 * Math.PI))
    .translate([width / 2, height / 2]);
```

Once we have the projection created, we can create an instance of the geographic path generator and set its `projection` attribute:

```
// Create and configure the geographic path generator
var path = d3.geo.path()
    .projection(equirectangular);
```

The path generator receives a GeoJSON feature or feature collection and uses the projection to compute the corresponding svg path string. Finally, we append a path element to the svg container, bind the feature collection to the selection, and set the path data string to be computed with the path generator:

```
// Append the path of the features to the svg container
svg.append('path').datum(geojson)
    .attr('class', 'land')
    .attr('d', path);
```

We will also add parallels and meridians to the figure. D3 has a generator that creates these lines. The `d3.geo.graticule()` method returns a configurable function that creates a feature collection that contains the graticule lines:

```
// Create the graticule lines
var graticule = d3.geo.graticule();

// Add the graticule to the figure
svg.append('path').datum(graticule())
    .attr('class', 'graticule')
    .attr('d', path);
```

A world map created with the Equirectangular projection is shown in the following screenshot:

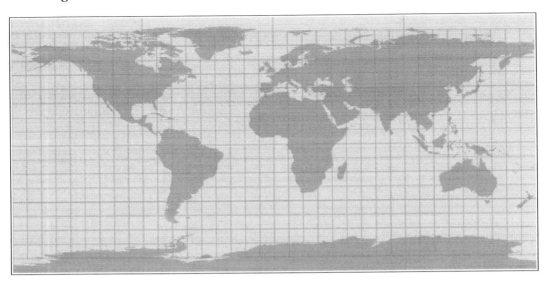

The Conic Equidistant projection

The Conic Equidistant projection maps the sphere into a cone whose axis coincides with the axis of the Earth. The cone can be tangent to the sphere in one parallel or secant in two parallels, which are called standard parallels. In this projection, the poles are represented with arcs, and the local shapes are true among the standard parallels. In the Conic Equidistant projection, the distances among meridians are proportionally correct. They are better suited to represent regions that have a small range of latitude, such as regional maps or small countries.

The process to generate a world map with this projection is the same as the previous process, except that this time, we need to create and configure an instance of the d3.geo.conicEquidistant projection. For this projection, computing the exact scale will be more difficult, but it's easy to adjust it until it has the correct size:

```
// Create and configure an instance of the projection
var conic = d3.geo.conicEquidistant()
    .scale(0.75 * width / (2 * Math.PI))
    .translate([width / 2, height / 2]);
```

The world map created with the Conic Equidistant projection is shown in the following screenshot:

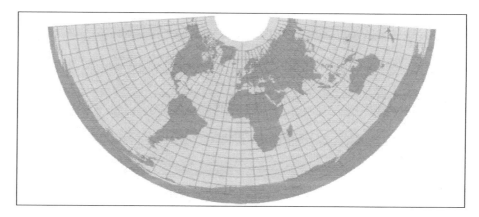

As we mentioned earlier, this projection is not appropriate to display the world map, but it can represent small areas accurately. We can rotate the projection to center it around New Zealand and set a bigger scale. We set the standard parallels to 5 degrees north and 15 degrees south. This will minimize the distortion among these parallels:

```
// Create and configure an instance of the projection
var conic = d3.geo.conicEquidistant()
    .scale(0.85 * width / (Math.PI / 3))
    .rotate([-141, 0])
    .translate([width / 2, height / 2])
    .parallels([5, -15]);
```

The map of New Zealand using the Conic Equidistant projection is shown in the following screenshot:

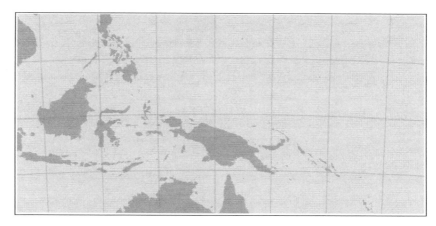

The Orthographic projection

The Orthographic projection is a perspective projection that shows the Earth as seen from space. This gives us the illusion of a three-dimensional view. Only one hemisphere can be seen at a time without overlapping. This has minimal distortion near the center and huge distortion towards the horizon.

To use this projection, we need to set the scale and translation of the projection and use it to configure the path generator:

```
// Create an instance of the Orthographic projection
var orthographic = d3.geo.orthographic()
    .scale(height / 2)
    .translate([width / 2, height / 2]);
```

An orthographic view of the Earth is shown in the following screenshot:

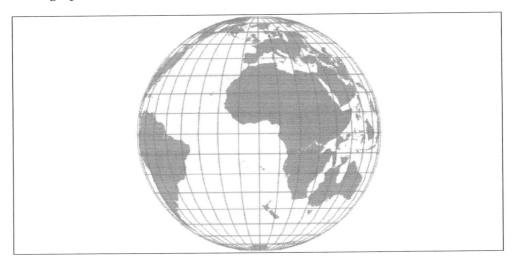

To avoid overlapping, we would need to display only the features that are on the same side as the observer. To do this, we need to clip the projection to hide the features that are at the other side of the Earth. The clipAngle method allows us to clip the features beyond the clipping angle. Setting this angle to 90 will modify the geometry of the features whose angular distance is greater than 90 from the center of the projection; so, they are not shown in the image:

```
// Create an instance of the Orthographic projection
var orthographic = d3.geo.orthographic()
    .scale(height / 2)
    .translate([width / 2, height / 2])
    .clipAngle(90);
```

The following screenshot shows us Earth from the side of the observer:

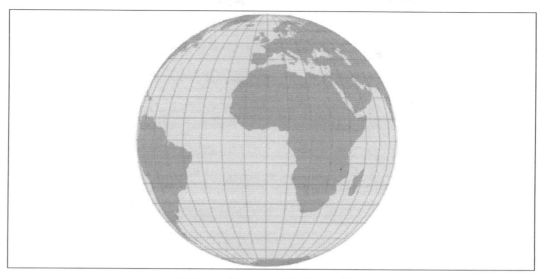

An Orthographic view of Earth with clipping

The projections shown in this section are only a small sample of the projections available in the geographic module of D3. As we can see, the pattern of use of different projections is always the same, but the parameters of each projection should be adjusted to get the desired result. In the next section, we will learn how to use the drag behavior to rotate the globe.

Creating a rotating globe

The Orthographic projection displays the Earth like a 3D object, but it only shows us one side at a time, and only the center is shown accurately. In this section, we will use this projection and the zoom behavior to allow the user to explore the features by rotating and zooming in on the globe.

The code of this example is available in the `chapter11/02-rotating` file of the code bundle. We will begin by drawing a globe using the Orthographic projection. As we did in the previous section, we load the TopoJSON data and construct the GeoJSON feature collection that represents the `ne_50m_land` object:

```
d3.json('/chapter11/data/land.json', function(error, data) {

    // Handle errors getting or parsing the data
```

```
        if (error) { console.error(error); }

        // Construct the GeoJSON feature collection using TopoJSON
        var geojson = topojson.feature(data,
          data.objects.ne_50m_land);

        // Create the svg container...
    });
```

We set the width and height of the svg element and use these dimensions to create and configure an instance of the Orthographic projection. We also select the container div and append the svg container to the map:

```
    // Width and height of the svg element
    var width = 600,
        height = 300;

    // Create an instance of the Orthographic projection
    var orthographic = d3.geo.orthographic()
        .scale(height / 2)
        .translate([width / 2, height / 2])
        .clipAngle(90);

    // Append the svg container and set its size
    var div = d3.select('#map-orthographic'),
        svg = div.append('svg')
            .attr('width', width)
            .attr('height', height);
```

We create an instance of the geographic path generator and set its projection to be the Orthographic projection instance:

```
    // Create and configure the geographic path generator
    var path = d3.geo.path()
        .projection(orthographic);
```

We will add features to represent the globe, the land, and lines for the parallels and meridians. We will add a feature to represent the globe in order to have a background for the features. The path generator supports an object of the Sphere type. An object of this type doesn't have coordinates, since it represents the complete globe. We will also append the GeoJSON object that contains the land features:

```
    // Globe
    var globe = svg.append('path').datum({type: 'Sphere'})
        .attr('class', 'globe')
```

```
    .attr('d', path);

// Features
var land = svg.append('path').datum(geojson)
    .attr('class', 'land')
    .attr('d', path);
```

We will also add the graticule, which is a set of parallels and meridian lines, in order to give us a more accurate reference for the orientation and rotation of the sphere:

```
// Create the graticule generator
var graticule = d3.geo.graticule();

// Append the parallel and meridian lines
var lines = svg.append('path').datum(graticule())
    .attr('class', 'graticule')
    .attr('d', path);
```

The preceding code will show us the Earth with the same aspect as the previous section. The strategy to add rotation and zoom to the globe will be to add an invisible overlay over the globe and add listeners for the pan and zoom gestures using the zoom behavior. The callback for the zoom event will update the projection rotation and scale and update the paths of the features using the path generator configured earlier. To keep the state of the zoom behavior and the projection in sync, we will store the current rotation angles and the scale of the projection in the state variable:

```
// Store the rotation and scale of the projection
var state = {x: 0, y: -45, scale: height / 2};
```

We will update the configuration of the projection to use the attributes of this variable, just for consistency:

```
// Create and configure the Orthographic projection
var orthographic = d3.geo.orthographic()
    .scale(state.scale)
    .translate([width / 2, height / 2])
    .clipAngle(90)
    .rotate([state.x, state.y]);
```

The zoom and pan should be triggered only when the user performs these gestures over the globe, not outside. We will create an overlay circle of the same size as the globe and set its fill-opacity attribute to zero. We will bind the state variable to the overlay in order to modify it in the zoom callback:

```
// Append the overlay and set its attributes
var overlay = svg.append('circle').datum(state)
```

```
    .attr('r', height / 2)
    .attr('transform', function() {
        return 'translate(' + [width / 2, height / 2] + ')';
    })
    .attr('fill-opacity', 0);
```

We need to create an instance of the zoom behavior and bind it to the overlay. This will add event listeners for the pan and zoom gestures to the overlay. We will limit the scale extent to between 0.5 and 8:

```
// Create and configure the zoom behavior
var zoomBehavior = d3.behavior.zoom()
    .scaleExtent([0.5, 8])
    .on('zoom', zoom);

// Add event listeners for the zoom gestures to the overlay
overlay.call(zoomBehavior);
```

When the user zooms or pans the overlay, a zoom event is triggered. The current event is stored in the d3.event variable. Each event type has its own attributes. In the case of the zoom event, the zoom translation vector and the scale are accessible through the d3.event.translate and d3.event.scale attributes. We need to transform the scale and the translation vector to the appropriate projection scale and rotation:

```
function zoom(d) {

    // Compute the projection scale and the constant
    var scale = d3.event.scale,
        dx = d3.event.translate[0],
        dy = d3.event.translate[1];

    // Maps the translation vector to rotation angles...
}
```

The zoom event will be triggered several times when the user performs the drag gesture. The translate array accumulates the horizontal and vertical translations from the point where the drag gesture originated. If the user drags the globe from the left-hand side to the right-hand side, the globe should be rotated 180 degrees, counterclockwise. We will map the horizontal position of the translation vector to an angle between 0 and 180 degrees:

```
// Maps the translation vector to rotation angles
d.x = 180 / width * dx;    // Horizontal rotation
d.y = -180 / height * dy;  // Vertical rotation
```

If the user drags the North Pole towards the bottom of the image, we will want the globe to rotate forward. As the latitude is measured from the equator to the poles, we need to rotate the projection by a negative angle in order to have a rotation forward from the point of view of the observer. With the rotation angle computed, we can update the projection's `rotate` and `scale` attributes. The zoom scale is a relative zoom factor, and we need to multiply it by the original size of the map to obtain the updated scale of the projection:

```
// Update the projection with the new rotation and scale
orthographic
    .rotate([d.x, d.y])
    .scale(scale * d.scale);
```

To update the image, we need to reproject the features and compute the svg paths. The path has a reference to the projection instance, so we need to just update all the paths in the svg with the updated projection:

```
// Recompute the paths and the overlay radius
svg.selectAll('path').attr('d', path);
overlay.attr('r', scale * height / 2);
```

We also updated the overlay radius so that the dragging area coincides with the globe, even if the user changes the zoom level. The globe can be rotated and zoomed as shown in the following screenshot:

The globe can be rotated and zoomed with mouse or touch gestures, allowing the user to explore every part of the globe in detail. The strategy to add rotation and zoom behaviors can be used with any projection, adapting the mapping between the zoom translation and scale to rotations and scale of the projection. Depending on the level of detail of the features, there can be some performance issues during the rotation. The projection and path generation are being done on each rotation step. This can be avoided by rendering simpler features during the rotation, or even showing just the graticule when rotating and rendering the features when the user releases the mouse.

The rotation of the globe is not perfect, but it's a good approximation of what we would expect. For a better (but more complex) strategy, see the excellent article from Jason Davies at `https://www.jasondavies.com/maps/rotate/`.

In the next section, we will use the Stereographic projection and the zoom behavior to create an interactive star map.

Creating an interactive star map

In this section, we will use the Stereographic projection and a star catalog to create an interactive celestial map. The Stereographic projection displays the sphere as seen from inside. A star map created with the Stereographic projection is shown in the following screenshot:

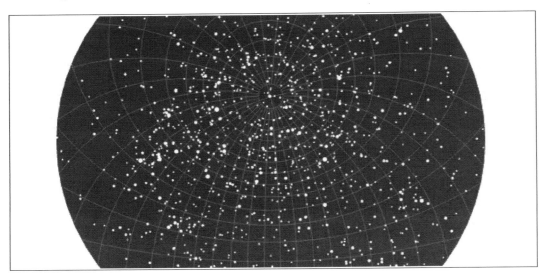

Celestial coordinate systems describe positions of celestial objects as seen from Earth. As the Earth rotates on its axis and around the Sun, the position of the stars relative to points on the surface of the Earth changes. Besides rotation and translation, a third movement called precession slowly rotates the Earth's axis by one degree every 72 years. The Equatorial coordinate system describes the position of stars by two coordinates, the **declination** and the angle from the projection of the Earth's equator to the poles. This angle is equivalent to the Earth's longitude. The **right ascension** is the angle measured from the intersection of the celestial equator to the ecliptic, measured eastward. The ecliptic is the projection of the Earth's orbit in the celestial sphere. The right ascension is measured in hours instead of degrees, but it is the equivalent of longitude.

Choosing our star catalog

To create our star map, we will use the HYG database, which is a celestial catalog that combines information from the Hipparcos Catalog, the Yale Bright Star Catalog, and the Gliese Catalog of Nearby Stars. This contains about 120,000 stars, most of which are not visible to the naked eye. The most recent version of the HYG database is available at `https://github.com/astronexus/HYG-Database`.

As we did in the previous sections, we will add targets to `Makefile` in order to download and parse the data files that we need. In order to filter and process the stars of the catalog, we wrote a small Python script that filters out the less bright stars and writes a GeoJSON file that translates the declination and right ascension coordinates to equivalent latitudes and longitudes. Note that due to the rotation of the Earth, the equivalent longitude is not related to the Earth's longitude, but it would be useful to create our visualization. We can compute a coordinate equivalent to the right ascension using the `longitude = 360 * RA / 24 - 180` expression. The generated GeoJSON file will have the following structure:

```
{
  "type": "FeatureCollection",
  "features": [
    {
      "geometry": {
        "type": "Point",
        "coordinates": [-179.6006208, -77.06529438]
      },
      "type": "Feature",
      "properties": {
```

```
          "color": 1.254,
          "name": "",
          "mag": 4.78
        }
      },
      ...
    ]
  }
```

In this case, every feature in the GeoJSON file is a point. We will begin by creating a chart using the Equirectangular projection to have a complete view of the sky while we are implementing the map and change the projection to stereographic later. We begin by loading the GeoJSON data and creating the svg container for the map:

```
d3.json('/chapter11/data/hyg.json', function(error, data) {

    // Handle errors getting and parsing the data
    if (error) { console.log(error); }

    // Container width and height
    var width = 600, height = 300;

    // Select the container div and creates the svg container
    var div = d3.select('#equirectangular'),
        svg = div.append('svg')
            .attr('width', width)
            .attr('height', height);

    // Creates an instance of the Equirectangular projection...
});
```

We create and configure an instance of the Equirectangular projection, setting the scale to display the entire sky in the svg container:

```
    // Creates an instance of the Equirectangular projection
    var projection = d3.geo.equirectangular()
        .scale(width / (2 * Math.PI))
        .translate([width / 2, height / 2]);
```

Drawing the stars

We will represent the stars with small circles, with bigger circles for brighter stars. For this, we need to create a scale for the radius, which will map the apparent magnitude of each star to a radius. Lower magnitude values correspond to brighter stars:

```
// Magnitude extent
var magExtent = d3.extent(data.features, function(d) {
    return d.properties.mag;
});

// Compute the radius for the point features
var rScale = d3.scale.linear()
    .domain(magExtent)
    .range([3, 1]);
```

By default, the path generator will create circles of constant radius for features of the Point type. We can configure the radius by setting the path's `pathRadius` attribute. As we might use the same path generator to draw point features other than stars, we will return a default value if the feature doesn't have the `properties` attribute:

```
// Create and configure the geographic path generator
var path = d3.geo.path()
    .projection(projection)
    .pointRadius(function(d) {
        return d.properties ? rScale(d.properties.mag) : 1;
    });
```

With our path generator configured, we can append the graticule lines and the features for the stars to the svg container:

```
// Add graticule lines
var graticule = d3.geo.graticule();

svg.selectAll('path.graticule-black').data([graticule()])
    .enter().append('path')
    .attr('class', 'graticule-black')
    .attr('d', path);

// Draw the stars in the chart
svg.selectAll('path.star-black').data(data.features)
    .enter().append('path')
    .attr('class', 'star-black')
    .attr('d', path);
```

We obtain the following celestial map, which shows us the graticule and the stars as small black circles:

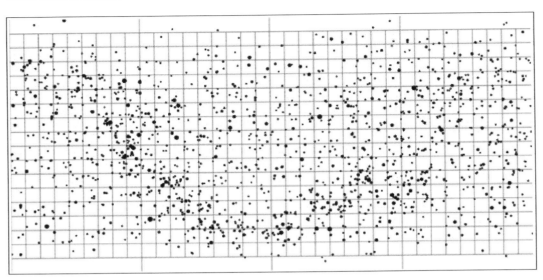

Celestial map created with the Equirectangular projection

Changing the projection and adding rotation

We will replace the Equirectangular projection with the Stereographic projection and add styles to the elements of the map to make it more attractive. We will use the drag behavior to allow the user to rotate the chart. As we did with the rotating globe, we will create a variable to store the current rotation of the projection:

```
// Store the current rotation of the projection
var rotate = {x: 0, y: 45};
```

We can create and configure an instance of the Stereographic projection. We will choose a suitable scale, translate the projection center to the center of the svg container, and clip the projection to show only a small part of the sphere at a time. We use the rotation variable to set the initial rotation of the projection:

```
// Create an instance of the Stereographic projection
var projection = d3.geo.stereographic()
    .scale(1.5 * height / Math.PI)
    .translate([width / 2, height / 2])
    .clipAngle(120)
    .rotate([rotate.x, -rotate.y]);
```

We won't duplicate the code to create the svg container, graticule, and features because it's very similar to the rotating globe from earlier. The complete code for this example is available in the `chapter11/03-celestial-sphere` file. In this example, we also have an invisible overlay. We create and configure a drag behavior instance and add event listeners for the drag gesture to the invisible overlay:

```
// Create and configure the drag behavior
var dragBehavior = d3.behavior.drag()
    .on('drag', drag);

// Add event listeners for drag gestures to the overlay
overlay.call(dragBehavior);
```

The `drag` function will be invoked when the user drags the map. For `drag` events, the `d3.event` object stores the gesture's x and y coordinates. We will transform the coordinates to horizontal and vertical rotations of the projection with the same method as the one used in the previous section:

```
// Callback for drag gestures
function drag(d) {
    // Compute the projection rotation angles
    d.x = 180 * d3.event.x / width;
    d.y = -180 * d3.event.y / height;

    // Updates the projection rotation...
}
```

We update the projection rotation and the paths of the stars and graticule lines. As we have clipping in this example, the path will be undefined for stars outside the clipping angle. In this case, we return a dummy svg command that just moves the drawing cursor to avoid getting errors:

```
// Updates the projection rotation
projection.rotate([d.x, d.y]);

// Update the paths for the stars and graticule lines
stars.attr('d', function(u) {
    return path(u) ? path(u) : 'M 10 10';
});
lines.attr('d', path);
```

In the style sheet file, `chapter11/maps.css`, we have included styles for this map to display a dark blue background, light graticule lines, and white stars. The result is a rotating star map that displays a coarse approximation of how the stars look from Earth.

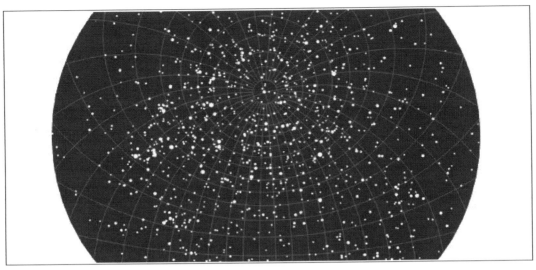

Rotating star map created with the Stereographic projection

Adding colors and labels to the stars

We will create a fullscreen version of the star map. The source code for this version of the map is available in the `chapter11/04-fullscreen` file in the code bundle. For this example, we need to set the body element and the container div to cover the complete viewport. We set the width and height of the body, HTML, and the container div to 100 percent and set the padding and margins to zero. To create the svg element with the correct size, we need to retrieve the width and height in pixels, which are computed by the browser when it renders the page:

```
// Computes the width and height of the container div
var width = parseInt(div.style('width'), 10),
    height = parseInt(div.style('height'), 10);
```

We create the projection and the path generator as done earlier. In this version, we will add colors to the stars. Each star feature contains the attribute color, which indicates the color index of the star. The color index is a number that characterizes the color of the star. We can't compute a precise scale for the color index, but we will use a color scale that approximates the colors:

```
// Approximation of the colors of the stars
var cScale = d3.scale.linear()
    .domain([-0.3, 0, 0.6, 0.8, 1.42])
    .range(['#6495ed', '#fff', '#fcff6c', '#ffb439',
      '#ff4039']);
```

We will set the color to the features using the `fill` attribute of the paths that correspond to the stars:

```
// Add the star features to the svg container
var stars = svg.selectAll('path.star-color')
    .data(data.features)
    .enter().append('path')
    .attr('class', 'star-color')
    .attr('d', path)
    .attr('fill', function(d) {
        return cScale(d.properties.color);
    });
```

We will also add labels for each star. Here, we use the projection directly to compute the position where the labels should be, and we also compute a small offset:

```
// Add labels for the stars
var name = svg.selectAll('text').data(data.features)
    .enter().append('text')
    .attr('class', 'star-label')
    .attr('x', function(d) {
        return projection(d.geometry.coordinates)[0] + 8;
    })
    .attr('y', function(d) {
        return projection(d.geometry.coordinates)[1] + 8;
    })
    .text(function(d) { return d.properties.name; })
    .attr('fill', 'white');
```

The star map visualization in fullscreen is shown in the following screenshot:

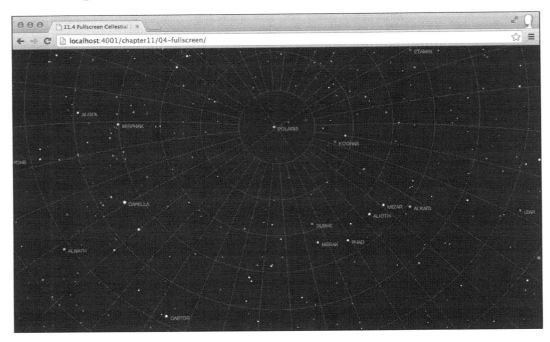

We create the overlay and the drag behavior and configure the callback of the zoom event as earlier, updating the position of the labels in the zoom function. Now we have a fullscreen rotating star map.

Projecting raster images with D3

Until now, we have used svg to create maps. In this section, we will learn how to use D3 to project raster images in canvas elements. This will allow us to use JPG or PNG images to generate orthographic views of these images. A raster image reprojected using the Orthographic projection is shown in the following screenshot:

Rendering an image of Earth using the Orthographic projection (or any other projection) involves manipulating two projections. First, for each pixel in the original image, we compute its corresponding geographic coordinates using the image inverse projection. Then, we use the geographic coordinates of each pixel to render them using the Orthographic projection. Before beginning the implementation of these steps, we will discuss the `inverse` method of a projection.

Projections are functions that map geographic coordinates to points on the screen. The **inverse** projections do the reverse operation; they take coordinates on the two-dimensional surface and return geographic coordinates. In the `chapter11/05-raster` file, there is an interactive example that computes the geographic coordinates of the point under the mouse. Note that not all projections in D3 have an inverse operation. Computing the geographic coordinates of a point under the mouse is shown in the following screenshot:

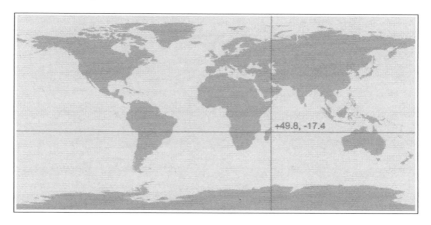

To obtain the geographic coordinates that correspond to a point under the cursor, we can add a callback to the `mouseover` event over an element:

```
// Callback of the mouseover event
rect.on('mousemove', function() {
    // Compute the mouse position and the corresponding
    // geographic coordinates.
    var pos = d3.mouse(this),
    coords = equirectangular.invert(pos);
})
```

The **Next Generation Blue Marble** images are satellite images of Earth captured, processed, and shared by NASA. There are monthly images that show Earth with a resolution of 1 pixel every 500 meters. These images are available in several resolutions at the NASA Earth Observatory site at `http://earthobservatory.nasa.gov/Features/BlueMarble/`. We will use a low-resolution version of the Blue Marble image in this section.

Rendering the raster image with canvas

This time, we won't use svg to create our visualization, because we need to render individual pixels in the screen. Canvas is more suitable for this task. We will begin by creating a canvas element, loading the Blue Marble image, and drawing the image in the canvas element. We select a container div and append a canvas element, setting its width and height as follows:

```
// Canvas element width and height
var width = 600,
    height = 300;

// Append the canvas element to the container div
var div = d3.select('#canvas-image'),
    canvas = div.append('canvas')
        .attr('width', width)
        .attr('height', height);
```

The canvas element is just a container. To draw shapes, we need to get the 2D context. Remember that only the `2d` context exists:

```
// Get the 2D context of the canvas instance
var context = canvas.node().getContext('2d');
```

Then, we create an instance of `Image`. We set the image source and set a callback that can be be invoked when the image is fully loaded:

```
// Create the image element
var image = new Image;
image.onload = onLoad;
image.src = '/chapter11/data/world.jpg';
```

In the `onLoad` function, we use the canvas context to draw the image. The arguments of the `drawImage` method are the image, the offset, and size of the source image and the offset and size of the target image. In this case, the original image size is 5400 x 2700 pixels; the target image size is just 600 x 300 pixels:

```
// Copy the image to the canvas context
functiononLoad() {
    context.drawImage(image, 0, 0, image.width, image.height,
      0, 0, width, height);
}
```

The Blue Marble image rendered in a canvas element is shown in the following screenshot:

As the Blue Marble image was created using the Equirectangular projection, we can create an instance of this projection and use the `invert` method to compute the longitude and latitude that corresponds to each pixel:

```
// Create and configure the Equirectancular projection
var equirectangular = d3.geo.equirectangular()
    .scale(width / (2 * Math.PI))
    .translate([width / 2, height / 2]);
```

Computing the geographic coordinates of each pixel

We can add an event listener for the mousemove event on the canvas element. The d3.mouse method returns the position of the mouse relative to its argument, in this case, the canvas element:

```
// Add an event listener for the mousemove event
canvas.on('mousemove', function(d) {

    // Retrieve the mouse position relative to the canvas
    var pos = d3.mouse(this);

    // Compute the coordinates of the current position
});
```

We can use the invert method of the projection to compute the geographic coordinates of the point under the cursor. To display the geographic coordinates that correspond to the position of the cursor, we clear a small rectangle of the canvas content and add fillText to add the label in the upper-left corner of the image:

```
// Compute the coordinates of the current position
var coords = equirectangular.invert(pos);

// Create a label string, showing the coordinates
var label = [fmt(coords[0]), fmt(coords[1])].join(', ');

// Cleans a small rectangle and append the label
context.clearRect(2, 2, 90, 14);
context.fillText(label, 4, 12);
```

Using the invert method to compute geographic coordinates is shown in the following screenshot:

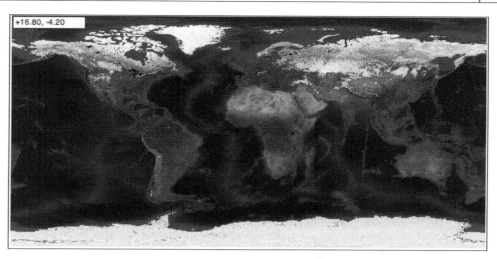

Reprojecting the image using the Orthographic projection

Until now, we have learned how to copy an image element in canvas and how to use the `invert` method of a projection to compute the geographic coordinates that correspond to a pixel in the canvas element. We will use this to **reproject** the raster image using the Orthographic projection instead of the original Equirectangular projection. The strategy to project the image into a different projection is as follows:

- Insert the source image in the canvas element, setting its width and height.

- Create an instance of the source projection (the projection used to generate the image) and configure it in a way that if it were used to project the world, it would fit exactly with the source image.

- Create an empty target image. The size of this image should fit the target projection.

- Create and configure an instance of the target projection. In this case, we will use an instance of the Orthographic projection.

- For each pixel in the target image, use the `invert` method of the target projection to compute the geographic coordinates that correspond to that pixel. Using the source projection, compute the pixel coordinates of that location, and copy the pixel data to the pixel in the target image.

The procedure sounds a little convoluted, but it's basically about copying the pixels from the source image to the target image using the geographic coordinates in order to know where each pixel can be copied to.

We begin by drawing the source image in the canvas element once the image is fully loaded. Images in canvas are represented as arrays. We read the data array of the source data and created an empty target image and got its data:

```
// Copy the image to the canvas context
function onLoad() {

    // Copy the image to the canvas area
    context.drawImage(image, 0, 0, image.width, image.height);

    // Reads the source image data from the canvas context
    var sourceData = context.getImageData(0, 0, image.width,
      image.height).data;

    // Creates an empty target image and gets its data
    var target = context.createImageData(image.width,
      image.height),
    targetData = target.data;

    // ...
}
```

Note that the target image is not shown yet, but we will use it later. In canvas, images are not stored as matrices; they are stored as arrays. Each pixel has four elements in the array, which are its red, green, blue, and alpha components. The rows of the image are stored sequentially in the image array. With this structure, for an image of 200 x 100 pixels, the index of the red component of the pixel 23 x 12 will be *4 * (200 * 11 + 23) = 844*.

To make things easier, we will iterate the image data as if it were a matrix, computing the index of each pixel with the aforementioned expression. We iterate in columns and rows of the target image and compute the corresponding coordinates of the current pixel using the `invert` method of the target projection:

```
// Iterate in the target image
for (var x = 0, w = image.width; x < w; x += 1) {
    for (var y = 0, h = image.height; y < h; y += 1) {

        // Compute the geographic coordinates of the current pixel
```

```
var coords = orthographic.invert([x, y]);

// ...
    }
}
```

The inverse projection could be undefined for a given pixel; we need to check this before we try to use it. We can now use the source projection to compute the pixel coordinates of the current location in the source image. This is the pixel that we need to copy to the current pixel in the target image:

```
// Source and target image indices
var targetIndex, sourceIndex, pixels;

// Check if the inverse projection is defined
if ((!isNaN(coords[0])) && (!isNaN(coords[1]))) {

    // Compute the source pixel coordinates
    pixels = equirectangular(coords);

    // ...
}
```

Knowing which source pixel we need to copy, we need to compute the corresponding index in the source and target image data arrays. The projection could have returned decimal numbers, so we will need to approximate them to integers. We will also ensure that the indices of the red channel for both images should be exactly divisible by four:

```
// Compute the index of the red channel
sourceIndex = 4 * (Math.floor(pixels[0]) + w *
  Math.floor(pixels[1]));
sourceIndex = sourceIndex - (sourceIndex % 4);

targetIndex = 4 * (x + w * y);
targetIndex = targetIndex - (targetIndex % 4);
```

We can copy the color channels using the indices that were just computed:

```
// Copy the red, green, blue and alpha channels
targetData[targetIndex]     = sourceData[sourceIndex];
targetData[targetIndex + 1] = sourceData[sourceIndex + 1];
targetData[targetIndex + 2] = sourceData[sourceIndex + 2];
targetData[targetIndex + 3] = sourceData[sourceIndex + 3];
```

When we finish iterating, the target image data array should be complete and ready to be drawn in the canvas container. We can clear the canvas area and copy the target image:

```
// Clear the canvas element and copy the target image
context.clearRect(0, 0, image.width, image.height);
context.putImageData(target, 0, 0);
```

We obtain the Blue Marble image that is displayed using the Orthographic projection. The Blue Marble image rendered using the Orthographic projection is shown in the following screenshot:

There is more to know about reprojecting raster images. For instance, Jason Davies has a demo on projecting raster tiles and adding zoom behavior at http://www. jasondavies.com/maps/raster/. Also, Nathan Vander Wilt has a well-documented demo on how to use WebGL to reproject raster images using the GPU at http:// andyet.iriscouch.com/world/_design/webgl/demo2.html.

Summary

In this chapter, we used several cartographic projections to create interactive maps that can be zoomed and rotated. We created a globe that can be rotated and zoomed using the zoom behavior and the Orthographic projection. We used the Stereographic projection and the HYG combined catalog to create an interactive star map.

We also learned how to use the canvas elements and a combination of projections to project raster images of the Earth using arbitrary projections, creating realistic views of the Earth.

In the next chapter, we will learn how to add social media to our visualization projects and how to have several users interact with our visualizations at the same time.

12
Creating a Real-time Application

In this chapter, we will create a real-time application to explore the distribution of geotagged tweets containing user-defined topics. Creating this visualization will involve implementing a server-side application and a client-side application.

The server-side application will handle connections from the clients, receive topics to be heard on Twitter, and send tweets matching the topics to the corresponding clients.

The client-side application will connect with the streaming server, send it topics as the user enters the streaming server, receive tweets, and update the visualization as the tweets arrive.

We will begin this chapter by learning the basics of real-time interaction in client-side applications. We will use the HDI Explorer application from *Chapter 8, Data-driven Applications*, a service that provides the necessary backend to implement real-time applications.

We will then implement the server-side application using Node, Twit, and **Socket. IO**, a library that provides real-time communication support. Lastly, we will use Backbone, Socket.IO, and D3 to create the client-side application.

Collaborating in real time with Firebase

In some visualization projects, it can be convenient to have the application state shared among users so that they can collaborate and explore the visualization as a group.

Adding this feature would usually imply the installation and configuration of a server and the use of WebSockets or a similar technology to manage the communication between the server and client-side code in the browser. Firebase is a service that provides real-time data storage and synchronization between application instances using the client-side code. If the data changes at one location, Firebase will notify the connected clients so that they can update the state of the application. It has libraries for several platforms, including OS X, iOS, Java, and JavaScript. In this section, we will use Firebase's JavaScript library to add real-time synchronization to the HDI Explorer application.

Adding synchronization to HDI Explorer doesn't make sense in most cases; it would be weird if a user is seeing the evolution of the Human Development Index for one country and it suddenly changes to a different country. On the other hand, if several users were seeing the same visualization on their respective computers and discussing it, this would be useful because changing the selected country would update the visualization for the rest of the users as well, so they would all see the same content. To differentiate between the two scenarios, we will create a new page of the HDI Explorer application with synchronization and leave the index and share pages as they are now. The examples of this section are in the `firebase.md` file of the `hdi-explorer` repository.

Configuring Firebase

To add real-time support to our application, we need to create a Firebase account. Firebase offers a free plan for development, allowing up to 50 connections and 100 MB of data storage, which is more than enough for our application. Once we have created our Firebase account, we can add a new application. The name of our application will be `hdi-explorer`. This name will be used to generate the URL that identifies our application, in our case, `http://hdi-explorer.firebaseio.com`. By accessing this URL, we can see and modify the application data. We will create a single object with the `code` attribute to store the country code of the HDI Explorer application. Once we have our account and initial data configured, we can install the JavaScript library with Bower:

```
$ bower install --save-dev firebase
```

This will install Firebase in the `bower_components` directory. We will also update the `Gruntfile` to concatenate the Firebase library along with the other dependencies of our application in the `dependencies.min.js` file. Firebase data for the HDI Explorer application is shown in the following screenshot:

We can connect to the Firebase application using the Firebase client. We will create a script element at the end of the `firebase.md` page that contains the synchronization code and create an instance of the Firebase reference to our data:

```
<script>
    // Connect to the Firebase application
    var dataref = new Firebase('https://hdi-explorer.firebaseio.
com/');

    // Application callbacks...
</script>
```

Integrating the application with Firebase

Before integrating Firebase, we will review the structure of the HDI Explorer application. We used Backbone to organize the components of the application and the REST API of the World Bank as the data source for our models.

Our application has three models, that is, the `ApplicationModel`, `CountryTrend`, and `CountryInformation` models. The application model manages the application state, which is defined by the three-letter code of the country selected by the user. The country trend model contains the time series of the aggregated Human Development Index, and the country information model contains information about the main components of the index: education, life expectancy, and average income.

The `Countries` collection contains instances of the `CountryTrend` model. This collection has two views, the search view and the chart of the HDI trends. The `CountryInformation` model has one associated view, the table of indicators at the right-hand side of the page. The HDI Explorer application is shown in the following screenshot:

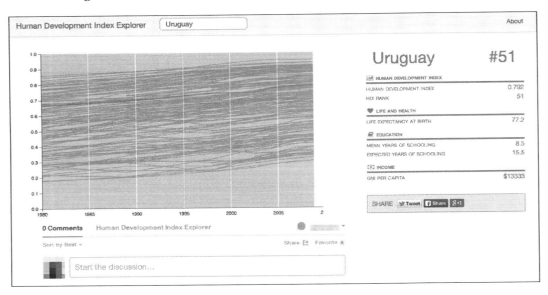

All these elements are initialized in the `app/setup.js` file; instances are created and the callbacks for the `change:code` event in the application model are defined. The views will update themselves when the user selects a country in the search field. To synchronize the application state among the connected users, we need to synchronize the country code.

We can read the data from Firebase through asynchronous callbacks. These callbacks will be invoked in the same way for both the initial state and for the changes in the data. Events will be triggered if any object under the current location is changed, added, removed, or moved. The `value` event will be triggered for any of these modifications. We will use this event to update the application state as follows:

```
// Update the application state
dataref.on('value', function(snapshot) {
    app.state.set('code', snapshot.val().code);
});
```

When something changes under the current location (such as the country code), the value event will be triggered, and the callback will be called with a **snapshot** of the current data as the argument. The snapshot will contain the most up-to-date object, representing the state of our application. We can access the object by calling the val() method of the snapshot and get the value of the current country code.

If we modify the value of the code in Firebase, users connected to the same URL will have their application instances updated. We also want to synchronize the state from the application to Firebase. We will add an event listener to the application model in order to update the Firebase data:

```
// The model will update the object with the selected country code.
app.state.on('change:code', function(model) {
    dataref.set({code: model.get('code')});
});
```

The set method will update the contents of the Firebase location, triggering an update of all the views of the local application instance and any other client connected to the firebase page.

In this section, we learned how to add real-time interaction to the application created in *Chapter 8, Data-driven Applications*. We learned how to change the state of the client-side application by adding callbacks for the events triggered at the backend.

Creating a Twitter explorer application

In this section, we will create an application to explore the distribution of geotagged tweets at a given time. Users can enter topics in the input box. The topics will be sent to the server-side application, which will begin to send tweets that match the topic to the client-side instance of the corresponding user. This application can be used to track the geographic distribution of a set of topics. For instance, a user might be interested to know which kind of meal is being discussed in different regions of the world, to monitor the Twitter stream for earthquake-related words, or to track the mentions of a particular brand. Our application will support multiple users to be connected at the same time, allowing each user to add up to five topics.

A screenshot of the client application is shown as follows:

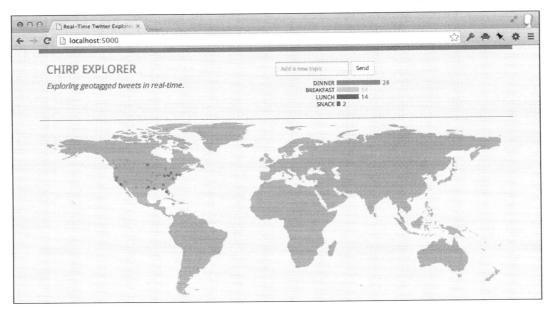

Our application will consist of two components, the streaming server and the client-side application. The streaming server will handle the connection with clients, a global list of topics to track, connect to the Twitter-streaming API, and deliver tweets that match the topics to the corresponding client. When a client disconnects, the server will remove the client's topics from the topics list. We will implement the streaming server in Node using Socket.IO to handle the connection with the user and send them tweets, and the **Twit** module to handle the connection to the Twitter-streaming API.

The client-side application will establish the connection with the streaming server, send new topics as they are added, and update the bar chart and the map components. We will use Backbone, Bootstrap, Socket.IO, and D3 to implement the client-side application.

We will begin by learning how to use the Twitter-streaming API and Socket.IO to implement the streaming server and then implement the client application.

Creating the streaming server

In this section, we will use Node to create the streaming server. The server will handle the client connections and the connection to the Twitter-streaming API; it will also manage the list of topics for all the clients who deliver tweets as they arrive.

We will begin by creating Twitter authentication tokens; we will learn how to use the Twit module to manage the connection to the Twitter API, and how to use Socket.IO to handle real-time communication between the server and the client application.

To follow the examples in this section, open the `chirp-server` project directory in the terminal and run the following command to install the project dependencies:

```
$ npm install
```

This will create the `node_modules` directory and download the project dependencies. If you haven't installed Node, download the binaries for your platform from `http://nodejs.org/download/` and follow the instructions on the page.

Using the Twitter-streaming API

Twitter provides a streaming API that allows developers to access Twitter's global stream of tweets through several endpoints. The following endpoints allow access to different streams:

- `statuses/sample`: This allows access to a small random sample of public statuses. All the applications connected to this endpoint will receive the same tweets.

- `statuses/filter`: This returns public statuses that match one or more predicates. We will use this endpoint in the project.

- `statuses/firehose`: This returns all the public statuses. This endpoint requires special access.

Also, there are the `statuses/user` and `statuses/site` endpoints, which allow you to access the public tweets of a particular user or website. When applications establish a connection with the Twitter endpoint, they are delivered a feed of tweets.

To run the examples in this chapter, you need to go to the Twitter Application Management page (`https://apps.twitter.com/`), create a new application, and generate API keys for the application. You will need the consumer key, the consumer secret, the access token, and the token secret.

The `credentials.js` file in the root directory of the project contains placeholders for the authentication tokens of the application. You can either replace the placeholder strings in this file with your own keys or create a new file with the same structure. In either case, make sure that the keys remain a secret. It would be a good idea to add this file to the `.gitignore` file in order to avoid accidentally pushing it to GitHub:

```
// Authentication tokens (replace with your own)
module.exports = {
    "consumer_key":        "xxx",
    "consumer_secret":     "xxx",
    "access_token":        "xxx",
    "access_token_secret": "xxx"
}
```

Using Twit to access the Twitter-streaming API

As mentioned earlier, we will use the Twit Node module (you can access the documentation in the project's repository at `https://github.com/ttezel/twit/`) to connect to the Twitter-streaming API. Twit handles both the REST and streaming APIs, keeping the connection alive and reconnecting automatically if the connection drops. The `01-twitter-sample.js` file contains the code to connect to the `statuses/sample` stream. We begin by importing the `twit` module and loading the configuration module:

```
// Import node modules
var Twit  = require('twit'),              // Twitter API Client
    config = require('./credentials.js');  // Credentials
```

The `config` object will contain the authentication tokens from the `credentials.js` file. We can now set the Twitter credentials and connect to the `statuses/sample` stream as follows:

```
// Configure the Twit object with the application credentials
var T = new Twit(config);

// Subscribe to the sample stream and begin listening
var stream = T.stream('statuses/sample');
```

The `stream` object is an instance of `EventEmitter`, a built-in Node class that allows you to emit custom events and add listener functions to these events. To begin listening to tweets, we can just attach a listener to the `tweet` event:

```
// The callback will be invoked on each tweet.
stream.on('tweet', function(tweet) {
    // Do something with the tweet
});
```

The `tweet` object will contain information about the tweet, such as the date of creation, tweet ID in the numeric and string formats, tweet text, information about the user who generated the tweet, and language and tweet entities that may be present, such as hashtags and mentions. For a complete reference to the tweet attributes, refer to the Field Guide at https://dev.twitter.com/docs/platform-objects/tweets. A typical tweet will have the following structure, along with many other attributes:

```
{
  created_at: 'Thu May 15 22:27:37 +0000 2014',
  ...
  text: 'tweet text...',
  user: {
    name: 'Pablo Navarro',
    screen_name: 'pnavarrc',
    ...
  },
  ...
  coordinates: {
    type: 'Point',
    coordinates: [ -76.786264, -33.234588 ]
  },
  ...
  entities: {
    hashtags: [],
    ...
  },
  lang: 'en'
}
```

You may have noticed that the `coordinates` attribute is a GeoJSON object, in particular, a GeoJSON point. This point is an approximation of where the tweet was generated. Less than 10 percent of the tweets in the sample stream contain this information, but the information is still useful and interesting to explore.

The `stream` object will emit other events that we might need to handle. The `connect` event will be emitted when Twit attempts to connect to the Twitter-streaming API:

```
stream.on('connect', function(msg) {
    console.log('Connection attempt.');
});
```

If the connection is successful, the `connected` event will be triggered. Note that when the application is running, the connection to the Twitter stream can be interrupted several times. Twit will automatically try to reconnect following the reconnection guidelines from Twitter:

```
// The connection is successful.
stream.on('connected', function(msg) {
    console.log('Connection successful.');
});
```

If a reconnection is scheduled, the `reconnect` event will be emitted, passing the request, response, and interval within milliseconds of the next reconnection attempt as follows:

```
// Emitted when a reconnection is scheduled.
stream.on('reconnect', function(req, res, interval) {
    console.log('Reconnecting in ' + (interval / 1e3) + '
        seconds.');
});
```

Twitter creates a queue with the tweets to be delivered to our application. If our program doesn't process the tweets fast enough, the queue will get longer, and Twitter will send a warning message to the application notifying us about the issue. If this happens, Twit will emit the `warning` event, passing the warning message as an argument to the callback function:

```
// The application is not processing the tweets fast enough.
stream.on('warning', function(msg) {
    console.warning('warning')
});
```

Twitter can disconnect the stream for several reasons. Before actually dropping the connection, Twitter will notify us about the disconnection, and Twit will emit the corresponding event as well. The complete list of events can be consulted in the Twit project repository at `https://github.com/ttezel/twit`.

In the project repository, there are examples of connections to the `statuses/sample` and `statuses/filter` streams. In the `01-twitter-sample.js` file, we configure the Twitter credentials and use the `statuses/sample` endpoint to print the tweets in the terminal screen. To run this example (remember to add your credentials), type the following command in the root directory of the project:

```
$ node 01-twitter-sample.js
```

This will print the tweets on the console as they are received. As mentioned earlier, there are more streaming endpoints available. The `statuses/filter` stream allows you to track specific topics. The stream object receives a list of comma-separated strings, which should contain the words to be matched. If we pass the topics `good morning` and `breakfast`, the stream will contain tweets that match either the word `breakfast` or both `good` and `morning`. Twit allows us to specify the topics that need to be matched as a list of strings.

In the `02-twitter-filter.js` file, we have the same setup as in the first example; however, in this case, we define the list of topics to track and configure the stream to connect to the `statuses/filter` endpoint, passing along the list of topics to track:

```
// List of topics to track
var topics = ['good morning', 'breakfast'];

// Subscribe to a specific list of topics
var stream = T.stream('statuses/filter', {track: topics});
```

To determine a match, Twitter will compare the tracking topics with the tweet text, the user name, screen name, and entities, such as hashtags and URLs. Note that the tweets won't include information about which term was matched; as our application will need this information, we will check which terms were matched in the `tweet` callback.

Using Socket.IO

Socket.IO is a JavaScript library that allows real-time communication between the client and the server. The library has two parts, the client-side library that runs in the browser and the server-side library for Node.

In this example, we will create an application that will allow you to send text messages to the server, which will send a text message back to inform you that the message was received. To follow the code in this example, open the `03-socketio-example.js` file for the server-side code and the `socketio-example.html` file for the client-side code. A screenshot of the client-side application is shown as follows:

We will begin by implementing the server-side code. In the server-side code, we import the `socket.io` module. This will expose the Socket.IO server:

```
// Import the Socket.IO module
var IOServer = require('socket.io');
```

We can now create an instance of the Socket.IO server. We can either use the built-in server or an instance of a different server, such as those provided by the HTTP or express modules. We will use the built-in version, passing along the port number for the server:

```
// Start the server, listening on port 7000
var io = new IOServer(7000);
```

The server is ready to receive connections and messages. At this point, the server won't do anything other than listen; we need to attach a callback function for the `connection` event. The callback will receive a socket object as the argument. The socket is the client-side endpoint of the connection. Refer to the following code:

```
// Listen for connections from incoming sockets
io.on('connection', function(socket) {

    // Print the socket ID on connection
    console.log('Client ' + socket.id + ' connected.');

    // Attach listeners to socket events...
});
```

This callback will display a log when a client connects to the server, displaying the socket ID:

```
$ node 03-socketio-example.js
Client ID pk0XiCmUNgDVRP6zAAAC connected.
```

We can now attach event listeners to the socket events. We will add a callback for the `disconnect` event, which will display a log message:

```
// Displays a log message if the client disconnects.
socket.on('disconnect', function() {
    console.log('client disconnected.');
});
```

We can attach listeners for custom events as well, and send JavaScript objects that can be serialized as arguments for the callback. Socket.IO also supports the sending of binary data. We will add a callback for the `client-message` custom event:

```
// The server will emit a response message.
socket.on('client-message', function (data) {
    socket.emit('server-message', {
        msg: 'Message "' + data.msg + '" received.'
    });
});
```

The callback for the `client-message` event will just send a message back to the client, indicating that the message was received. If we want to send a message to all the connected clients, we can use `io.emit('event name', parameters)`.

Socket.IO will serve the client-side library, which can be very useful. We can use either this version or download the client-side library separately. We can use the served version by adding `/socket.io/socket.io.js` to the server's URL. To follow the client-side code, open the `socketio-example.html` file from the project directory. In this example, we will use the served version, adding the following line in the header:

```
<script
  src="http://localhost:7000/socket.io/socket.io.js"></script>
```

Note that if you want to use the server from an external device, you should replace `localhost` with the URL of the server. We will add an input element in the page, where the user will type the messages to the server. Under the input element, a list will display the messages both from the client and the server. The older messages will be displaced to the bottom as new messages are received. Refer to the following code:

```
<div class="container">

<h1>Socket.IO Example</h1>

<!-- Input element to send messages -->
<form role="form" class="form-horizontal" id="msgForm">
  <div class="form-group">
    <label for="msgToServer" class="col-sm-1">Message</label>
    <div class="col-sm-9">
      <input type="text" class="form-control input-sm"
id="msgToServer" placeholder="Send a message to the server.">
    </div>
```

```
    <button type="submit" class="btn btn-default btn-sm">Send</button>
  </div>
</form>

<!-- List with messages -->
<ul id='msg-list' class='list-unstyled'></ul>

</div>
```

We will add a script with the code, which will establish the connection with the server and update the messages list. We will include D3 to handle the user input and to update the list of messages. We begin by opening a connection with the socket server:

```
// Open a connection with the Socket.IO server
var socket = io('http://localhost:7000');
```

Note that in this case, the `socket` variable refers to the server's endpoint. The client API is almost identical to the server API; the `socket` object will also trigger the `connect` event once the connection with the server is established:

```
// The callback will be invoked when the connection establishes
socket.on('connect', function() {
    console.log('Successful connection to the server.');
});
```

We will store each message, sender, and message timestamp in an array to display the messages in a list. We will also create a time formatter to display the timestamp of each message in a friendly format:

```
// Declare variables for the message list and the time formatter
var messages = [],
    dateFmt = d3.time.format('[%H:%M:%S]');
```

We will select the input element with the `#message` ID and attach a listener for the `submit` event. The callback for the event will retrieve the content of the input element and send the message to the server. We use `d3.event.preventDefault()` to prevent the form from trying to submit the form values to the server:

```
d3.select('#msg-form).on('submit', function() {

    var inputElement = d3.select('#message).node(),
        message = inputElement.value.trim();

    // Check that the message is not empty
    if (message) {
```

```
        // Sends the message to the server...
    }

    d3.event.preventDefault();
});
```

We retrieve the contents of the input element and verify that the message is not empty before we send the `client-message` signal. We also reset the input element value so that the user can write a new message without having to erase the message already sent:

```
// Check that the message is not empty
if (message) {
    // Sends the message to the server
    socket.emit('client-message', {msg: message});

    // Append the message to the message list
    messages.push({
        from: 'client',
        date: new Date(),
        msg: message
    });

    // Update the list of messages
    updateMessages();

    // Resets the form, clearing the input element
    this.reset();
}
```

In the `updateMessages` function, we will sort the messages by date, create a selection for the `li` elements, and append them on to the `enter` selection. The `li` elements will contain the time of the message, who sent the message, and the contents of the message. We will also add a class indicating who sent the message in order to set different colors for the server and the client:

```
// Update the message list
function updateMessages() {

    // Sort the messages, most recent first
    messages.sort(function(a, b) { return b.date - a.date; });

    // Create the selection for the list elements
    var li = d3.select('#msg-list')
```

```
            .selectAll('li').data(messages);

    // Append the list elements on enter
    li.enter().append('li');

    // Update the list class and content.
    li
        .attr('class', function(d) { return d.from; })
        .html(function(d) {
            return [dateFmt(d.date), d.from, ':', d.msg].join(' ');
        });
}
```

The message list will be updated when the user sends a message to the server and when the server sends a message to the client. The application allows the sending and receiving of messages to the server, as shown in the following screenshot:

Implementing the streaming server

In the previous sections, we learned how to use the `Twit` module to connect and receive tweets from the Twitter-streaming API's endpoints. We also learned how to implement bidirectional communication between a Node server and the connected clients using the `Socket.IO` module. In this section, we will use both the modules (`Twit` and `Socket.IO`) to create a server that allows multiple clients to track their own topics on Twitter in real time.

When the user accesses the application, a connection with the streaming server is established. Socket.IO will manage this connection, reconnecting and sending heartbeats if necessary. The user can then add up to five words to be tracked by the streaming server.

The streaming server will manage connections with the connected clients and one connection with the Twitter-streaming API. When a client adds a new topic, the streaming server will add it to the topics list. When a new tweet arrives, the server will examine its contents to check whether it matches any of the terms in the topic list and send a simplified version of the tweet to the corresponding client.

The code of the streaming server is in the `chirp.js` file in the top level of the project directory. We will begin by importing the Node modules and the `credentials.js` file, which exports the Twitter authentication tokens:

```
// Import the Node modules
var Twit    = require('twit'),
    IOServer = require('socket.io'),
    config   = require('./credentials.js');
```

To keep track of the correspondence between the topics and clients, we will store the topic and a reference to the topic in the topics list. For instance, if the client with `socket` adds the word `'breakfast'`, we will add the {word: `'breakfast'`, client: socket} object to the topics list:

```
// List of topics to track
var topics = [];
```

As mentioned in the previous sections, we can use either the `statuses/sample` or the `statuses/filter` endpoints to capture tweets. We will use the `statuses/filter` endpoint in our application, but instead of filtering by topic, we will filter by location and language (tweets in English only). We will set the `locations` parameter to `'-180,-90,180,90'`, meaning that we want results from anywhere in the world, and set the `language` parameter to `'en'`. Passing a list of words to the `statuses/filter` endpoint will force us to reset the connection when the user adds a new topic. This is a waste of resources, and Twitter could apply rate limits if we open and close connections frequently. We will use the `statuses/filter` endpoint to listen to anything in the stream and filter the words we want. This will allow you to add or remove words from the topics list without having to reset the connection. We will initialize the `Twit` object, which will read the Twitter credentials and store them to create the streaming requests to Twitter. We will also create the stream to the `statuses/filter` endpoint and store a reference to it in the `twitterStream` variable. We will filter only using the language (English) and location (the world), and match the items by comparing the topic word with the tweet contents:

```
// Configure the Twit object with the application credentials
var T = new Twit(config);

// Filter by location (the world) and tweets in English
var filterOptions = {
```

```
        locations: '-180,-90,180,90',
        language: 'en'};

    // Creates a new stream object, tracking the updated topic list
    var twitterStream = T.stream('statuses/filter', filterOptions);
```

We will define functions to handle the most important `Twit` stream events. Most of these callbacks will just log a message in the console, stating that the event has occurred. We will define a callback for the `connect` event, which will be triggered when a connection is attempted, and a callback for the `connected` event, which will be emitted when the connection to the Twitter stream is established:

```
    // Connection attempt ('connect' event)
    function twitOnConnect(req) {
        console.log('[Twitter] Connecting...');
    }


    // Successful connection ('connected' event)
    function twitOnConnected(res) {
        console.log('[Twitter] Connection successful.');
    }
```

We will display a log message if a reconnection is scheduled, indicating the interval in seconds:

```
    // Reconnection scheduled ('reconnect' event).
    function twitOnReconnect(req, res, interval) {
        var secs = Math.round(interval / 1e3);
        console.log('[Twitter] Disconnected. Reconnection scheduled in
          ' + secs + ' seconds.');
    }
```

We will also add callbacks for the `disconnect` and `limit` events, which will occur when Twitter sends a `disconnect` or `limit` message, respectively. Note that Twit will close the connection if it receives the `disconnect` message, but not if it receives the `limit` message. In the `limit` callback, we will display a message and stop the stream explicitly:

```
    // Disconnect message from Twitter ('disconnect' event)
    function twitOnDisconnect(disconnectMessage) {
        // Twit will stop itself before emitting the event
        console.log('[Twitter] Disconnected.');
    }


    // Limit message from Twitter ('limit' event)
    function twitOnLimit(limitMessage) {
```

```
        // We stop the stream explicitely.
        console.log('[Twitter] Limit message received. Stopping.');
        twitterStream.stop();
    }
```

Adding log messages for these events can help debug issues or help us know what is happening if we don't receive messages for a while. The event that we should certainly listen for is the `tweet` event, which will be emitted when a tweet is delivered by the streaming endpoint. The callback of the event will receive the `tweet` object as the argument.

As mentioned earlier, we will only send geotagged tweets to the connected clients. We will check whether the tweet text matches any of the terms in the topics list. If a term is found in the tweet text, we will send a simplified version of the tweet to the client who added the term:

```
// A tweet is received ('tweet' event)
function twitOnTweet(tweet) {

    // Exits if the tweet doesn't have geographic coordinates
    if (!tweet.coordinates) { return; }

    // Convert the tweet text to lowercase to find the topics
    var tweetText = tweet.text.toLowerCase();

    // Check if any of the topics are contained in the tweet text
    topics.forEach(function(topic) {

        // Checks if the tweet text contains the topic
        if (tweetText.indexOf(topic.word) !== -1) {

            // Sends a simplified version of the tweet to the
            //   client
            topic.socket.emit('tweet', {
                id: tweet.id,
                coordinates: tweet.coordinates,
                word: topic.word
            });
        }
    });
}
```

As we are not using the tweet text or its creation date, we will send just the tweet ID, the coordinates, and the matched word to the client. We can now attach the listeners to their corresponding events as follows:

```
// Add listeners for the stream events to the stream instance
twitterStream.on('tweet',       twitOnTweet);
twitterStream.on('connect',     twitOnConnect);
twitterStream.on('connected',   twitOnConnected);
twitterStream.on('reconnect',   twitOnReconnect);
twitterStream.on('limit',       twitOnLimit);
twitterStream.on('disconnect', twitOnDisconnect);
```

We have initialized the connection to the Twitter-streaming API, but as we don't have any topics in our list, nothing will happen. We need to create the Socket.IO server to handle connections with clients, which can add topics to the list. We will begin by defining the port where the Socket.IO server will listen and creating an instance of the server. Note that we can create an instance of the Socket.IO server with or without the new keyword:

```
// Create a new instance of the Socket.IO Server
var port = 9720,
    io = new IOServer(port);

// Displays a message at startup
console.log('Listening for incoming connections in port ' + port);
```

The io server will begin listening for incoming connections on port 9720. We can use other port numbers too; remember that ports between 0 and 1023 are privileged, as they require a higher level of permission to bind.

When a client connects, the connection event will be emitted by the io server, passing the socket as an argument to the event callback. In this case, we will display a log message in the console, indicating that a new connection was established, and add listeners for the socket events:

```
// A client's established a connection with the server
io.on('connection', function(socket) {

    // Displays a message in the console when a client connects
    console.log('Client ', socket.id, ' connected.');

    // Add listeners for the socket events...
});
```

The socket object is a reference to the client endpoint in the communication. If the client adds a new topic, the add custom event will be emitted, passing the added topic to the event callback. In the callback for this event, we will append the word and a reference to the socket to the topic list and display a log message in the console:

```
// The client adds a new topic
socket.on('add', function(topic) {
    // Adds the new topic to the topic list
    topics.push({
        word: topic.word.toLowerCase(),
        socket: socket
    });

    console.log('Adding the topic "' + topic.word + '"');
});
```

When the client disconnects, we will remove its topics from the list and display a log message in the terminal:

```
// If the client disconnects, we remove its topics from the
  list
socket.on('disconnect', function() {
    console.log('Client ' + socket.id + ' disconnected.');
    topics = topics.filter(function(topic) {
        return topic.socket.id !== socket.id;
    });
});
```

At this point, the server is capable of handling multiple clients connected at the same time, each adding their own terms to the topic list. When we implement (and access) the client-side application, we will have the streaming server generate logs such as the following:

```
$ node chirp.js
Listening for incoming connections in port 9720
[Twitter] Connecting...
[Twitter] Connection successful.
Client 4WDFIrqsbxtf_NO_AAAA connected.
Adding the topic "day"
Adding the topic "night"
Client 4WDFIrqsbxtf_NO_AAAA disconnected.
```

```
Client P8mb97GiLOhc-noLAAAB connected.

Adding the topic "coffee"

Adding the topic "tea"

Adding the topic "milk"

Adding the topic "beer"

[Twitter] Disconnected. Reconnection scheduled in 0 seconds.

[Twitter] Connecting...

[Twitter] Connection successful.

Client P8mb97GiLOhc-noLAAAB disconnected.

Client p3lFgVrxGI0bLPOFAAAC connected.

   ...
```

In the next section, we will use the client-side Socket.IO library, D3, and Backbone to create a visualization that shows the geographic distribution of tweets matching the user-defined topics.

Creating the client application

In the previous section, we implemented the streaming server. The server application allows other applications to send words that you can listen to from the `statuses/ sample` endpoint from Twitter. When the server receives geotagged tweets containing the words tracked by a client, it will deliver the client a simplified version of the tweet. The server doesn't enforce what the client applications do with the tweets; the client application could just count the tweets, visualize the frequency of each term in time with a heat map, or create a network chart showing the co-occurrence of the terms.

In this section, we will implement a client application. The application will display a map showing the location of the tweets that match each term in a world map, and will display a bar chart that will display the count for each term. As we did in *Chapter 6, Interaction between Charts*, we will use Backbone and D3 to structure our application. A screenshot of the application is shown as follows:

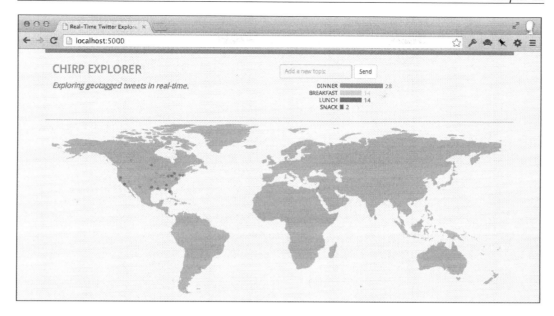

The code of the application is available in the `chapter12/chirp-client` folder. We will begin by describing the project structure, and then implement the project components.

The application structure

As mentioned earlier, we will use Backbone to structure the application's components. As we want to visualize the places where different topics are mentioned in the world at any given time, we will define a topic as the main component of our application. A topic will contain a word (the string that we want to track in Twitter), a color to visualize it, and a list of matching tweets. We will create a `Topic` model containing these attributes.

We will create a collection for the topics. The collection will be in charge of creating the topic instances when the user adds words in the input element and appending the tweets to the corresponding topic instance as they arrive. We will provide our collection with three views: the world map view, the barchart view, and the input element, where the user can add a new topic.

The code for the application components will be in the `src/app` directory in the project folder. We will have separate directories for the models, collections, and views of our application; we will have the `app.js` and `setup.js` files to define the application namespace and to set up and launch our application:

```
app/
    app.js
    models/
    collections/
    views/
    setup.js
```

We will encapsulate the components of our application under the `App` variable, which is defined in the `app/app.js` file. We will add attributes for the collections, models, and views to the `App` object, as follows:

```
// Define the application namespace
var App = {
    Collections: {},
    Models:      {},
    Views:       {}
};
```

To run the application, run the server application and go to the `chirp-client` directory and start a static server. The `Gruntfile` of the project contains a task to run a static server in the development mode. Install the Node modules with the following command:

$ npm install

After installing the project dependencies, run `grunt serve`. This will serve the files in the directory as static assets and open the browser in the correct port. We will review the application models and views.

Models and collections

The main component of our application will be the `Topic` model. A `Topic` instance will have a `word`, `color`, and an array of simplified tweets matching the topic's word. We will define our model in the `app/models/topic.js` file. The `Topic` model will be created by extending the `Backbone.Model` object:

```
// Topic Model
App.Models.Topic = Backbone.Model.extend({

    // The 'word' attribute will uniquely identify our topic
```

```
idAttribute: 'word',

// Default model values
defaults: function() {
    return {
        word:    'topic',
        color:   '#555',
        tweets: []
    };
},


// addTweet method...
});
```

The word string will uniquely identify our models in a collection. The topics will be given a color to identify them in the bar chart and the map views. Each topic instance will contain an array of tweets that match the word of the topic. We will add a method to add tweets to the array; in this method, we will add the topic's color. Array attributes (such as the tweets property) are treated as pointers; mutating the array won't trigger the change event. Note that we could also create a model and collection for the tweets, but we will use an array for simplicity.

We will trigger this event explicitly to notify potential observers that the array has changed:

```
// Adds a tweet to the 'tweets' array.
addTweet: function(tweet) {

    // Adds the color of the topic
    tweet.color = this.get('color');

    // Append the tweet to the tweets array
    this.get('tweets').push(tweet);

    // We trigger the event explicitly
    this.trigger('change:tweets');
}
```

Note that it is not necessary to define the default values for our model, but we will add them so that we remember the names of the attributes when describing the example.

We will also create a collection for our topics. The `Topics` collection will manage the creation of the `Topic` instances and add tweets to the corresponding collection as they arrive from the server. We will make the `socket` endpoint accessible to the `Topics` collection, passing it as an option when creating the `Topic` instance. We will bind the `on` socket event to a function that will add the tweet to the corresponding topic. We also set a callback for the `add` event to set the color for a topic when a new instance is created, as shown in the following code snippet:

```
// Topics Collection
App.Collections.Topics = Backbone.Collection.extend({

    // The collection model
    model: App.Models.Topic,

    // Collection Initialization
    initialize: function(models, options) {

        this.socket = options.socket;

        // Store the current 'this' context
        var self = this;

        this.socket.on('tweet', function(tweet) {
            self.addTweet(tweet);
        });

        this.on('add', function(topic) {
            topic.set('color', App.Colors[this.length - 1]);
            this.socket.emit('add', {word: topic.get('word')});
        });
    },

    // Add tweet method...
});
```

The `addTweet` method of the collection will find the topic that matches the tweet's `word` attribute and append the tweet using the `addTweet` method of the corresponding topic instance:

```
addTweet: function(tweet) {

    // Gets the corresponding model instance.
```

```
    var topic = this.get(tweet.word);

    // Push the tweet object to the tweets array.
    if (topic) {
        topic.addTweet(tweet);
    }
}
```

Implementing the topics views

In our application, we only need views for the `Topics` collection and for the application itself. We will have a view associated with the bar chart, a view for the map of tweets, and a view for the input element, which will be used to create new topic instances. The code for each of these views is in the `src/app/views` directory in the `topics-barchart.js`, `topics-map.js`, and `topics-input.js` files, respectively.

The input view

The input element will allow the user to add a new topic. The user can write a new topic in the input box and click on the **Send** button to send it to the server and add it to the list of watched topics. The input element is shown in the following screenshot:

To render this view, we will create a template with the markup of the form. We will add the template under the body tag in the `index.html` document:

```html
<!-- Input Element Template -->
<script type='text/template' id='topics-template'>
  <form role="form" class="form-horizontal form-inline" id="topic-
    form">
    <div class="form-group">
      <label for="msgToServer" class="sr-only">Message</label>
      <input type="text" class="form-control input-sm" id="new-
        topic" placeholder="Add a new topic">
      <button type="submit" class="btn btn-default btn-
        sm">Send</button>
    </div>
  </form>
</script>
```

We will implement this view by extending the `Backbone.View` object. The `template` attribute will contain the compiled template. In this case, the template doesn't have placeholder text to be replaced when rendering, but we will keep `_.template()` to allow the use of template variables in the future:

```javascript
// Topic Input
App.Views.TopicsInput = Backbone.View.extend({

    // Compile the view template
    template: _.template($('#topics-template').html()),

    // DOM Events
    events: {
        'submit #topic-form': 'addOnSubmit',
    },

    initialize: function (options) {
        // The input element will be disabled if the collection
        //   has five or more items
        this.listenTo(this.collection, 'add', this.disableInput);
    },

    render: function () {
        // Renders the input element in the view element
        this.$el.html(this.template(this.collection.toJSON()));
        return this;
    },

    disableInput: function() {
        // Disable the input element if the collection has five or
        //   more items
    },

    addOnSubmit: function(e) {
        // adds a topic when the user press the send button
    }
});
```

We will allow up to five topics by a user to avoid having too many similar colors in the map. We have limited space for the bar chart as well, and having an unlimited number of topics per user could have an impact on the performance of the server. When a new topic instance is created in the collection, we will invoke the `disableInput` method, which will disable the input element if our collection contains five or more elements:

```
disableInput: function() {
  // Disable the input element if the collection has five or
    more items
  if (this.collection.length >= 5) {
      this.$('input').attr('disabled', true);
  }
},
```

To add a new topic, the user can type the terms in the input element as soon as the **Send** button is pressed. When the user clicks on the **Send** button, the submit event is triggered, and the event is passed as an argument to the `addOnSubmit` method. In this method, the default action of the form is prevented as this would cause the page to reload, the topic is added to the topics collection, and the input element is cleared:

```
addOnSubmit: function(e) {

    // Prevents the page from reloading
    e.preventDefault();

    // Content of the input element
    var word = this.$('input').val().trim();

    // Adds the topic to the collection and cleans the input
    if (word) {
        this.collection.add({word: word});
        this.$('input').val('');
    }
}
```

The bar chart view

The bar chart view will encapsulate a reusable bar chart made in D3. We will describe the view and then comment on the implementation of the chart. For now, we will just need to know about the interface of the chart. The code for the bar chart view is available in the `src/app/views/topics-barchart.js` file. A bar chart showing the tweet count for a set of topics is shown in the following screenshot:

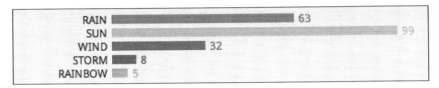

We begin by extending and customizing the `Backbone.View` object. We add the `chart` attribute, which will contain a configured instance of the `charts.barChart` reusable chart. The bar chart will receive an array of objects that will be used to create the bars. The `label` attribute allows you to set a function to compute the label for each bar. The `value` attribute will allow you to configure the value that will be mapped to the bar's length, and the `color` attribute will allow you to configure the color of each bar. We set functions for each one of these attributes, assuming that our array will contain elements with the `word`, `count`, and `color` properties:

```
// Bar Chart View
App.Views.TopicsBarchart = Backbone.View.extend({

    // Create and configure the bar chart
    chart: charts.barChart()
        .label(function(d) { return d.word; })
        .value(function(d) { return d.count; })
        .color(function(d) { return d.color; }),

    initialize: function () {
        // Initialize the view
    },

    render: function () {
        // Updates the chart
    }
});
```

In the `initialize` method, we add a callback for the `change:tweets` event in the collection. Note that the `change:tweets` event is triggered by the topic instances; the collection just echoes the events. We will also render the view when a new topic is added to the collection:

```
initialize: function () {
    // Render the view when a tweet arrives and when a new
      topic is added
    this.listenTo(this.collection, 'change:tweets',
      this.render);
    this.listenTo(this.collection, 'add', this.render);
},
```

The `render` method will construct the data array in the format required by the chart, computing the `count` attribute for each topic; this method will select the container element and update the chart. Note that the `toJSON` collection method returns a JavaScript object, not a string representation of an object in the JSON format:

```
render: function () {

    // Transform the collection to a plain JSON object
    var data = this.collection.toJSON();

    // Compute the tweet count for each topic
    data.forEach(function(item) {
        item.count = item.tweets.length;
    });

    // Compute the container div width and height
    var div = d3.select(this.el),
        width  = parseInt(div.style('width'), 10),
        height = parseInt(div.style('height'), 10);

    // Adjust the chart width and height
    this.chart.width(width).height(height);

    // Select the container element and update the chart
    div.data([data]).call(this.chart);
    return this;
}
```

The topics map view

In the topics map view, the tweets from all the topics will be drawn as points in a map, with each tweet colored as per the corresponding topic. The code of this view is in the `src/app/topics-map.js` file. Tweets for each topic in a world map is shown in the following screenshot:

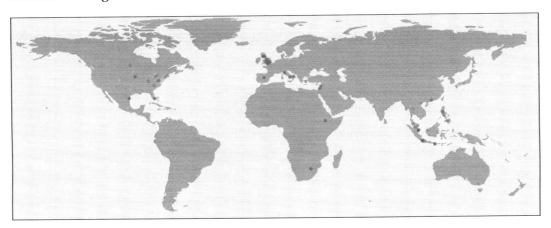

To create this view, we will use the `charts.map` reusable chart, which will render an array of GeoJSON features and a GeoJSON object base. This chart uses the equirectangular projection; this is important to set the width and height in a ratio of 2:1. In the `initialize` method, we set the base GeoJSON object provided in the options object. In this case, the `options.geojson` object is a feature collection with countries from Natural Earth. We will render the view only when a tweet arrives:

```
// Topics Map View
App.Views.TopicsMap = Backbone.View.extend({

    // Create and configure the map chart
    chart: charts.map()
        .feature(function(d) { return d.coordinates; })
        .color(function(d) { return d.color; }),

    initialize: function (options) {
        // Sets the GeoJSON object with the world map
        this.chart.geojson(options.geojson);

        // Render the view when a new tweet arrives
        this.listenTo(this.collection, 'change:tweets',
        this.render);
```

```
        },

        render: function () {

            // Gather the tweets for all the topics in one array
            var tweets =  _.flatten(_.pluck(this.collection.toJSON(),
                'tweets'));

            // Select the container element
            var div = d3.select(this.el),
                width  = parseInt(div.style('width'),  10);

            // Update the chart width, height and scale
            this.chart
                .width(width)
                .height(width / 2)
                .scale(width / (2 * Math.PI));

            // Update the chart
            div.data([tweets]).call(this.chart);
            return this;
        }
    });
```

In the `render` method, we gather the tweets for all the topics in one array, select the container element, and update the chart. The geotagged tweets will be drawn as small points on the world map.

Creating the application view

We will create a view for the application itself. This is not really necessary, but we will do it to keep things organized. We will need a template that contains the markup for the application components. In this case, we will have a row for the header, which will contain the page title, lead paragraph, input element, and bar chart. Under the header, we will reserve a space for the map with the tweets:

```
<!-- Application Template -->
<script type='text/template' id='application-template'>

    <div class="row header">
        <!-- Title and about -->
        <div class="col-md-6">
```

```
        <h1 class="title">chirp explorer</h1>
        <p class="lead">Exploring geotagged tweets in real-time.</p>
      </div>

      <!-- Barchart -->
      <div class="col-md-6">
        <div id="topics-form"></div>
        <div id="topics-barchart" class="barchart-block"></div>
      </div>
    </div>

    <div class="row">
      <div class="col-md-12">
        <div id="topics-map"></div>
      </div>
    </div>
  </div>
</script>
```

The application view implementation is in the src/app/views/application.js file. In this case, we don't need to compile a template for the view, but we will compile it if we add template variables as the application name or lead text:

```
// Application View
App.Views.Application = Backbone.View.extend({

    // Compile the applicaiton template
    template: _.template($('#application-template').html()),

    // Render the application template in the container
    render: function() {
        this.$el.html(this.template());
        return this;
    }
});
```

In the render method, we will just insert the contents of the template in the container element. This will put the markup of the template in the container defined when instantiating the view.

The application setup

With our models, collections, and views ready, we can proceed to create the instances and wire things up. The initialization of the application is in the `src/app/setup.js` file. We begin by creating the `app` variable to hold the instances of collections and views. When the DOM is ready, we will invoke the function that will create the instances of our views and collections:

```
// Container for the application instances
var app = {};

// Invoke the function when the document is ready
$(function() {
    // Create application instances...
});
```

We begin by creating an instance of the application view and setting the container element to the div with the `application-container` ID. The application view doesn't have an associated model or collection; we can render the view immediately as shown in the following code:

```
// Create the application view and renders it
app.applicationView = new App.Views.Application({
    el: '#application-container'
});
app.applicationView.render();
```

We can create an instance of the `Topics` collection. At the beginning, the collection will be empty, waiting for the user to create new topics. We will create a connection to the streaming server and pass a reference to the server endpoint as well as to the collection of topics. Remember that in the initialization method of the `Topics` collection, we add a callback for the `tweet` event of the socket, which adds the tweet to the corresponding collection. Remember to change `localhost` to an accessible URL if you want to use the application on another device:

```
// Creates the topics collection, passing the socket instance
app.topicList = new App.Collections.Topics([], {
    socket: io.connect('http://localhost:9720')
});
```

As we have an instance of the `Topics` collection, we can proceed to create instances for the topic views. We create an instance of the `TopicsInput` view, the `TopicsBarchart` view, and the `TopicsMap` view:

```
// Input View
app.topicsInputView = new App.Views.TopicsInput({
```

```
        el: '#topics-form',
        collection: app.topicList
    });

    // Bar Chart View
    app.topicsBarchartView = new App.Views.TopicsBarchart({
        el: '#topics-barchart',
        collection: app.topicList
    });

    // Map View
    app.topicsMapView = new App.Views.TopicsMap({
        el: '#topics-map',
        collection: app.topicList
    });
```

In the map chart of the `TopicsMap` view, we need a GeoJSON object with the feature or feature collection to show as the background. We use `d3.json` to load the `TopoJSON` file containing the world's countries and convert it to the equivalent GeoJSON object using the `TopoJSON` library. We use this `GeoJSON` object to update the map chart's `geojson` attribute and render the view. This will display the map that shows the world's countries:

```
    // Loads the TopoJSON countries file
    d3.json('dist/data/countries.json', function(error, geodata) {

        if (error) {
            // Handles errors getting or parsing the file
            console.error('Error getting or parsing the TopoJSON
              file');
            throw error;
        }

        // Transform from TopoJSON to GeoJSON
        var geojson = topojson.feature(geodata,
          geodata.objects.countries);

        // Update the map chart and render the map view
        app.topicsMapView.chart.geojson(geojson);
        app.topicsMapView.render();
    });
```

Finally, we render the views for the `topicList` collection:

```
// Render the Topic Views
app.topicsInputView.render();
app.topicsBarchartView.render();
app.topicsMapView.render();
```

At this point, we will have the input element, an empty bar chart, and the world map without tweet points. As soon as the user adds a topic, the server will begin to deliver tweets, which will appear in the views. The application and rendered topic views can be seen in the following screenshot:

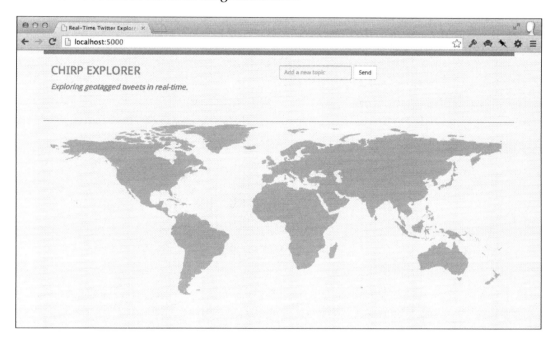

Let's recapitulate how the client application works. Once the views are rendered, the user can add topics by typing words in the input box. When the *Enter* key is pressed, the contents of the input element will be added as the word attribute of a new topic instance. The collection will send the word to the streaming server, which will add the topic and a reference to the client in the topics list. The server will be connected to the Twitter-streaming API. Each time the server receives a geotagged tweet, it will compare the tweet text with the topics in the list; if a match is found, a simplified version of the tweet will be sent to the client. In the client, the tweet will be added to the `tweets` array of the topic that matches the tweet text. This will trigger the views to render, updating the bar chart and the map. Here, we can guess where people are having their breakfast and where they are having dinner, as shown in the following screenshot:

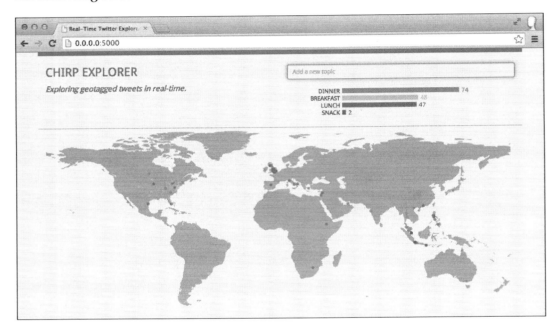

The streaming server can be used with any application that can send the add event and receive the tweets when the server emits the tweet event. We chose to create a client to visualize the geographic distribution of tweets, but we could have implemented a different representation of the same data. If you want to experiment, use the streaming server as a base component to create your own client visualization. Here are some suggestions:

- The time dimension was neglected in this application. It might be interesting to display a heat map that shows how the tweet count varies in time or makes the old tweets fade away.

- Adding zoom and pan to the map chart could be useful to study the geographic distribution of tweets at a more local level.

- The user can't remove topics once they are created; adding a way to remove topics can be useful if the user decides that a topic was not interesting.

- Use brushing to allow the user to select tweets only from a particular region of the world. This would probably involve modifying the server such that it sends the tweets from that location to the client who selected it.

- Use a library of sentiment analysis and add information on whether the topic was mentioned in a positive or negative way.

- Add the ability to show and hide topics so that the overlapping doesn't hide information.

Summary

In the last chapter of the book, we learned how to use D3 and Socket.IO to create a real-time visualization of geotagged tweets. In this chapter, we described two applications: the streaming server and the client application.

We implemented the streaming server in Node. The streaming server keeps a persistent connection to the Twitter-streaming endpoints and supports several connected users at the same time, with each user adding topics to be tracked on the Twitter-streaming API. When the tweets match one of the user topics, they are delivered to the corresponding client.

In the client application, we used Backbone, Socket.IO, and D3 to create a visualization of where the topics are defined by the user in the world. The user can add topics at any given time; the server will add the topic to its list and begin to send tweets that match the topic to the client.

Through this book, we learned how to use D3 to create several kinds of charts, but mostly, we learned how to create visual components that can be reused across several projects. We learned how to integrate D3 and reusable charts with other libraries to structure applications better, how to deploy web applications, and how to add real-time updates to the charts. As we have seen in the examples of this book, D3 is powerful and flexible, making it especially attractive for tinkerers and creative developers.

Index

Thank you for buying
Mastering D3.js

About Packt Publishing

Packt, pronounced 'packed', published its first book "*Mastering phpMyAdmin for Effective MySQL Management*" in April 2004 and subsequently continued to specialize in publishing highly focused books on specific technologies and solutions.

Our books and publications share the experiences of your fellow IT professionals in adapting and customizing today's systems, applications, and frameworks. Our solution based books give you the knowledge and power to customize the software and technologies you're using to get the job done. Packt books are more specific and less general than the IT books you have seen in the past. Our unique business model allows us to bring you more focused information, giving you more of what you need to know, and less of what you don't.

Packt is a modern, yet unique publishing company, which focuses on producing quality, cutting-edge books for communities of developers, administrators, and newbies alike. For more information, please visit our website: www.packtpub.com.

About Packt Open Source

In 2010, Packt launched two new brands, Packt Open Source and Packt Enterprise, in order to continue its focus on specialization. This book is part of the Packt Open Source brand, home to books published on software built around Open Source licenses, and offering information to anybody from advanced developers to budding web designers. The Open Source brand also runs Packt's Open Source Royalty Scheme, by which Packt gives a royalty to each Open Source project about whose software a book is sold.

Writing for Packt

We welcome all inquiries from people who are interested in authoring. Book proposals should be sent to author@packtpub.com. If your book idea is still at an early stage and you would like to discuss it first before writing a formal book proposal, contact us; one of our commissioning editors will get in touch with you.

We're not just looking for published authors; if you have strong technical skills but no writing experience, our experienced editors can help you develop a writing career, or simply get some additional reward for your expertise.

Data Visualization with d3.js

ISBN: 978-1-78216-000-7   Paperback: 194 pages

Mold your data into beautiful visualizations with d3.js

1. Build blocks of web visualizations.

2. Learn visualization with detailed walkthroughs.

3. Learn to use data more effectively.

4. Animate with d3.js.

5. Design good visualizations.

Data Visualization with D3.js Cookbook

ISBN: 978-1-78216-216-2   Paperback: 338 pages

Over 70 recipes to create dynamic data-driven visualization with D3.js

1. Create stunning data visualization with the power of D3.

2. Bootstrap D3 quickly with the help of ready-to-go code samples.

3. Solve real-world visualization problems with the help of practical recipes.

Please check **www.PacktPub.com** for information on our titles

Real-time Web Application Development using Vert.x 2.0

ISBN: 978-1-78216-795-2   Paperback: 122 pages

An intuitive guide to building applications for the real-time web with the Vert.x platform

1. Get started with developing applications for the real-time web.

2. From concept to deployment, learn the full development workflow of a real-time web application.

3. Utilize the Java skills you already have while stepping up to the next level.

4. Learn all the major building blocks of the Vert.x platform.

Practical Data Analysis

ISBN: 978-1-78328-099-5   Paperback: 360 pages

Transform, model, and visualize your data through hands-on projects, developed in open source tools

1. Explore how to analyze your data in various innovative ways and turn them into insight.

2. Learn to use the D3.js visualization tool for exploratory data analysis.

3. Understand how to work with graphs and social data analysis.

4. Discover how to perform advanced query techniques and run MapReduce on MongoDB.

Please check **www.PacktPub.com** for information on our titles